Real Possibilities

MAR 2 4 2016

D0370813

Juggling Life, Work, and Caregiving

Amy Goyer

Defending Liberty
Pursuing Justice
AMERICAN BAR ASSOCIATION

19 18 17 16 15   5 4 3 2 1

Library of Congress Cataloging-in-Publication Data

Goyer, Amy, author.

Juggling life, work, and caregiving / Amy Goyer.

pages cm

ISBN 978-1-63425-163-1 (softcover : alk. paper) -- ISBN 978-1-63425-164-8 (e-book) 1. Older people--Long term care--Law and legislation--United States. 2. Caregivers--United States--Handbooks, manuals, etc. I. Title.

KF3737.G69 2015

362'.0425--dc23   2015011900

Dedication

I dedicate this book to my parents, Robert and Patricia Goyer; my sister Karen Goyer; and my grandparents, Genevieve and C. V. Goyer and Harold and Clara Stutz: Thank you for teaching me how to lovingly care for others.

I want to extend my heartfelt appreciation to my sisters, Karen, Susie, and Linda, for their support of my work, input into this book, and help caring for our parents.

A special thanks goes to Bill, who supports me in all that I do.

And for Jackson, for being my four-legged partner in caregiving.

In loving memory of Shaelee McDaniel, Anne Samaan, Patricia Goyer, and Karen Goyer.

Contents

Foreword

Freda Lewis-Hall, M.D., Executive Vice President and Chief Medical Officer, Pfizer Inc.

Caregiving, in my family, is an act of love and honor—and an expectation. When I was a child, my uncle, who was severely affected by polio, lived with my family. The rhythm of his care saw me lace his intricate leg and back braces in the morning and my mother handle his doctors' visits in the daytime. Come night, my father—dead-tired from long days and evenings driving a taxi—would lift his brother onto his back and carry him up the stairs to bed.

When my mother died suddenly from a stroke after my first year in medical school, there was no question about who would care for my aging grandparents. In my mid-20s, I quickly came to understand both the nobility and the intensity of caregiving. I balanced medical school and the launch of my medical career with the demands of caring for my elders and starting a family of my own. The pressure only increased as my Alzheimer's-stricken grandmother declined before my eyes.

We all have mixed feelings about caregiving. We hear it described as the pinnacle of human compassion—and we take heart in that. But we also struggle to manage caregiving and career, especially given a tight economy, a highly mobile society, and our own aging and health challenges. Millions of us have both young children and aging parents staking claims to our time, energy, aspirations, and relationships. We often find ourselves in uncharted territory, fearing loss of control.

Juggling Life, Work, and Caregiving from AARP and the American Bar Association will help you stay in control, especially at the important decision points of your life. Author Amy Goyer, a well-respected professional in this arena and a caregiver for her own parents, offers practical advice on the caregiving challenge and helps you deal with the essential details of managing finances, medical care, and daily work, as well as the crises that inevitably come with caregiving.

This publication affirms the worth of caregiving but also speaks to the powerful, often confusing emotions that come with it. *Juggling Life, Work, and Caregiving* fully recognizes the importance of taking care of *you* and helps you do so without guilt.

Pfizer sponsored the first iteration of this book, *Juggling Work and Caregiving,* because we believe that caregivers are both essential to our society and underappreciated within it. We honor caregivers and advocate for them. You will find this publication highly useful on its own and as a gateway to other helpful resources. These include AARP's Caregiving Resource Center at www.aarp.org/caregiving and two Pfizer-sponsored sites, www.getold.com and www.gethealthystayhealthy.com. Whatever your situation, *Juggling Life, Work, and Caregiving* makes it clear: You are not alone. Pfizer and AARP care, and we want to help.

Acknowledgments

My thanks to the AARP experts—Laura Bos, Elizabeth Bradley, Mary Liz Burns, Debbie Chalfie, Rita Choula, Jon Dauphine, Lynn Feinberg, Allyson Funk, Jordan Green, Dorothy Howe, Sally Hurme, Carol Kaufmann, Justin Kirkland, Marcie LeFevre, Amy Levner, Heather Nawrocki, Leslie Nettleford, Susan Reinhard, Rhonda Richards, Lindsay Sena, Patti Shea, Yolanda Taylor, Nancy Thompson, Gena Wright, and Lisa Yagoda, among others—and experts Bronwyn Belling, Karen Kolb Flude, and Debra Sellers—for their input, review, and help in connecting caregivers to this book.

Special appreciation goes to Jodi Lipson for her guidance, flexibility, empathy, and expert editing; to Michelle Harris for her eagle eye and skilled fact-checking and editing; and to Kevin Donnellan, Myrna Blyth, and Bob Stephen for their leadership and support. My appreciation also goes to Pfizer's Freda Lewis-Hall for passionately championing the caregiving cause as well as writing the foreword for this book, and to Bob Miglani for his input, wisdom, and enthusiasm.

My unending gratitude goes to Danielle Romesburg, Kelly McGinnis, Maria Trejo, Debbie Bachler, Debbie Bear, Dee Marriage, and my sister Linda Goyer Lane, who helped care for my parents, making it possible for me to write this book.

My deepest admiration and thankfulness go to all the friends and caregivers who provided anecdotes and insight for this book, including Laurette Bennhold-Samaan, Robin Hungerford Burgess, Bill Carter, Dave Conover, Monda De-Weese, Laura George, Chris Jennings, Susan Sligo

Karageorge, Therese Fieler Lackey, Susan Roche, Jenny Samaan, Maureen Statland, and Kim Ward.

My thanks go to my two favorite coffee shops, where much of this book was written in an atmosphere of peace and community: St. Elmo's in Alexandria (Del Ray), Virginia, and Bergies in Gilbert, Arizona.

To all of you family caregivers I meet online, on the radio or television, at my speaking engagements, in doctors' offices and hospitals, and throughout my everyday life, thank you for sharing your stories and support with me. We are stronger together. Remember to create and notice the joy.

About the Author

Amy Goyer has more than 30 years of experience in this field. She started her career as a music therapist, activities director, and administrator in adult day services centers and nursing homes. Later, she worked for the Ohio Department of Aging, monitoring home- and community-based programs serving older Americans and leading statewide senior volunteer and intergenerational initiatives. She then joined the staff of AARP, heading up its intergenerational efforts and its program supporting grandparent caregivers. Now she is an aging and families author and consultant, specializing in caregiving, grandparenting, and multigenerational relationships and issues. A passionate champion for caregivers, she has been one her entire adult life, first for her grandparents and then for her sisters and parents. She serves as AARP's family and caregiving expert (www.aarp.org/amygoyer), a role that includes talking to the media and live audiences, writing columns and a blog, and creating online videos (www.aarp.org/takingcare) that document her personal caregiving journey and provide actionable tips for families and caregivers.

Learn more about Amy's work at www.amygoyer.com. Connect with her on Twitter at @amygoyer and on Facebook at AmyGoyer1.

Introduction

My Caregiving Journey

I've been a caregiver my entire adult life.

First I helped care for my grandparents. Then I helped with my mom when she had a stroke at age 63, some 25 years ago, making frequent cross-country trips from Washington, D.C., to Arizona. But when Dad showed increasing signs of Alzheimer's disease in 2008, that wasn't enough. So I adapted my work, choosing jobs that let me telecommute, and began working from Arizona a week or two a month.

When Dad stopped driving and my parents, with their service dog, Jackson, moved to a senior-living community, they needed even more support. So I reversed my life, basing myself in Arizona. I moved into the house they moved out of, worked from home, and began traveling to the D.C. area a week or so a month, where most of my work is based and where most of my friends and my boyfriend live. As my parents' health changed and they needed 24-hour care, though, they couldn't afford to stay in the senior community, so they moved back into the house with me. I rented an office nearby and hired a professional live-in caregiver. To augment that support, my sister Linda comes from Ohio to help as one of our paid caregivers when I am away on business travel. She plans to eventually move to Phoenix to take on more of the care. Susie, my sister who lives in Los Angeles, comes when she can to help. Karen, my oldest sister, lived in Maryland and developed Cushing's Disease. I became her long-distance caregiver; yet even when she was very sick, she helped as best she could by calling every day.

In January of 2012, we lost my niece Shaelee to suicide after her long battle with bipolar illness. In October of 2013, Mom passed on. We miss her terribly. Dad's Alzheimer's disease continues to progress, and it's much harder for him to stay oriented without Mom. She was his north star. Then in December 2014, my sister Karen passed on. Grief and loss have been devastating and unceasing elements of our caregiving journey.

How do I manage my role as a caregiver? I've always been organized, but I've learned to be even more efficient. I'm getting better at mindfulness, fully focusing my attention on whatever my task is at that moment—helping Mom comb her hair, singing with Dad, writing a blog post, or giving a media interview. I'm fortunate because I am in the field of aging and families, working with clients who truly get it when it comes to caregiving. They tend to be extremely flexible and understanding about all that I'm juggling and the odd hours that work gets done.

Have I missed opportunities and struggled with the unique challenges of being self-employed? Absolutely. Have I sacrificed aspects of my personal relationships, hobbies, interests, and health? Indeed. Am I sometimes frustrated and overwhelmed? Yes. But here's what sustains me: I believe that I'm doing the right thing, and I create and notice joy in the act of caring for others. Every day I've made a conscious *choice* to care for others, especially my parents, just as they have cared for our family, so I've adapted my work and personal goals. People ask me how I do it; I wonder, how could I *not* do it? I wouldn't have it any other way. I succeed because I want to and because I believe so strongly in what I'm doing.

In my heart of hearts, I know that I'm growing and benefiting from this experience too. Perhaps the most important lesson I've learned is that my goal as a caregiver is not to prevent change; it will invariably happen. My goal, instead, is to ride the waves of change. I am increasingly aware of what I can control and the ways in which I am powerless. My true success as a caregiver lies in being resilient and being fully, lovingly present with my loved ones in this unpredictable journey.

Are You a Caregiver?

At any given time, more than a quarter of the U.S. adult population—
some 42 million people—are caring for adults. More than eight out of
ten are caring for friends or relatives over the age of 50, according to a
2011 AARP Public Policy Institute study, "Valuing the Invaluable." The
estimated economic value of their annual unpaid effort is $450 billion—
more than the total annual sales of Wal-Mart stores! If you're a caregiver,
you are making a valuable contribution.

- The statistically typical family caregiver is a woman, age 49, who is
  caring for her mother. She provides 20 hours of unpaid care per week
  and does so for nearly five years. She also holds down a paid job.
- Sixty-five percent of family caregivers are women.
- More than half of caregivers are involved in medical/nursing tasks—
  including caring for wounds, managing numerous medications, and
  dealing with incontinence—for those with multiple chronic physical
  and cognitive conditions.
- Nearly half of U.S. family caregivers are caring for loved ones with
  Alzheimer's or serious mental illness (cognitive or behavioral health
  disorders). The number of people with Alzheimer's disease will nearly
  triple by the year 2050.
- One in five family caregivers is a spouse or partner, and compared to
  other family caregivers they are often more vulnerable, have fewer
  resources, and get less help from family and friends.
- Ten percent of family caregivers are African-American; about half of
  African-Americans are or have been family caregivers.
- Eleven percent of family caregivers are Hispanic; more than one in
  three Hispanic households includes a family caregiver.
- As Baby Boomers age, family caregivers will increasingly have fewer
  people to share the care. In 2010, there were seven potential caregivers between the ages of 45 and 65 to care for one person age 80 or
  older. By 2030, that ratio will decline sharply to 4:1 and by 2050, 3:1.
- Family caregivers are vulnerable and at risk themselves in terms of
  their finances, mental and physical health, relationships, and careers.

Many of us are primary caregivers: We lead the support team for the people we care for and often provide most of the care and coordination. Others play a role as part of the caregiving team with family, friends, paid professional therapists, health-care practitioners, and care providers.

You may not think of yourself as a caregiver per se. But if you help out with, provide support for, care for, or check up on a friend, neighbor, parent, spouse, grandparent, or other family member or loved one, you are indeed a caregiver. Whether you do these things every few months, once a week, or every single day, you are a caregiver. Whether you are the only person providing support or you share responsibilities with others, you are a caregiver. If you ever do any of these things to help loved ones, you are a caregiver:

- Help with household tasks, such as cleaning, doing repairs, and caring for the yard.
- Chauffeur them to stores, doctors, faith-community meetings, volunteer activities, the senior center, friends' or relatives' homes, or restaurants.
- Help with researching health conditions and treatment options and making health choices or medical decisions.
- Advocate or provide care in a health-care crisis, such as a hospitalization.
- Order and pick up medications.
- Perform complex medical tasks, such as caring for wounds and giving injections.
- Sort mail.
- Pay bills.
- Oversee investments.
- Understand insurance coverage and manage claims.
- Monitor or help with bathing, toileting, grooming, and dressing.
- Buy groceries and run other errands.
- Prepare meals and monitor nutrition.
- Explain, coordinate, and handle complicated personal, financial, or business matters.
- Help them make decisions about where to live.

- Cover their expenses.
- Coordinate unpaid and professional paid caregivers, therapists, or other support.
- Provide emotional support.
- Initiate or receive phone calls to check in.
- Visit them to see how they are doing.

You may have started helping just now and then, increasing your support over time. Or you may have become a caregiver instantly because of a crisis. You know caregiving is becoming a big part of your life when—

- You squeeze in other friends and family members, recreational activities, exercise, your own medical appointments, and even work only if you find time *after* you take care of your loved ones.
- You are more familiar than they are with their health, finances, and personal affairs.
- You are so worried about their needs that you become anxious and even lose sleep.
- You have their birth dates, Social Security numbers, and insurance information memorized.
- You are on a first-name basis with their pharmacist.
- You are greeted at the hospital emergency room with "welcome back!"
- You are tired from the juggling and the emotional toll. All the time.

If you're doing these things while working a paid job—full-time or part-time, ongoing or seasonal, in an office or factory or store or from home—you are a working caregiver with an extra level of demands. And each aspect of your life comes with a unique set of circumstances to juggle. (You'll find specific resources for working caregivers in Chapter 5.)

A Community of Caregivers

You are in the company of millions of other caregivers, whether you know it or not. The community of caregivers that I've cultivated has been the driving force keeping me going. Throughout this guide, I tap into this community to help you navigate your journey of caregiving.

For many of us, caregiving is a gift of love; others struggle with difficult relationships but still step up to the plate because they feel responsible. Regardless of the motivation, we all struggle at times, and we also have a lot to learn from one another. Our situations may be similar or not, but either way we are each other's most valuable support. I encourage you to connect with other caregivers—talk with your friends, join a support group, or go online through social media such as Facebook or Twitter or online support groups and caregiving websites.

Your Job Description

If you have working experience in paid or volunteer jobs, you've likely had a job description. Your job as a caregiver is just as important. Sometimes you get experience on the job or through trial and error. But caregiving requires hard-earned skills, and you have them all! Look for job descriptions at the end of every chapter in this guide, updating the talents and abilities you hone throughout your tenure as a caregiver. Congratulations—you have earned the title caregiver. Here is your overall caregiving job description.

Job Title: Caregiver

Reports to: Self, conscience, care recipients, primary caregiver or team leader, employer (if working), higher power.

Hours: Unpredictable; days, evenings, nights, weekends, and holidays.

Qualifications: None required but many preferred: compassion, caring, love, patience, stability, humor, humility, ingenuity, energy, commitment, tenacity, strong communication and observational skills, proficiency with technology and medical/legal terminology, ability to perform medical/nursing tasks, attention to detail, organizational skills, and excellent crisis management abilities.

Summary of duties and responsibilities: Assists with or manages loved ones' mental and physical health and care, legal and financial matters, living environment, business matters, activities of daily living (ADLs), and quality of life; serves as advocate for those who are vulnerable. Other duties as assigned with no prior notice. Juggles caregiving with duties and responsibilities from family, personal life, and paid or volunteer work.

Special and challenging demands: Prolonged commitment; sleep deprivation; financial uncertainty; exposure to intense emotions, from great sadness to great joy; precarious personal relationships. Some travel may be required.

Pay: Salary range from $0 to personal rewards such as a clear conscience, smiles, hugs, appreciation, and lots of love. (Some family caregivers may be paid—see Chapter 5.) Potential for bonus of good karma depending on duties performed.

In This Guide

This guide aims to provide you with practical resources and tips that will help you be successful too. Whether you're caregiving day-to-day, planning for future needs, or experiencing a crisis, the resources in this book will be quick and easy to find when you need them. Here are some topics you'll learn about:

- **Reviewing your current situation.** I help you take a 360-degree look at yourself and the people you care for. You'll get a clear picture of needs and resources and create a preliminary plan of action.
- **Caring for yourself.** You may *understand* the need to care for yourself so that you'll be able to care for others, but taking the time to do so is another story. You'll find tips for infusing much-needed time and energy into your own interests and needs.
- **Creating a caregiving team.** No one is caregiving in a vacuum; we all need somebody to lean on, right? Whether you can see it or not, you have—or can form—a team to help you, with team members contributing what and when they can. I help you build your team.
- **Getting—and staying—organized.** Organizing my personal, work, and caregiving lives is the only way I stay sane. You'll learn about

low- and high-tech ways to organize paperwork, information, and environments to save you time, money, and energy.

- **Balancing work and caregiving.** You'll get the scoop on communicating with your employer, taking full advantage of employer benefits such as flexible work schedules and counseling, keeping your career on track, and managing work-life balance.

- **Navigating the legal maze.** Better to deal with tricky legal issues early on than wait for a crisis. I help you understand, in plain language, the basics, including advance directives, powers of attorney, and estate planning.

- **Managing money matters.** From budgets and bill paying to bank accounts and debt, you'll learn to discern when the people you care for need help and how to take steps to increase income and lower expenses.

- **Handling health and medical care.** I spend 90 percent of my caregiving time dealing with health and medical issues. I help you navigate the rough waters of helping your loved ones get and stay happy and healthy (and hopefully *prevent* doctor appointments!), and I offer tips on how to manage complicated medical scenarios.

- **Dealing with living situations.** The people you care for may live in their own or relatives' homes, senior communities, group homes, or independent living, assisted living, or nursing facilities. I help you evaluate their living situation and manage care wherever they live.

- **Getting through a crisis.** Sooner or later, most caregivers deal with an emergency. Crises may occur regularly. You'll find ways to prepare that should decrease your stress in the long run. And I help you manage when you're in the middle of a catastrophe.

- **Experiencing the end of life.** For many of us, caregiving isn't a "short-term and then they get better" scenario. It's a journey that often leads to the end of your loved ones' lives. I provide you with information and resources about how to support the people you care for sensitively through their final days—and how to get through it yourself.

- **Grieving and moving forward.** At some point, your role as a caregiver will probably change. It will transition into a different role because loved ones get better or move or other caregivers step in. Or it will end because your loved ones pass on. Either way, you may experience a sense of loss, guilt, and myriad other feelings. I help you deal with these changes and find your way to the next phase of your life.

- **Finding help.** In addition to helping you connect with other caregivers, I help you draw on a network of national, state, and local organizations that exist to assist caregivers. And I point you to professional caregivers and other services that may be needed for complicated personal, financial, and legal issues. This guide will help you choose the right people to help you *and* the people you care for.

In addition to this book, you may also want to consult *Checklist for Family Caregivers: A Guide to Making It Manageable* by Sally Hurme, also from AARP and the American Bar Association (AARP.org/ChecklistCaregivers). A companion guide to this book, *Checklist for Family Caregivers* walks you through getting and staying organized.

CHAPTER 1

YOUR CAREGIVING PLAN

The first time I got a good sense of my parents' overall situation and spoke with them about their long-term plans was when Dad, then 72, retired. They were in pretty good health, despite Mom's stroke about seven years prior. Dad was a strong, independent man whose greatest desire was to take care of Mom and enjoy life. Mom's priority was to stay in their home, and they had a financial adviser who was helping them do so. Dad soon became an active AARP volunteer, so he had plenty of intellectual stimulation and socialization, and Mom joined him frequently for meetings and events. They owned long-term care insurance, should they ever need it. And they had advance directives (a living will and powers of attorney) and a living trust.

My three sisters and I also assessed our situations and made a simple plan: We would visit more, help as needed when our parents traveled, support them when major health issues or other challenges arose, and monitor their medications and safety.

Since then, all our needs and situations have changed, as has our family's plan. As my parents' health declined, we got them more help with house and yard work. They spent time every summer with my sister Linda in Ohio. My sister Karen, in Maryland, visited them when she could. For a time, my sister Susie managed their health care, and I managed their finances from a distance. When Dad's dementia worsened, I moved to Arizona to take on an increased role, and since then my sisters' roles have also changed.

1

Every time I think we have a solid plan in place, our health or financial circumstances change. That means our caregiving plan is a moving target, involving a constant process of reevaluating and adapting. The one constant is this: At every step, my parents' health, desires, and quality of life are the primary drivers.

Introduction

Whether you are suddenly thrust into a caregiving role or gradually take on increasing responsibilities, it's crucial that you take the time to create a caregiving plan. Your plan will be a "living" document, as it will change over time, but it provides a clear framework to go back to and revise as needs change. Having this in place will save you time, money, and a lot of stress.

Vital first steps are reviewing yours *and* your loved ones' needs—both initially and then periodically as circumstances change. It's so easy to get caught up in just doing the next thing or responding to other people's needs as they arise. No one can do it all, so this process will help you determine what you can realistically give and help you better communicate with other team members what you can and can't do. The 360-degree assessments of you and your loved ones also help you identify any additional assistance that is needed. Then you can make a game plan for going forward.

In this chapter you'll learn how to:
- Review your situation.
- Get a handle on your loves ones' needs, living situations, and options for care.
- Identify available resources.
- Determine how you can help, where there are gaps, and how others might help.
- Create a simple caregiving plan.

Your Five-Step Caregiving Plan

You have a big job to do, and many caregivers tell me they are over-whelmed and just don't know where to start. You'll need a plan to juggle life, caregiving, and any paid job you may have.

You can create a viable caregiving plan in five simple steps. I recommend that you make a chart, table, or spreadsheet to lay out your plan so you can track all the components easily. I used large flip charts with my parents so they could easily see all the options and make choices. Keep digital copies on your computer or mobile device so you can readily access the plan, review and revise it, and share it with others. You'll find more on incorporating technology in Chapter 4.

Below are the key components of the caregiving plan:

Step 1: Conduct a 360-degree review of your own needs, abilities, and goals.

Step 2: Conduct a 360-degree review of your loved ones' needs, abilities, and goals.

Step 3: List goals, needs, resources, and gaps.

Step 4: Determine how to fill the gaps.

Step 5: Create a realistic budget to support the caregiving plan.

Step 1: Conduct a 360-Degree Review of Your Own Needs, Abilities, and Goals

When it comes to caregiving, your instinct might be to start with an evaluation of the people you are caring for, but I suggest you start with yourself. If you do, you're more likely to be aware of how much you have to offer and to feel good about what you are doing. You're also more likely to be cognizant of your strengths and your limits, where you could benefit from training, and where additional help is needed.

A self-assessment is a process of stepping back and taking an honest look at yourself as objectively as possible. The self-assessment, along with your loved ones' evaluation, will help you develop your overall caregiving plan. You will also use the information you gather here in many other ways throughout your caregiving journey, from juggling your life, family, work, and caregiving responsibilities to taking care of yourself, to making decisions about your loved ones' care, to handling the end of their lives and eventually moving on from caregiving.

In a work setting, a 360-degree assessment usually involves getting input from your surrounding colleagues, including those who report to you and your supervisors. For your caregiving review, it can be helpful to ask key people in your life—such as your partner, relatives, and friends—to provide input. But because you're likely feeling very vulnerable right now, be as specific as possible when you ask them questions, and be clear that you are not inviting them to dump on or criticize you; you simply want their productive thoughts and ideas to help you gain a 360-degree view of your entire situation.

You can keep this review simple by reading sample questions I've listed below and contemplating your responses. Or you can create a document or start a journal to record your reactions and any other thoughts that come up. I recommend that, if possible, you use your computer or mobile device and create a digital document that can be copied, periodically updated, or shared with others. (See Chapter 4 for more suggestions.) Don't let the questions overwhelm you; you may not have all the answers right now. Use them to jump-start your thinking, and go back to reassess throughout your caregiving journey, because these aspects of your life will undoubtedly change over time.

Your Personal Life

Your personality: Your personality is an important piece of the equation when it comes to caregiving. Some people are more suited to certain caregiving tasks than others. Ask yourself: What are your attitudes about caring for others? What are your individual traits? What makes you happy, frustrated, bored, or exhausted? Are you generally upbeat, positive, and optimistic? Are you a worrier? Do you make decisions easily or take more time? What do you need from others? Do you get energized interacting with other people (an extrovert) or being alone (an introvert)? Are you a risk-taker? Are you more flexible or do you like to have a plan and be in control?

Your values: Your values will have a strong influence on how you approach caregiving. Ask yourself where your priorities fall—being with and supporting family and friends? Your work? Your religious beliefs? Other interests and beliefs? Which do you value more, independence and autonomy or interpersonal relationships? Are you willing to make sacrifices to live out your values?

Your religious or faith beliefs: Many caregivers say their faith is a big help throughout their caregiving experience. Ask yourself: Is religion a foundation in your life? Are you active in your faith community? Does it host caregiver or other types of support groups or programs? Are there volunteers through your faith community who can help support you and your loved ones? Would it be helpful to reconnect with past faith practices?

Your skills and abilities: You bring a lifetime of experience to your caregiving role. Ask yourself: What skills do you have that might be useful to caregiving? Are you good at cleaning, helping others, organizing, communicating, tracking paperwork, nurturing, observing, note-taking, researching, shopping, maintaining and fixing cars, caring for animals, listening, cooking, handling money? What other abilities might come in handy?

Your learning and adapting styles: Caregiving may involve learning new skills, and people adjust differently. Ask yourself: Do you learn new skills easily or does it take time and effort? How do you learn best—by reading, doing, watching, or listening? Online or in person? Do you jump into new things or assimilate slowly? Do you find new or unfamiliar things intimidating or exciting?

Your interests and activities: You may have interests and experience that will contribute to your caregiving in surprising ways. It's also important to keep up with some activities that nurture you when caregiving depletes your energies. Ask yourself: What do you gain the most fulfillment from? What are your hobbies? How do you prefer to spend free time? Do the people you care for share your interests? Are there things you can do that your loved ones would enjoy learning or watching you do? What do you do to relax? What gets you excited?

Your short- and long-term goals and priorities: When caregiving, it's easy to lose sight of your own goals, and your priorities often change. Take stock of what you want in life; even if you need to adjust your goals, don't lose sight of them completely. Ask yourself: What are your dreams and desires? Have you been planning a vacation? Are you moving? Retiring? Dating or getting married? Spending time with children or grandchildren? Buying a new car or house? Building your career or starting a new job? Writing a book or a blog? Losing weight? Starting a new exercise program? Planting a garden? Learning about investments? How do you prioritize your goals? Where do the people who need care fit into your priorities?

Your family, friends, and significant relationships: Your family and friends are a big part of your life and support system. You don't want other relationships to suffer when you're caregiving. But realistically, adjustments may be necessary. Ask yourself: Who are you responsible for and what are their needs? Who are you closest to? Who do you have a difficult relationship with? Where are your loved ones living? Are your relationships suffering because of the stress of care? Which relationships make you happiest? Also, be sure to take an honest look at your relationship with the person you are caring for and how it affects your perspective on providing care.

Your responsibilities: Caregiving doesn't happen in a vacuum; the rest of life goes on. Consider *all* that is on your plate—it may illuminate why you feel so overwhelmed at times and help you feel freer to seek assistance. Ask yourself: What are your top responsibilities—family, work (see more below), home and other real estate properties, animals, partnerships, vehicles, friends or neighbors, volunteer activities, financial obligations? Do you anticipate additional new responsibilities coming up? How would you prioritize your responsibilities?

Your support system: Every caregiver needs support. We all have a different mix of people who sustain us and help care for our loved ones. Ask yourself: Who supports you, both emotionally and in practical, day-to-day ways? Who in your immediate family is involved in your loved ones' care? Do you ask for help? Can you count on them to complete a task adequately and on time? Is it more stressful for you to do it all or to sometimes be disappointed by people who make promises but don't come through? Who would you like to become more involved? Who and where are your closest friends? Can your friends help you in person or from a distance? Can you make new friends and build your support system in other ways? Are there professional people you count on (such as professional caregivers, counselors, mediators, financial managers, cleaning professionals, organizers, and assistants)? Do you participate in a caregiver support group?

Your hygiene and home care: It's amazing the extent we caregivers can neglect our own personal needs. Ask yourself: Are you taking care of yourself in general? Do you bathe often enough, get your hair washed and cut, manicure your nails? Are you keeping up with laundry and wearing clean clothes that fit you? Is your appearance appropriate when you show up for work? Is there shopping you need to do? Do you change the bedding regularly? Is your house clean? Is there moldy food in your refrigerator? Is there any food at all in your refrigerator?

Physical health: Many caregivers put their own physical health needs aside while focusing on the people they care for. Ask yourself: Are you keeping up with your treatment plans for specific health challenges? Do you have physical limitations that affect your caregiving abilities? Are you sleeping well and long enough? Are you getting your routine health exams, screenings, and immunizations? Are you taking your prescribed medications? Have you gained or lost weight? Are you eating well? Are you exercising?

Mental health: Caregiving can be mentally and emotionally exhausting. Many struggle with the emotional roller coaster. And if you already have a mental illness, it can be intensified. Ask yourself: Are you managing your mental health issues in appropriate and healthy ways? Are you feeling hopeless or depressed? Do you frequently feel anxious and overwhelmed? Are you crying a lot? Feeling alone? Experiencing mood swings? Do you have healthy coping mechanisms? Could you benefit from some professional mental health help?

Your finances and legal affairs: Your own financial security is, of course, very important for you to keep up when you are caregiving. Compared to people who aren't caregiving, many of us have less money coming in but have to spend more. Ask yourself: What is the state of your financial security? Do you have savings you can tap into? Are you on track for your retirement savings? Are you paying bills and taxes on time? Do have adequate income to cover your expenses? Do others depend on you financially? Is there any flexibility in the budget to help support your loved ones or to pay for additional help you are unable to provide? Can your budget handle less income if you have to make a change in your work? Do you have adequate insurance? Do you have a will or living trust and advance directives? (You'll find more on legal affairs and finances in Chapters 6 and 7.)

Your caregiving responsibilities: Since you may already be in the throes of caregiving, be sure to include an inventory of ways you are already supporting your loved ones. Ask yourself: Are you helping with their finances or home? Are you helping with "activities of daily living" (more on this below), such as bathing, grooming, eating, and toileting? Are you cooking or cleaning for them? How much time are you spending on caregiving?

Your Work Life

Your work history and current job: Look back over your work history and, if you are currently working, at your current job (or jobs) to get a handle on your breadth of experience. Ask yourself: What kinds of jobs have you held? What are your key work skills? Do you enjoy your work? Is it stressful? Do you feel you are on the right career path? Would you like to make a change in your work life? Have you not been working but need to start again? Do you feel that work is a healthy break from caregiving? Has work been a big part of your self-identity?

Your current workplace realities: If you are currently working, it's a good idea to have an accurate view of the limits and boundaries in your current job. Ask yourself: What hours or shifts are you working? Is there any flexibility in your work schedule or could you change hours? Do you have paid vacation, personal or sick leave? Can you use Family and Medical Leave Act (FMLA) time? Are you getting all of your work done on time? Are you able to make personal phone calls from work at any time? Could you work a compressed schedule (longer days but fewer days), telecommute from home or work remotely, or share your job with someone else? Does your company have an office closer to your loved ones' home from which you could work? Is it possible to go from full- to part-time work within your company, or work different hours? Might another position in your company work better for you? Is it more important to you to make more money or to work fewer hours? Are there ways you could do both? Do you feel comfortable being honest with your colleagues and manager about being a caregiver or do you keep it to yourself?

Your employer's policies regarding working caregivers: Some employers support work-life balance. If you're currently working, or if you're looking for a job, find out if your current or prospective employer has any resources in place that may be helpful to you. Ask yourself: Does your employer know you are caregiving? Does your employer support work-life balance in principle and in practice? Is your direct supervisor willing to be flexible so you can meet both your work and caregiving responsibilities? Are there any specific supports for families, caregivers, or eldercare? Does your employer offer an Employee Assistance Program (EAP)? Can you use your sick leave to care for loved ones? How much leave do you accumulate? Can co-workers donate their vacation or sick leave to you?

You'll find more about work issues while caregiving in Chapter 5.

Step 2: Conduct a 360-Degree Review of Your Loved Ones' Needs, Abilities, and Goals

Before Maureen Statland's father became ill, she had just a vague idea of his financial situation, his health, and his plans for the future. Only when his liver disease became acute did she and her sister begin to frequently discuss with him his state of affairs and desires in detail. "The legal paperwork he had in place was very general," Maureen says, "but conversations about what he wanted—and especially what he didn't want—along with what was important to him in life made it so much easier for us to evaluate and continuously revise our plan as caregiving intensified."

You'll want to take a good look at your loved ones' overall situation, just as you evaluated yours. A clear, comprehensive review of their health, living situation, needs, and abilities helps identify risks and determine their safety and level of independence. An understanding of their financial and other resources will help you know how to pay for their housing and care. Accurate perspectives of their opinions, philosophies, beliefs, goals, wishes, likes, and dislikes will guide decision-making about the kind of care they receive and the quality of life that is important to them.

Remember to always keep in mind: Your role as a caregiver is to support your loved ones' overall health, safety, and financial well-being, but equally important is their quality of life. Your focus may be on helping them stay healthy and alive, but you're also helping to make their life worth living.

Unless health conditions of the people you care for preclude their participation, it's vital that you involve them in assessments and discussions about their care. (For suggestions on broaching this topic, see Tips for Challenging Conversations in the appendix.) Their involvement will give them more control over their lives and help them feel more comfortable with the caregiving plans. I suggest you start by talking with them first, if possible. Document your views as well, and also get perspectives from other key people, including family members, friends, and professionals who work with your loved ones (and who may have completed more formal evaluations that can inform your own caregiving-plan process). Then you can go back again and discuss these issues with the people you care for, sharing additional perspectives and input if they were not able to participate in the other conversations.

You can coordinate this review yourself or you can hire someone, such as a geriatric care manager, case manager, or social worker. (Contact your local area agency on aging, the National Association of Professional Geriatric Care Managers or the Case Management Society of America to find someone locally to help with an assessment. See Resources for contact information.) Your employer may have eldercare supports or contracts with companies that provide discounted or free evaluations.

Their Personal Lives

I urge you to first take a look at who your loved ones *are* before considering what they can or can't *do*. We often get so caught up in the basics of care that we forget they are people too: human beings with experiences, desires, dreams, and goals.

Just as you looked at yourself, take stock of your loved ones by referring to the same questions I outlined above in your self-assessment regarding these areas:

- **Their personalities:** Personality drives us and will help determine how your loved ones receive care and deal with aging, loss, and illnesses.
- **Their values:** What do your loved ones feel strongly about? Their values may differ from yours, and if they do, it doesn't mean either one of you is right or wrong. Just different.
- **Their faith:** Religious beliefs and practices may become increasingly important to the people you care for. They may benefit from connection to their faith; their care facilities, volunteers, or service providers may help maintain that.
- **Their learning and adapting styles:** The people you care for are having new experiences. Understanding how they adapt to new situations and learn new skills can help you coordinate their care.
- **Their skills and abilities:** Remember that your loved ones have a lifetime of experience too. They may have skills and abilities that they aren't fully using but that you can bring out in them.
- **Their interests and activities:** Just because the people you care for need care or support doesn't mean they can't still enjoy their interests and activities. You can help incorporate them into daily life, even if adaptations are necessary.
- **Their short- and long-term goals and priorities:** Become aware of their goals and priorities so you can help them achieve their dreams. For example, if staying in their home or being near family or friends is a top priority, you can have that in mind as you look at possible living situations.
- **Their family, friends, and significant relationships:** Making a list of significant people in your loved ones' lives can help you understand who they view as important, who has the ability to affect their quality of life, and who you might include in your caregiving team. (See Chapter 3.)

- **Their responsibilities:** The people you care for may need support, but they may still have responsibilities for their home, volunteer activities, and loved ones. We began supporting Dad when he was still caring for Mom.
- **Their support system:** Who is helping your loved ones? Getting a handle on the people and resources they view as supportive and who you actually see helping them can provide important perspectives.

Their Living Situation

Their home setting will have a bearing on the types of support and care they need and how it is delivered. Evaluate the safety of their environment (don't assume they are safe just because they are living in a facility), including accessibility, smoke and other safety alarms, and safety from intruders and door-to-door telemarketers and scammers. Your assessment will differ depending on their living situation. If the people you care for live in a facility, personally assess the situation to be sure what is promised is actually delivered. (You'll find more about living situations in Chapters 9 and 10.)

- **In their own home:** Are they living alone or with a spouse or others? Do they have full responsibility for the care of the home? What, if any, in-home professional services and support do they receive? Do they drive or use public transportation?
- **Independent living:** Your loved ones may live in an independent living facility, where they have their own apartment and live independently, with some services provided, such as meals, housecleaning, and activities. What other services do they receive, perhaps for a fee, such as medication reminders or help with bathing and laundry? Do your loved ones drive, or does the facility provide transportation to activities and medical appointments?
- **Assisted living:** This is an increased level of care from independent living. Services and costs can vary greatly. Generally, staff provide assistance in the morning and evening with bathing and dressing as well as medication management, meals, and some activities. What services are provided, for a fee or included? Be sure to personally

assess the situation. Don't assume someone will be checking on your loved ones all day, or that staff will be at their beck and call. A resident will have a call button to get help, but I've observed that response time can be as much as half an hour. It's really not 24-hour, hands-on care or attention. For most facilities, residents can still come and go as they please, so don't assume someone will know if your loved ones leave the facility.

- **Skilled nursing facility:** If your loved ones live in a skilled nursing facility (sometimes called a nursing home), they probably require a higher level of medical care. The facility will provide meals and activities like other levels of care, but with more supervision and hands-on care (at least in theory). Your loved ones may be bedridden or they may be up and about. They will likely have call buttons, but again, make a personal assessment. I've found these facilities are often short-staffed (even if they meet state standards) and not able to provide as much attention to your loved ones as you might like or they might need.

- **Memory care facility:** If your loved ones have dementia, they may be in a special program geared for those with memory impairment. These facilities offer meals, activities, and assistance with bathing, dressing, and medications, and there is generally a higher staff-to-resident ratio and more supervision and security measures to ensure that a confused resident doesn't leave the grounds and get lost. But again, assess the situation carefully. Don't expect that the people you care for will have someone constantly by their side unless you hire a private-pay aide.

- **Continuing care retirement communities (CCRCs):** These usually, but not always, include all the previous levels of care on one campus. If your loved ones live in a CCRC, they can move between levels of care as their health situations change. You'll want to separately assess the services in each level of care—for example, you might find the independent living meets your qualifications but the skilled nursing falls short.

- **Group homes or board-and-care homes:** Your loved ones may live in a neighborhood home setting in which several people are cared for by the homeowner or live-in staff. These facilities are labeled differently across the states. The services offered vary greatly, but they offer meals and usually help with bathing, dressing, and medications. Some activities may be offered. They may provide more one-to-one care because they are smaller, or they may offer *less* because they have fewer staff. The attention your loved ones receive may vary a great deal from home to home.

Activities of Daily Living

When assessing your loved ones' abilities and needs, you'll want to evaluate how much help they need to complete "activities of daily living" (ADLs) or "instrumental activities of daily living" (IADLs), including:

- Caring for themselves, including bathing, shaving, washing and styling their hair, dressing, brushing their teeth, grooming, caring for nails, toileting and dealing with incontinence.
- Preparing meals, feeding and eating, including getting food to their mouths, chewing, and swallowing.
- Managing their health care, including making and attending doctor appointments, scheduling tests, tracking results and instructions, and keeping records of their health issues.
- Taking the correct prescription and over-the-counter medicines and supplements in the correct dosages and at the proper times.
- Communicating, including being able to convey ideas and deal with an emergency.
- Ambulating or mobility, including getting out of a chair and walking or getting around using an assistive device, such as a walker or wheelchair.
- Driving or managing transportation to doctors, shopping, their faith community, and other places.
- Completing housework and chores.
- Managing money, including handling bills and bank, investment, and retirement accounts.
- Shopping for clothing, groceries, household goods, and other items.
- Using technology, such as a telephone, computer, mobile phone, security system, or other devices.

- Taking care of pets, including feeding, exercising, and cleaning up after them.
- Staying safe from crime and falls or injuries in their living environment, and being able to handle an emergency.

Physical Health

Understand the basics of the medical history and current health situation of the people you care for. (You'll find more about how to help them manage their health in Chapter 8.) In addition to their basic ability to handle the activities of daily living described above, ask these questions, which can help point to the level of care they need now or will need in the future:

- Do they have a written or digitally stored medical history?
- Do they have a list of all their doctors and contact information?
- What are their major medical issues? Include chronic conditions and illnesses (such as diabetes, heart disease, arthritis, COPD, dementia, and high blood pressure) as well as any current acute medical conditions.
- Are they keeping up with treatment of current conditions?
- What is their pain level? Is pain kept under control? Do they have unusual swelling?
- Are they getting routine health exams, immunizations, and tests?
- Do they have any dental problems? Do they have dentures?
- Do they have visual conditions, such as glaucoma, macular degeneration, or cataracts? Do they wear glasses and are prescriptions up to date?
- Do they have a hearing impairment? Do they wear or need hearing aids or another type of hearing device?
- Are they eating well?
- Have they gained or lost an unusual amount of weight?
- Are they sleeping well and long enough?
- Do they get adequate exercise?
- What prescribed and over-the-counter medications are they taking? Are they taking them regularly as prescribed? Do they organize their medications or is someone helping them? Do they get medication

reminders or does someone administer their medications to them? Has a doctor and/or pharmacist reviewed their comprehensive list of medications and supplements to screen for any adverse interactions?

Mental Health

Your loved ones' emotional and mental health needs are just as important as their physical health, and the two interact constantly. It's not uncommon for older adults to develop depression or other mental health problems, sometimes concurrent with health issues such as stroke, heart disease, or dementia. Ask these questions:

- Are your loved ones isolated? Do they have opportunities to socialize and interact?
- Do they feel sad, hopeless, depressed, anxious, or overwhelmed? Do they cry a lot?
- Do they experience mood swings?
- Do they exhibit rage or angry outbursts?
- Have they been unusually forgetful lately?
- Are they maintaining their interests?
- Have they been diagnosed with dementia or any mental illnesses?
- Do they have professional mental health help?
- Are they taking any prescription medications for mental illness?
- Do they feel they have a purpose in life? Do they engage in purposeful activities?
- Do they feel they have a good quality of life?

Health, Disability, and Long-Term Care Insurance

You'll learn more about insurance in Chapter 7. Meanwhile, assess what insurance coverage your loved ones have so you can help manage claims and make sure they are receiving all possible benefits and coverage. Find out about their policies for physical and mental health, dental, vision, disability, and long-term care insurance. Keep in mind they may have more than one insurance policy.

Legal Affairs

You'll learn more about legal issues in Chapter 6. For now, simply find out if the people you care for have any of the following in place:

- Advance directives (living will, power of attorney for health care, power of attorney for mental health care, do not resuscitate orders, or other advance health-care orders).
- Power of attorney for finances and digital power of attorney.
- Estate-planning documents (will, living trust, or others).

Finances

You'll need to assess your loved ones' abilities to manage their finances and pay for their expenses and care. You'll find out more about helping with finances in Chapter 7. For now, determine the basics:

- Are they paying their bills and taxes on time?
- Do they have enough income and savings to pay for their monthly expenses now and in the future?
- Is anyone helping them with finances?
- Is there flexibility in their budget to pay professional caregivers to help with tasks you are unable to do?

Paid or Volunteer Services Your Loved Ones Receive

Finish your loved ones' assessment by listing volunteer or professional services they currently receive, either at home or in a facility. Services may include:

- Help with personal care
- Meal preparation or home-delivered meals
- Housework, chores, or yard care
- Transportation
- Adult health or care services at a daytime facility
- Financial management
- Legal assistance

- Physical, speech, occupational, recreation, music, or creative arts therapy
- Hydrotherapy
- Massage therapy
- Friendly visits or companionship
- Transportation
- Hair and nail care.

Step 3: List Goals, Needs, Resources, and Gaps

Next you'll use the information you gathered in your assessments to make simple lists of goals, needs, and resources. If you create a chart, spreadsheet, or table electronically—or use paper or a flip chart—you can easily see how needs and resources line up and where the gaps are.

Goals and Needs

Drawing from your loved ones' assessments, write out clear goals that came up. Are they on track with their goals? Then record the unmet needs or changes that are needed for them to stay in line with their goals while being safe, healthy, happy, and as independent as possible for as long as possible. In what ways do your loved ones need more support or care? Do they need minimal personal assistance but more help managing finances and projects? Are they managing their lives but feeling isolated and depressed? There may be a wide range of needs, such as researching medical conditions, going out for fun more often, getting transportation to medical appointments, managing paperwork and finances, connecting via technology, or getting hands-on care with personal needs. Your list should include their needs pertaining to these areas:

- Activities of daily living
- Health
- Safety
- Housing
- Socialization
- Transportation
- Finances
- Legal

Existing Resources

Again, drawing from your 360-degree reviews, make a list of all existing resources that are available to address your loved ones' needs. Be realistic about how far the money can go and what you and other team members can contribute. Which current resources can be used to meet their needs and bring about necessary changes? Include all these types of resources and anything else that can help meet needs, such as:

- Funds
- People: yourself, other friends or family, and volunteer and paid professionals (see Chapter 3 for more ideas on who can contribute on your caregiving team)
- Housing
- Transportation
- Technology and equipment

Gaps

Take a look at the goals and needs you've listed and line them up with existing resources. Do you already have all the resources needed to fill the gaps or are new resources needed? Determine gaps between goals and needs and resources. For example, perhaps your loved ones' goal is to stay in their home as they age. You'll look at existing resources. Maybe they have enough for home maintenance and housekeeping, but the house needs modifications to be safe, and they don't have adequate funds to pay for the changes. Or perhaps your loved ones need more socialization to prevent isolation, and the nearby senior center offers free transportation to activities that could meet that need, but your loved ones aren't signed up for this service. This step will help you see more clearly where to focus your energies.

Step 4: Determine How to Fill the Gaps

This is where you'll identify additional resources that are needed. The gaps will likely require a mix of resources, such as people to provide care, coordinate services, or assist you in finding solutions; a change in your loved ones' living situation; technology to ensure their safety, decrease isolation, or improve mobility; services such as transportation, yard care, personal care, or housekeeping; and money to pay for it all.

List needed resources, and then prioritize. Remember, there will likely be more than you alone can do, so you'll need your caregiving team to help accomplish the plan. (See Chapter 4 for more on working with a caregiving team.) Identify the top three priorities and start there.

Your Contributions

First, compare the gaps that need to be filled with what you learned in your self-assessment. Given your life situation, what resources can you offer? Are you able to address all their unmet needs? Can you offer hands-on care? Is long-distance support an option? Can you coordinate care, but do you need help from others to implement it? List the things that you can realistically do to help.

Reevaluating the Gaps

Now that you've filled in what you're able to do to help, are there still gaps? Do your loved ones need help from other sources? Do you need help in your personal or work life to free you up so you can focus more on the people you care for? Does someone else need to be the team leader?

Additional Help

Go back to your assessments and look at family, friends, and work and community resources. Who can take on broader responsibilities and who can complete smaller, specific tasks? After you've exhausted all those possibilities, determine how much professional paid help is needed.

Team Members and Their Roles

To complete this step of the caregiving plan, list everyone (including you) who is providing support, their broad or specific responsibilities, specific tasks, and time lines for accomplishment. Share a copy with everyone on the team so they can understand their unique roles and how everyone is working together. You'll also be able to see how balanced the plan is, in terms of both how your loved ones' needs are met and each person's load. (See Chapter 3 for more on teamwork.)

Step 5: Create a Realistic Budget to Support the Caregiving Plan

A budget that includes income and expenses associated with your loved ones' care will help you establish and monitor financial resources. Do your loved ones have financial resources to pay for all that you and other family members and friends cannot accomplish? How long will the money last? Can you or another family member help pay? Is it time to begin collecting long-term care insurance benefits? Are there veteran's or other benefits available? (See Chapter 7 for more about increasing income.)

Review, Adapt, Revise . . . Repeat

Once you've implemented your plan, you'll probably find you need to fine-tune it as you go along. Even seemingly minor adjustments such as insurance changes, vacations, or extra work will demand changes to the plan. Sometimes a health condition or illness can throw the whole plan off kilter, and you'll have to create new goals. Financial needs and resources may change. Team members may drop off. Others may be able to take on more responsibility.

I recommend that you view the caregiving plan as a framework—a place to start. I thought we had a plan in place when my parents moved to a continuing care retirement community. But when their care needs increased and we realized we couldn't afford the facility plus the additional care they needed, the plan went out the window and they moved back to their home with me. I learned the importance of not getting too tied to the plan. At first, I felt I'd failed to plan well, but then I realized that a plan is like a map, and sometimes we decide to go to another destination, get thrown off course by a roadblock, or take detours. Having a base to come back to is crucial to keep yourself on track when changes and crises occur. Just "winging it" over time will cause you more stress, and you'll be thrown off course more easily. Your goal as a caregiver is to be resilient; a plan will help you bounce back and focus more efficiently on needed changes when caregiving takes you to your knees. Accepting the fact that the plan will change helps me be more flexible and adaptable, which lowers my stress levels. You can always make a change later.

Your Job Description: Planner

Congratulations! You've taken an honest look at your own personal and work situations, coordinated a review of your loved ones' complicated status, and created a plan. You've earned another new job description:

Collects a range of data regarding self, loved ones, family, friends, and community. Reviews data and assesses needs versus resources. Conducts difficult family conversations with diplomacy and respect. Prepares broad strategies and specific task-oriented plans based on assessments. Coordinates team evaluation, review of plans, and periodic revisions. Implements plan directly or coordinates implementation by team members.

CHAPTER 2

CARING FOR YOU, THE CAREGIVER

I lay there wide awake in the roll-away bed, springs from the mattress poking me between the ribs. My chest felt tight, my heart was pounding, and I struggled to breathe. I just wanted to sleep, but my body wouldn't calm down. I got up and stretched, walked the hall a few times, sniffed lavender essential oil, and practiced a calming meditation. Nothing worked. The flashing lights didn't help much. Nor the constant beep-beep-beep of the machines. I began to panic.

I'd lost track of how many nights I'd slept next to Mom in her hospital bed—30? She'd had a bad fall and fractured her spine, developed an irregular heartbeat, contracted a horrible intestinal infection (C Diff.) in the hospital, gone into congestive heart failure, suffered a heart attack, became septic (her whole body, including her blood, was infected) . . . the list went on. She'd been through the wringer, and I'd been by her side almost the entire time. With my panic symptoms persisting, I began to wonder if I should walk down to the emergency room and get myself checked out. Maybe I was having a heart attack.

I eventually got a little sleep that night. But the incident scared me, so I went to see my doctor right away. Her diagnoses: stress to the point of burnout resulting in anxiety, insomnia, and exacerbated asthma. My body was reacting to the extended and intensive stressors of staying with Mom, making decisions about her care, losing sleep, worrying about her pain, fearing for her life, managing Dad's care and working at the same time. That night was a wake-up call for me. We all do what we have to do in crisis situations, but sooner or later we suffer the consequences. I knew I needed to take better care of myself.

Introduction

Let's face it: Caregiving can be a very rewarding experience, but it can also be draining. As caregivers, we give and give— so it should come as no surprise when we crash. Your intentions may be good, but if you don't take care of yourself, you will not be as good at taking care of someone else or, if you're also working a paid job, performing work duties. Think of the oxygen-mask analogy: First put on yours and then help those in need. You may feel at the mercy of the needs of your loved ones, but always remember: You do have choices. You've *chosen* to care for friends or family members, and you can also choose to take care of yourself. It's not an either/or decision. Look at yourself as you do your loved ones; you are equally important in the equation, and as a caregiver you are also vulnerable. What are your basic needs? What do you need to keep going? I often remind myself that I don't expect my car to run on an empty tank of gas, but I seem to expect myself to run on an empty tank of energy. What are you doing to keep your own tank full?

In this chapter you'll learn how to:
- Understand the wide range of emotions that working caregivers feel.
- Recognize stress and how it affects you.
- Develop coping mechanisms to deal with difficult emotions and stress.
- Find help so you can take a well-deserved break.
- Keep your finances in order and your career on track.

The Emotional Roller Coaster

Being a caregiver can be physically depleting, but I find that dealing with the emotions is my biggest challenge, especially when I'm tired (which is most of the time). Our minds and hearts can feel so depleted; we're weary to the bone. I want to be tough and not let things get to me, but sometimes I have a meltdown. We caregivers may look OK on the outside, and people marvel at us—what wonderful caregivers we are, how much we get done, how we keep doing our jobs while we are caregiving—but in reality we're not sure how we will make it through the day. It's total internal overload. And that's OK. Be gentle with yourself. Whatever you're feeling—and you're probably experiencing a range of feelings—is normal.

Love, Joy, and Happiness

First, keep in mind that caregiving is not all about difficult emotions. Happiness, love, warmth, closeness, and contentment are a vital part of our caregiving experience. I have worked very hard to create moments of great joy with my parents, as well as to be mindful and notice the more subtle everyday joys. I'll never forget the elation I felt when Mom took her first tentative steps after the surgery for her fractured spine—we had worried she might never walk again. Every time I enjoy a beautiful sunset with Dad, I feel tremendous peace and gratitude. I have felt happiness when we sing or play a game together. The smile on Mom's face as I tucked her into bed is still ever-present in my mind, and I'm so glad I stopped to enjoy that moment every night. Every time Dad relaxes and is visibly relieved when I come home to be with him fills me with a deep sense of love and the knowledge that I'm doing the right thing. Just knowing that I have helped my parents, who have done so much for their family, brings me a great sense of fulfillment. These are my caregiving triumphs, and I treasure them. These emotions are so real and significant, and yet we tend to give them short shrift.

Frustration and Anger

Frustration and anger come up often when we spend numerous hours dealing with the medical system and service providers. We may feel frustrated, resentful, hurt, and disappointed when members of our caregiving team don't live up to their responsibilities or support us. We may feel frustrated and angry with ourselves, too, when we make mistakes, don't get our work done, or forget things. If we are working while caregiving, we may feel frustrated with co-workers who don't understand the burdens we bear or, worse yet, do understand but just don't care, or make our work lives more difficult.

And often we lose patience or feel incredibly angry at the people we are caring for, perhaps when they give up or don't try to get better, complain, are difficult to please, or don't seem to appreciate or value us. We may get frustrated because they are dependent upon us and keep us from other parts of our lives. For some of us, our loved ones cause financial strain. Those caring for people with dementia may get frustrated when they repeatedly ask the same question or fail to understand what we are trying to convey.

Guilt

Once we've experienced anger at the very loved ones who need us so much, then the guilt kicks in. Guilt is our constant companion. We feel guilty when we are not with those we are caring for because we are working, taking care of ourselves, or spending time with other people. Yet when we are with our loved ones, we feel guilty because we are not doing those other things. We worry about decisions we make for the people we care for and feel guilty if things don't turn out the way we had hoped. We feel like we never do enough. We even feel guilty for feeling guilty!

Sadness

Inherently, caregiving is a process of loss. When our loved ones need support, it's never for a good reason. Even if it's temporary, they are experiencing changes that prevent them from complete independence. Whether the change is small, such as the inability to clean the house, or overwhelming, as for those who have dementia, it's still a loss. And for many, a slow process of loss continues over a long period of time. I often liken it to water torture—my parents' abilities slowly declining, one drip at a time. One small drip doesn't get to me, but over time it eats away at me and periodically sadness overwhelms me.

Discouragement

We often feel inadequate or incapable of handling caregiving tasks. We may feel discouraged or disheartened when we are unable to keep up with all that is on our plate. Sometimes we may even see ourselves as complete failures.

Fear and Worry

Caregivers have a lot to fret about. We know worrying doesn't help, but that doesn't stop us. We worry about making decisions and what will happen "if." We agonize about the future, the bills that must be paid, and the needs that must be met. We fear the loss of our loved ones, and yet we fear that caregiving will go on and on. We panic when we realize that someday we may also need this type of support; we wonder who will care for *us*.

Powerlessness

This is, perhaps, the most challenging emotion of all. We feel unable to stop the progression of a disease or solve the financial problems, unable to find the right treatment or medication to ease our loved one's pain, unable to stop the changes happening all around us, and unable to get everything done. The sense of powerlessness can be overwhelming, and it's difficult to accept that we cannot control everything.

Recognizing Stress

Believe it or not, stress is actually not all bad! In fact, there are many good stressors in our lives. Stress is simply your body's reaction to what is going on both internally (your emotions and thoughts) and externally (caregiving, your job, a sports event, a wedding). You may react positively to stress, from the simple drive to get out of bed in the morning to the excitement of winning a new account at work. Or you may react negatively, when you feel anxiety or despair as you witness your loved ones losing their cognitive or physical abilities. Positive stress may be seen simply as motivation: it is necessary for survival. Negative stress may be viewed as distress.

But our bodies can't differentiate between good and bad stress. Too much or prolonged stress of any kind can have negative consequences. It can suppress the immune system, cause headaches and tense muscles, overload your brain, and eliminate your sex drive. Our bodies store fat in reaction to stress, as if we are about to face a famine, making it harder for us to lose weight. Stress can undermine our emotional stability, causing panic attacks, insomnia, anxiety, and depression.

Between the never-ending set of strains of our paid jobs and our caregiving demands, it's no wonder we have stressful lives. Most of us have no idea how long the high stress levels will continue. So be aware that stress is a part of your life and watch for negative physiological or emotional symptoms; they're red flags that you need to make some changes before you have a catastrophic health situation to deal with on top of working and caregiving.

Burnout

In the extreme, stress results in burnout. As caregivers, we give and give and give. The prolonged stress builds up, we are robbed of energy, and sometimes we reach a point of total emotional, mental, and physical exhaustion. We may lose motivation completely or feel we just don't care—about our loved ones' care, our other relationships, or our work. We may feel that we've lost ourselves in the vastness of caregiving. Hopelessness is a hallmark of burnout—the feeling that nothing we can do will make a difference. We may see drastic changes in our health, including constant, severe fatigue. The inability to perform routine everyday tasks is also a red flag. If you feel like this most of the time, or you feel yourself shutting down, you may have reached burnout. Some caregivers are so depleted that they simply walk away from their loved ones without a backup plan. Be sure to reach out for help if you are experiencing burnout.

Learning How to Cope

You can't avoid the emotional roller coaster or the stresses of caregiving. If you try to hold your feelings in, they will likely come out suddenly and unexpectedly anyway. If you ignore stress building up, you'll likely suffer the repercussions emotionally and physically sooner or later. But caregivers have found many healthy ways to cope with these challenges.

Monitor Your Mind-Set
Acknowledge Emotions
Often emotions bubble up when you can't safely express them in healthy ways—maybe you're in the middle of caregiving, in a crisis, or at work. When that happens, you may have to contain your emotions temporarily, but don't deny them. Take deep breaths and actively acknowledge to yourself what you are feeling. If you can and it helps, quickly write your feelings down or share them with a trusted friend or relative.

Be Mindful
Caregivers are constantly multitasking and feeling distracted: We worry about our loved ones when we are grocery shopping or performing a task at work; when we are helping our loved ones with personal care, we worry about tomorrow's appointment or myriad other things. While multitasking can be useful at times, studies show that too much distraction leads to inefficiency. Practicing the technique of "mindfulness"—focusing fully on the current moment—has lowered my stress levels a great deal, and I get more accomplished in the long run. It also lets me experience each moment with my loved ones more fully. I notice more joy when I'm aware and mindful, and that helps me cope.

Ask Yourself Whether You're Operating from Fear or Love
When you experience difficult emotions, ask yourself if they're coming from a place of fear or love. If they are fear-based, try to view the situation from a place of love—for yourself and others—and see how your emotions adjust. One day, I got incredibly anxious and angry when Mom's doctor's office performed a lab test incorrectly. When I stopped

to evaluate my response, I realized I was coming from fear: The bottom line was I was terrified that she would get sicker, and I was desperate for answers and a course of treatment. I shifted to a love-based motivation, calmed down, and focused on getting her well. The anger dissipated, and I was able to reschedule the test. This process kept me moving forward and brought me a sense of peace.

Remember Why You Made the Choice to Care

Love, a sense of responsibility, the desire to do the right thing or give back—these are some of the reasons you are here. Even if you feel obligated or forced into caregiving, in actuality everything is a choice, so you *have* made a choice to do so—you could have walked away (some people do). Sometimes consciously revisiting the choice you've made can empower you and help you feel good about what you are doing, even when it's stressful.

Know What You Can Control

If you accept the fact that, in reality, the only things you have control over are your own behavior, reactions, and choices, you'll save yourself a great deal of stress. You can't control other people's motivations, consciences, actions, or choices. You cannot change others' personalities or lifetimes of behavior patterns. You cannot come up with all the answers, cure your loved ones' illnesses, or check off everything on the list. But you can control your own attitude.

Choose Positivity

When I begin to fall into the abyss of emotional despair, the thing that works the best for me is to replace negative with positive feelings. When I feel overwhelmed with all that I've not accomplished, I list things I *did* get done for my parents or my job. When I feel sad about Dad losing his cognitive abilities, I think about how great it is that his personality is still basically the same and that he can still experience happiness. When I feel stressed about an upcoming work deadline, I think about all the deadlines I've met and how much work I've accomplished since I started caregiving. When I feel discouraged about solving one of my parents' health challenges, I fix my sights on the rewards of caring for them. Yes, it's a conscious choice to switch to the glass half full. Sometimes it's a struggle, but it always makes me feel better and more able to press on.

Don't "Should" on Yourself

You are a caregiver, not a saint. As much as you try, you will never be perfect. You may always feel there is more you "should" be doing. But Anne Samaan, a wise friend who cared for her husband with Alzheimer's disease for more than 20 years, told me repeatedly: "Don't should on yourself." Second-guessing your decisions is simply unproductive; you know you can't go back. And piling on a list of additional tasks that you should be doing only leads to guilt. That doesn't mean you should be selfish, absolve yourself of responsibilities, dump the care on others, walk away from those who need you, and have a devil-may-care attitude. Just do your best and allow life to flow—it will be what it will be, and you will have a clear conscience.

Monda DeWeese, executive director of a correctional facility in Ohio, was primary caregiver for her mother, who battled Alzheimer's disease for many years. Monda says trying to meet the needs of her mom as well as those of her husband, teenage daughter, and job often felt insurmountable. "Attempting to be truly present in each aspect of a sandwich generation life is a challenge for a working caregiver," she says. "Some days it can feel like there is always some area that is shortchanged. Making peace with that feeling, realizing that you are doing the best you can, making the most of where you are and who you are with, is the only way that you, as well as those around you, receive the gift of your presence."

Know Your Best Outlets

Keep a Private Journal

Writing about your feelings, daily events, and the joys and challenges of caregiving can be cathartic. You can keep a handwritten or electronic journal. Articulating all the positive and negative emotions in one place can allow you to move on.

Use Technology

Write a blog, post on a social media venue such as Facebook or Twitter, or share with an online support group or message board. But when you do, remember that your post lives forever. Be judicious about what you share and who might be hurt by what you post. Posting your emotions about a sibling who won't help may get back to him or her and make the situation worse.

Talk It Out

Someone who is not deeply involved in your caregiving situation may be the ideal sounding board, but for some, a relative, spouse, or partner can play this role. You want someone who knows how to listen supportively without giving advice or judging. I know which friends can handle a quick call when I just need to vent—they are on speed dial!

Get Moving

The mind-body connection is a reality; you can help release your stress and overflowing emotions through your body. I talk more about exercise later in this chapter, but I want to mention a few quick suggestions here. For some, a vigorous workout or run does the trick. For others, dancing or aerobics lifts their spirits and works out emotions. Walking is an excellent, easily accessible way to ease stress, clear your mind, and boost your energy. This is one outlet you can often use with other people, including the loved ones you care for. Dad used to love going for a quick walk with me, which was good for both of us. (As his Alzheimer's progresses, he isn't as excited about taking walks.) And when I feel especially stressed out, I often just stop where I am and do squats, jumping jacks, or punch the air. It works!

Maintain Your Identity

Nurture Yourself

You have spent a lifetime developing your own identity—but it's easy to get so engulfed in caregiving that you lose yourself. Think about all the great things you laid out in your self-assessment in Chapter 1. You are a fantastic individual. Don't lose those important components of the most important person in your life: you. Take time to do things that nurture your soul, stimulate your personal growth, and excite you. It's absolutely necessary to keep your own tank full of energy.

Cultivate Your Interests and Hobbies

You may have to sacrifice some of your activities to fit in the demands of working and caregiving, but strive to engage in things you like to do at least occasionally to maintain balance in your life. If you find yourself often feeling sad and saying, "I used to like to do that, but I don't have time anymore," that's a clue you need to *make* time. And yes, you probably can make time.

Cultivate Your Relationships

Your relationships with your friends, spouse or partner, children, grandchildren, siblings, and other loved ones are part of who you are. As caregiving increasingly takes up your time, these relationships are often the first things to suffer. You may feel emotionally drained and unable to give in any other relationship. Your schedule may be so jam-packed you do not have time to make a phone call, much less spend a relaxing evening with those you love. Furthermore, they may not be able to identify or understand the extent to which you are barely able to keep up with the basics of your life. Realistically, something's gotta give! Still, do your best to stay in touch, prioritize time together, take vacations or breaks together, and be there for these important people. When your caregiving comes to an end, you'll want them in your life.

Sustain Your Professional Identity

If you work a paid job, volunteer, or have a hobby that you've been devoted to, your identity in those realms can be a great comfort. There are times when all caregivers feel inadequate or incompetent: We are not all trained or fully prepared for the tasks and challenges of caregiving. Balancing those feelings with the competence we feel in other areas of our lives can boost our confidence levels.

Watch Your Health

Sleep

I'm convinced that sleep deprivation is the biggest enemy of caregivers. When we are tired, we are robbed of the ability to cope, and we can't adequately process the myriad emotions we experience—we simply don't have the reserves to deal with them. Our cognitive functioning is also depleted, affecting our work and our ability to make good decisions. If you are not sleeping because of anxiety and worry, you might want to seek professional help from a therapist or doctor. If you sleep well but not enough, then it's time to adjust your work and caregiving schedules. When Mom came home from rehab after her fall, she was up every two hours all night long. Since it wasn't safe for her to go to the bathroom by herself, I got up with her. After two months of sleep deprivation, I could hardly function. I finally began to pay professional caregivers to take the night shift a few days a week so I could sleep. It was miraculous what a few good nights' sleep a week did for me in all areas of my life!

Eat Well

You're an on-the-go caregiver, and I bet you sometimes substitute quick-and-easy eating on the run, snacks, and comfort food for healthy meals. I gained a great deal of weight when I started intense caregiving for my parents, and I know I'm not alone. As I mentioned before, weight gain for caregivers isn't just about not eating well; it also can be about our body's reaction to stress levels and lack of sleep. Still, we know that letting our nutrition go is the first step on a downhill health slide. We have control over what we put in our mouths, so why don't we choose better for ourselves? Here are a few ways to approach our nutrition needs:

- Consult a nutrition professional. You don't always need to pay a lot of money on an ongoing basis to get results. One or a few consultations might be very helpful for you to identify negative eating patterns and get yourself back on track nutritionally.
- Join a group. Caregivers tend to find each other when they join Jenny Craig, Overeaters Anonymous, Weight Watchers, or other groups

focused on healthy eating. Many find the one-on-one support incredibly effective.

- Keep a food journal. Write down everything you eat for a week or two. You'll become much more aware of where the calories are coming from.
- Attend a nutrition seminar. Learn all you can about healthy nutrition.
- Address the psychological aspects of nutrition. Why do you eat the way you do? How are you handling stress? Are there triggers in your caregiving or work life that spur you to unhealthy eating? A food journal could help here, too. Next to what you eat, write down why you're eating—whether it's actual hunger or a response to emotions or stress.

Exercise

Staying physically active is vital to all aspects of your health, including your brain health. You need your full strength and a strong immune system when you're a caregiver. But regular exercise is one of the first things to drop off the list when work and caregiving converge. Find a regimen that works for you. Some get up early in the morning to work out; others exercise on their lunch hour, after dinner, or in short breaks throughout the day. Try armchair yoga, or stretchy bands for resistance, which are easy to stash in a desk drawer or suitcase if you travel for work. I try to work exercise into time I spend with Dad because he loves it and we can do it together, adapting difficulty for both of our abilities. If your workplace offers a gym, a trainer, discounts to health clubs, or other incentives to exercise, take advantage of them!

Visit Your Doctors

You may find yourself putting off your annual physical, vaccinations, and dental and vision appointments. After all, the people you care for are more vulnerable, and therefore their health needs are more important, right? Wrong. Studies show that the stress of caregiving makes you more vulnerable as well. I find that if I schedule regular doctor appointments ahead of time—even a year ahead—I am more apt to keep up with them. Get out your calendar and schedule those visits!

Be Practical

Set Limits

The needs of the people we care for can be so great that when we strive to meet them all, we set ourselves up to fail. Or maybe you have an employer that will keep taking and asking for more of your time than is reasonable. We all have to develop boundaries, and knowing our limits is something that is learned over time. Start by noticing when you feel uncomfortable about giving more than you really have to give. Think about setting some boundaries around your time as well as your responsibilities. Be clear when you've reached your limits at home, at work, and in your caregiving role. You can also set limits in your leadership role in caregiving—perhaps you don't mind being the primary caregiver, but that doesn't mean you have to do everything; learn to delegate. Finally, you can set boundaries around how you'll share information about the people you are caring for. Instead of spending time constantly sending out emails and making phone calls, post the information on a closed website and ask family members to seek it out. You'll find more on this in Chapter 4.

Just Say No

When you are overburdened but still keep adding tasks to your list, you put more stress on yourself; it's the perfect equation for a meltdown. And if you say "yes" but you don't follow through, you'll likely suffer repercussions. You can't add more time to your day, so be very judicious about saying "yes." That said, "no" may not be an option if you are being asked to live up to your basic caregiving or work responsibilities. If so, something else may have to be taken off your list instead.

Get Help

Accept Offers

How many times have friends or family told you, "If there is anything I can do, just let me know." Take them up on it. Many of us find it hard to ask for help, but when it's been offered, you have no excuse for going it alone. When I first moved to Arizona in 2009, two wonderful employees at our local grocery store offered to check on Mom and Dad when I went out of town. They had both been fond of my parents for many years, and

I knew both of them well enough to trust them. Another friend offered to do the same. So I took them up on it, and they often stopped by to bring bananas, share a meal, or just chat and monitor my parents' status while I was away. They didn't need to stay long, but it eased my worries immensely and gave my parents a lift as well. Unless you know people who offer to help very well, you'll want to check references and get a background check (contact the local police department to find out how to get one for free).

Get Support for Your Own Life

This is often the last thing caregivers think of, and the last thing others think to do to help a caregiver. But it should be the first. When you start to notice emotions, exhaustion, and stress building up, recruit friends, volunteers, or paid professionals to help you. Your first instinct may be to get help with caregiving, but consider channeling resources to support your own life, such as cleaning, mowing the lawn, running errands, or sorting mail. It's a huge relief to know these things are being taken care of so I can focus on my paid job and the tasks that only I can do for myself and for Dad. Concierge services can help, and you'd be surprised how affordable their prices are; even an hour or two a week can make a big difference in your stress levels. A growing number of both online and in-person concierge or personal assistant services are available; to find them, search online or check your local Yellow Pages. Be sure to check references and make sure they are insured for liability and bonded in case they cause any damages to your home or property.

Seek Professional Counseling or Medical Care

If you're experiencing overwhelming emotions, stress, or burnout, it may be time to get some help from a counselor, therapist, or doctor. You may experience mood swings, sleeplessness, or profound hopelessness or depression. Anxiety symptoms may manifest physically, such as tightness in your chest, a pounding heart, or difficulty breathing. If you notice any of these signs, or if your co-workers, family members, or friends are concerned about you, get an evaluation.

Try Mediation

Are you having trouble convincing your loved ones to accept care or change their living situation? Are anger and resentment building up toward your siblings or others who might not be helping out as expected ? You might consult with a professional mediator who specializes in family or eldercare mediation. Sometimes an objective third party is the best person to negotiate agreements about plans, roles, contributions, and responsibilities. Keep in mind, though, that all parties have to be willing to participate and communicate openly for mediation to work. No pulling punches in a mediation session or setting someone up to be ambushed.

Lean on Other Caregivers

No one will understand what you are going through quite like another caregiver. You can build friendships with other caregivers and talk, text, or email each other. You can connect online via caregiving support groups, message boards and groups (visit aarp.org/caregiving to find AARP's online groups), Facebook groups, and Twitter chats for caregivers. Or you can join a local caregiver support group to meet regularly in person. (See the Resources section for information about how to find a support group.)

Take Breaks

Grab Some Quick R & R

Caregivers are busy, and if we're also working a paid job, we are even more crunched. It's difficult to find time for substantial breaks, but it's amazing how quickly I can refresh my attitude and energy with just a short break in my routine. Here are some of the refreshers that work for me when I'm feeling stressed out or overwhelmed. Make a list of refreshers that work for you!

- **Relax.** Do something you enjoy just for the sake of enjoying it no matter how big or small. It may be getting a cup of coffee, watching a favorite TV program, going for a walk, cuddling a pet, savoring a piece of chocolate, watering your garden, meditating, or napping.
- **Have fun.** Laughter really is good medicine. Watch a humorous TV show or movie, read a funny book, peruse funny greeting cards, play

a game, or just be silly. This is something you can do with the people you care for, too.

- **Be creative.** Creating often brings out the best in us. Write a poem, sing a song, play an instrument, paint a picture, work on a scrapbook, make crafts, decorate your home—anything that gets your creative juices going.
- **Enjoy plants and flowers.** Watering plants can be calming, and even a single beautiful flower can be so cheerful. Look for the beauty around you.
- **Connect with animals.** Our furry friends can be therapeutic, and studies show they make us healthier and happier too.
- **Get intergenerational.** There is nothing like the laughter, energy, and enthusiasm of children to energize us and give us hope. Make sure you have opportunities to connect with other generations.

Arrange for Respite Care

Respite is a period of rest or relief from something difficult—in this case, a break from caregiving. It may be an ongoing or one-time arrangement for an hour or two to get together with friends, see your doctor, or run errands; an overnight so you can get some sleep; or a longer period of time to take a vacation, focus on work, or meet other family obligations. Here are a variety of ways to get respite care.

- Ask friends or relatives to care for your loved ones, either coming to their home or taking them out for dinner, shopping, or to a movie. It will be good for your loved ones to get out, and good for you to have some quiet time as well.
- Find a volunteer-staffed respite program in a faith-based organization or volunteer placement agency.
- Pay a professional from a home-health agency, or hire one directly yourself, to care for your loved ones in their home.
- Arrange a short-term stay for the people you care for at a hospice respite, assisted-living or nursing facility, or a group home.
- Have your loved ones attend an adult day services (or day health) center that offers group activities, services, and meals. These centers

are usually open five days a week, although some have weekend and overnight programs.

- Join with other caregivers in your community to create a respite cooperative in which you take turns caring for each other's loved ones.
- If your state has one, use a state voucher program in which you select the respite provider and the state supplies vouchers to pay them.

To locate an organized respite program in your community, contact your local area agency on aging (www.eldercare.gov), visit the respite locator (www.archrespite.org/respitelocator), or contact your local senior center, volunteer agency, or faith-based initiative.

Maintain Your Own Finances

We often get so caught up in caregiving and working that we neglect the basics of our own lives, including finances. Many caregivers suffer financially if they cut back on work or get so busy they forget to pay their bills or keep up with financial records or taxes. I often hear from caregivers that they manage their loved ones' finances meticulously, but their own finances are a mess. Frequently caregivers have to make financial sacrifices, but in the long run you won't do your loved ones any good if you are financially unstable. (See Chapter 7 for more tips on budgeting.) Take the time to keep up with the basics.

- Create and maintain your own budget, track expenses, pay off debt, and pay your bills. You might consider autopay for some of your bills; just make sure you always have enough money in your account to cover them.
- Keep up with your taxes. As a family caregiver, *you* may be able to take some deductions. If you are paying more than half of your family members' expenses and their income meets IRS requirements, you may be able to declare them as dependents on your tax return or take the Child and Dependent Care Credit. Consult a tax professional for more about how you can maximize deductions as a caregiver.

- Save for retirement. Usually, when caregiving makes the budget tight, saving is the first thing to go. But as a caregiver, you know better than anyone how important it will be to have savings when you are older and may need care yourself. If you don't have retirement savings goals, create them, and if you do have them, monitor your progress and prioritize your own future.
- Educate yourself about insurance policies, such as disability, life, and long-term care insurance. It may or may not be a good time to purchase these policies.

Take Care of Your Career

I go more deeply into this in Chapter 5, but if you are working or wish to return to work at a later date, I want to remind you that your work and career are an important part of who you are, so taking care of yourself includes keeping your career goals in sight. Given your caregiving responsibilities, it's understandable and perhaps admirable if you decide to make sacrifices and adjust your career goals. Despite your amazing multitasking skills, maybe you can't actually have it all. But try to adapt your career plans while you keep moving forward. Get creative. You may adapt your goals for now, or change fields, or get new training. You may need to postpone advancement, but perhaps making a change in your career path will actually end up advancing your career in unexpected ways.

Your Job Description: Self-Care Coach

Great work! You've mastered an understanding of the emotions and stress associated with working caregivers. You merit an additional component of your job description:

Observes and evaluates one's own emotions and stressors. Identifies personal vulnerabilities. Recognizes stress overload, identifies stressors, and takes action to ameliorate negative effects using proven coping mechanisms. Nurtures identity and maintains personal care.

CHAPTER 3
YOUR CAREGIVING TEAM

*E*ight months after I'd relocated to Phoenix to help my parents, I found *myself frozen, unable to drag myself out of bed and face my to-do list. I was emotionally exhausted and utterly overwhelmed. I leaned out of bed far enough to reach my laptop and emailed some friends. Dorothy emailed back, "Do not succumb to the bed!" Her message made me laugh in spite of myself, and it spurred me to thinking. Glancing at my list, I realized that single-handedly accomplishing everything on my list—organized by tasks for Mom and Dad, work, house, and personal (yes, as usual I was at the bottom of the list)—was humanly impossible. It was time to get more help.*

Still in bed, I wrote a list of all the people who helped support my parents: my sisters; friends; staff at the senior community where my parents lived at the time; their massage therapist, hair stylist, and manicurist; their doctors; people from the local grocery store who offered to check on my parents when I was out of town. Then I listed people who help me so I can support my parents: my boyfriend; long-distance friends (at the time I knew almost no one in Arizona except my sister); Dee, who cleaned our house; Brant, who cleaned our pool; our handyman; neighbors at my house in the D.C. area.

When I put my two lists side by side, it was instantly clear that we needed to expand our team to free me up to do the things only I could do: taking care of myself (including sleeping), working my paid job, and doing certain financial management and hands-on caregiving tasks with my parents, as well as spending quality time with them. I needed someone to help me with the mounds of paperwork, take care of my house and plants, organize house projects, run errands, and check on my parents when I was out of town.

So I searched online until I finally came across the White Glove Concierge, a company that could do everything from helping with paperwork to caring for my parents to running me to the airport. I called Debbie, the owner, and set up an appointment. That call changed my entire caregiving experience.

And then I was able to get out of bed.

Introduction

The only way to work while you're caregiving is to create a team. You can accomplish a lot by yourself, but you cannot do it all. You can take charge, coordinate, and streamline the operation, but you and the people you care for need help from others. I'm often asked what to do if other family members refuse to help with caregiving tasks. This chapter will help with that challenge. Even if nobody else currently helps, that doesn't mean you don't have a team or can't create one. Look around you. Team members can play a variety of roles and may be family members, friends, volunteers, or paid professionals—and don't forget those important animals who may comfort and provide a service for those you care for, or who keep you sane! Sometimes the team members support you, so you can be freed up to do your job as a caregiver; maybe it's someone who will drag you to a yoga class or brew a cup of tea when you're worn out. Other team members support your loved ones directly. You'll be a better caregiver if you have a diverse team—and your loved ones will do better, too.

In this chapter you'll learn how to:
- Build a caregiving team.
- Create roles, responsibilities, and tasks appropriate for each team member.
- Communicate effectively with team members.
- Deal with problems among your team.
- Recognize and reinforce team members.

Identifying Team Members

Who are the first people on the team roster? The people you care for! It's important to remember that they are members, and in fact leaders, of their own team—even if they are unable to make decisions or fully understand how the team functions. They should be included as much as possible, and they may have ideas about whom to include.

Then make a list of everyone who is currently involved in your loved ones' care and who supports you so you can be a caregiver. A good place to start building your list is to go back to your assessments and caregiving plan from Chapter 1. Once you've recorded all current team members, expand your thinking to who else could be more involved on your team. Consider the following:

- Family members
- Neighbors (your loved ones' and yours, if you live elsewhere)
- Friends (of yours, of the people you care for, and of other family members)
- Members of faith communities
- Paid or volunteer services, such as these:
  - House cleaner
  - Mail delivery person
  - Yard-/pool-care worker
  - Concierge, personal assistant, or other services
  - Pet-care professionals (groomers, veterinarian, dog walkers, pet sitters)
  - Handyman
  - Cook or meal-delivery services
  - Friendly visitor or companion
  - Hair stylist
  - Manicurist
  - Personal exercise trainer or fitness class teacher
  - Chore services
  - Grocery delivery

- Medical, health-care, social services, or geriatric professionals, such as these:
  - Social workers
  - Geriatric care managers
  - Nurses
  - Certified Nursing Assistants (CNAs) or home health aides
  - Doctors
  - Pharmacists
  - Therapists, such as physical, occupational, speech, music, recreation, activities, creative arts, hydrotherapies (water), and hippotherapy (horses)
  - Paid professional caregivers and home health aides
- Financial, legal, and technology advisers
- Gatekeepers (so-called because they interact regularly with your loved ones and may be the first to notice a change or problem—people such as such as mail carriers, yard workers, the electric company, police officers, firefighters and EMTs)

You also may want to add to your list people who say, "If there is ever anything I can do, let me know." You probably never take them up on it. Most people don't know how to help, so they make an open offer. They need specific tasks to accomplish. Next time you're in a fix, overwhelmed, or just need a task done that you can't get to, they will be on your list of people to ask for help. You will be giving them the gift of the opportunity to help another person. Take them up on their offer.

Debbie and her husband, Gary, have been an integral part of our caregiving team ever since 2010, when I called White Glove Concierge from my bed. They provide office assistance; sort mail, flagging urgent matters; make phone calls; track insurance claims; organize closets; make or find someone to make minor home repairs; help plan special celebrations; water plants; pack suitcases and drive me to the airport; and run errands. They have also helped Mom and Dad, sometimes taking them to appointments, fixing meals, walking with Dad, dog-sitting for Jackson, and more. Debbie even acts as my sounding board when I'm problem-solving and my sisters aren't available. Of course, not everyone can afford this kind of help, so I consider our family lucky (although it may be more affordable than you think—and just an hour here and there makes a huge difference in my life). I think I'd still be in bed if not for them!

Building the Team

Once you've got your list, it may be helpful to know what motivates team members. They may be family members who feel a sense of love and responsibility. Even within families, people are driven by different reasons for participating (or not) in caregiving. Some of us have strong convictions that we should care for others, so we make it a priority. Some believe family takes care of family first and foremost. Others feel an obligation to care for family members even if they don't like it. Many will participate only when pushed, making the least possible amount of personal sacrifice; others are bottomless fonts of generosity.

Some paid professionals who interact with the people you care for as a part of their jobs may not be interested in helping out in addition to their duties or communicating with you. Others are more than happy to go that extra step or give you a heads-up if they see a change you should be aware of. You never know until you ask, and most of the time I'm surprised and touched by the kindness of near-strangers. Mom's manicurist, Nancy, and her husband, William, were especially compassionate with my parents. They helped me coordinate Dad getting a massage in the same shopping center while Mom got her manicure (and sometimes I got a pedicure too). William helped Dad navigate his way to the nail shop with Jackson and brought them both water, letting Mom and me relax for a bit. They were invaluable members of our team for a time; it was a personal care and quality-of-life outing for all of us, but I couldn't have managed well without their cooperation.

Asking for Help

Whether because of pride, embarrassment that we can't handle everything by ourselves, or an assumption that people won't be willing, asking for help can be hard. My advice? Get over it. As I said, it's not humanly possible for one caregiver to do it all, and the truth is we are all in this together: If someone you're asking isn't a caregiver now, chances are they have been one or will become one eventually. So let people know you'll be happy to return the favor someday. When asking people to participate in the caregiving team, it's helpful to be as specific as possible about tasks they might do or roles they might perform. Some people will respond better to a specific, time-limited task. You don't have to make it sound like a big commitment; perhaps you won't even use the word "team." You may just ask them to do a specific task.

Team Roles

Your caregiving team includes a variety of people with all sorts of skills, personalities, time limits, interests, and levels of commitment. Everyone won't contribute at the same level. Typically, roles fall into one of these six general types, and some people play more than one role:

- **Big-picture team members:** These are generally family members or paid coordinators, such as geriatric care managers, who serve as primary caregivers or care managers, keeping an eye on your loved ones and communicating their overall planning and status.
- **Single-responsibility team leaders:** These people may coordinate one chunk of caregiving, such as managing finances, health care, or the household.
- **Ongoing interactors:** The people with whom you and your loved ones interact on an ongoing basis are important members of your team. Paid, volunteer, or family caregivers; service providers; neighbors; and friends may fall in this category. They are your eyes and ears who observe your loved ones. They help you with the everyday aspects.

- **Task-oriented achievers:** These people are happy to accomplish a single task but don't take on a bigger role. They can be helpful as long as you can give them specific time-limited jobs with clear instructions. These may be very practical tasks, such as cleaning the house every week, sorting mail periodically, conducting online research, scheduling appointments, visiting regularly, grocery shopping, or calling every day.
- **One-time contributors:** Some team members don't have ongoing roles but step in to help at times, such as for special projects or emergencies. Sometimes extended family, neighbors, and friends are willing to serve in this role.
- **Backup players:** Some may be unwilling to play ongoing or even one-time roles, but they will serve as backup in case your caregiving plan goes awry. These folks need to be apprised of the usual routine so they can step in at any moment in case of an emergency.

When doling out roles, keep in mind that some people are uncomfortable helping their father go to the bathroom or their mother bathe, but will valiantly spend untold hours making sure the bills are paid, taxes are done, and food is on the table. Team members will likely fall into one of the following two categories, although some are comfortable in both:

- **Hands-on:** Those who are comfortable with direct care. They are caring and compassionate and like personal interactions and helping others. They don't mind helping with bathing, toileting, grooming, dressing, or combing hair. They are able to identify and focus on another person's needs and act on them.
- **Hands-off:** Those who prefer hands-off supporting roles. They are more comfortable dealing with finances and paperwork; conducting research; making phone calls; cleaning; organizing; running errands; or doing other work to free up the hands-on caregivers.

It's OK that everyone isn't comfortable with both of these approaches; there has to be balance on the caregiving team, and there's plenty of work to go around. Problems occur, though, when the primary need is hands-on care, and you only have people who are hands-off. Or if the bills aren't getting paid even though mom and dad have excellent personal care and lots of visitors. Trouble also occurs when some team members are uncomfortable with hands-on care so they withdraw completely, refusing to contribute in any way. It's best to accept people as they are—you have enough to do without trying to change them. But you can work around personalities by having a variety of ways to contribute to the team.

Matching Team Members with Needs

When deciding on team roles, go back to your self-assessment and encourage other team members to do the same. Think about who is most comfortable with each of the roles or types of support needed. Is someone in your family less comfortable with personal care but organized and enjoys cleaning? That person would be great as a one-time or task-oriented contributor. Do you have a family member who is a great planner? Perhaps that relative fits best in a big-picture role. Discuss various roles and capacities, and get as clear as possible about what people can commit to.

Consider time limitations, too. Are there some on your team who aren't working outside the home and have more time to contribute? Which team members are in the "sandwich generation," raising their own children at the same time as caregiving? Who has a very demanding job or travel obligations? These are the realities of life and need to be taken into account when it comes to caregiving.

Long-Distance Caregiving

Long-distance caregiving carries its own unique challenges. If you are the primary caregiver, you'll need eyes and ears on the ground monitoring your loved ones. You may need to bear the expense of frequent visits to check on the people you care for. You'll worry about what is happening when you can't see for yourself. Caregivers at a distance may take on hands-off roles that they can easily deal with on the phone or using technology. One-time projects or ongoing task-oriented roles such as researching health or financial issues online, managing finances, or making phone calls might be appropriate for long-distance caregiving.

Therese Fieler Lackey says she and her siblings worked out caregiving roles that suit their skill sets, lifestyles, and personalities. "We chose to have the oldest child (my sister Laura, the accountant) take care of all things medical and paperwork, such as insurance and bills, as she is best suited," Therese says. "This is a very time-consuming responsibility that Laura takes care of outside of work, usually late at night or on weekends. Her job as treasurer of a school district does not allow her to take time off much." Therese handles all the "people stuff" involving face-to-face interactions, like appointments. Her schedule as a teacher was more flexible, allowing her to take sick and personal days plus late afternoons and all summer. For a while, she was retired and even more available. Even now that she has a part-time job, she still manages to take her mother to important appointments.

Team Communication

Are You the Hub?

Research indicates that most families have a person who serves as "the hub"—someone who keeps all family members in the loop, sending alerts when loved ones' status changes or help is needed. When it comes to caregiving for older parents, the hub tends to be the primary caregiver or the oldest child—but not always. I tend to be the hub in my family, though I'm the youngest of my siblings. For some families, the hub is the person who lives closest to loved ones, is very organized, has experience with caregiving, and is able to focus on others, or who has an outgoing, people-oriented personality. Or it may simply be the person who is willing to take on the responsibility. If you don't have a naturally occurring hub, it might be a good role to designate one for your caregiving team.

Logistics

Kim Ward is the oldest of three and the primary caregiver for her mother, who lives in a nursing facility in the community. Kim coordinates a caregiving team consisting of her husband, her 21-year-old daughter, her sister, her sister's three oldest children, her sister's husband, and her two aunts (who are in their late 70s). "I'm lucky. There is so much family nearby that my mom has a visitor three times a day," says Kim. "We communicate primarily by text message—even my aunts have mastered texting." Everyone texts their visiting time, impressions of how Kim's mom is doing, and if follow-up is needed. When her mom's care plan or medication changes, Kim sends out a mass text message. "It's simple, but it works!" she says.

I am so incredibly busy doing the day-to-day care, managing the finances, and handling my own complicated life that I don't always remember to send an email or make a phone call to update my sisters or our professional caregiving team members. That's why I do everything I can in the most efficient way possible. There are so many ways to communicate with team members; the key is finding out what is easiest and fastest and what team members will respond to. If you have teenagers on your team, texting may be the only way to communicate. If you have those who are proficient with technology, an app or website might do the trick. Team members who are more oriented to reading will prefer to have notes and updates in writing; others are more apt to respond to a telephone call. Start by asking about communication preferences, then take into account what people will actually respond to and what is doable for those communicating the information. Consider these options:

- **Text messaging:** Kim's family uses text messaging. It's quick and simple, but she is concerned that there is no record of updates and visits, so she's looking for other ways to communicate as well.
- **Phone trees:** Start the chain by calling one person and then that person calls the next person on the list and so on. You or someone on the team will need to organize the phone tree.
- **Apps and websites:** Many apps allow you to take and share notes as well as information and updates about health, finances, legal papers, and more. See Chapter 4 for more about how technology can help you stay organized and keep in touch. Technology is a big help to me, especially when it comes to sharing information such as medical

updates after doctor appointments or hospital stays. When I make notes for my records, I create them in a note-taking app and can quickly and immediately email a copy to key team members as I save and close the notes. The team appreciates the updates, and then it's one less thing for me to worry about. I also have a record of whom I've sent the notes to.

Communication

I speak with many caregivers, and almost every time I hear about a problem among their teams, it boils down to a communication issue. Communication is vital to keeping the team running smoothly.

I learned from Dad, who was a professor and communication researcher, that for communication to take place, you need four elements:

1. A message sender;
2. A method of sending the message (verbal, nonverbal, written, visual, or touch);
3. A message receiver; and
4. Feedback between sender and receiver ensuring that the message came through correctly and that the parties reach a mutual understanding.

If any of the four elements is missing, communication hasn't happened.

I've also found that even if we put the information out there, we cannot force people to read the notes, check the website, or open their mail or email, and that can be frustrating. All you can do is put it out there. You can bring a horse to water, but you can't make him drink (as my grandmother used to say)!

For example, you may send an email to your sister, who is scheduled to take your mother to a doctor's appointment, telling her the appointment time has been changed. If she doesn't read the email, there is no receiver: No communication occurs. Your mother misses her appointment, and you're angry with your sister. Better to find a mode of communication that will ensure your sister gets the message than deal with the fallout.

Communication Styles

We all have primary communication styles. It can be helpful to know your and your team members' styles and take them into consideration when interacting with the team.

- **Relaters:** These are the peacemakers, considerate and cooperative. They are warm, "touchy-feely," and good listeners. They are team players, cooperative, and all about people and relationships. With a relater, take your time, empathize, be sincere, and say thank you.
- **Expressives:** Social and spirited, expressives are all about being accepted in relationships. They're talkative and speak quickly, with big gestures. Enthusiasm is their trademark. Expect a fast-paced conversation with open body language, and have patience when they stray off the point. Stay on the big picture, and don't give too many details.
- **Thinkers:** Analytical and systematic, thinkers feel grounded when they have data and facts. Often perfectionists, they have a strong drive to achieve results. They are not spontaneous. Thinkers respond to well-planned conversations, less talk, and more results.
- **Directors:** Bold and straightforward, they are honest and plainspoken. They are confident go-getters. Directors have strong opinions, are decisive, and see things as right or wrong. They are organized and goal-oriented, and they can be competitive. With directors, be straightforward and brief.

Communication Tips

When communicating with team members, you'll avoid confusion, conflict, and miscommunication if you keep these tips in mind (and check out my Tips for Challenging Conversations in the appendix).

- **Identify communication styles:** Recognize individual communication styles for yourself, your loved ones, and your fellow team members. Learn how to adapt when interacting with people who have different styles.
- **Listen:** The Greek philosopher Epictetus once said, "We have two ears and one mouth so that we can listen twice as much as we speak."

Some people are natural listeners, but for most of us, listening is a learned skill. To improve your skills, practice reflective listening:

1. Listen.
2. Paraphrase what you heard, and repeat it back to them.
3. Check to see if the message you received is accurate.

- **Notice nonverbal cues and body language:** If you are sitting back in your chair with your arms crossed and looking around the room while your fellow caregiver is relating an incident with your loved ones, she'll get the message that you don't care. Be sensitive to the nonverbal cues you are conveying and receiving.

- **Minimize the drama:** Notice your feelings, but avoid reacting emotionally—instead, stop, breathe, and reflect. When you're angry, avoid communicating in any form. If you don't, it may be a conversation some family members will never let you forget.

- **Use "I" statements:** Starting a sentence with "You" can put people on the defensive. Instead of saying, "You did [that]," say, for example, "I feel [this way] when you [say or do this] because I [have this reason]. Next time, will you please [do this]?"

- **Make no judgments:** Stick to the facts. If you really want to have open communication with members of your team, they need to feel you won't be critical or tell them what you think they should do or how they should act.

Dennis and his sister had been supporting their father, who has been on dialysis for many years, with hands-on assistance, help around the house, and financial management. When their father's condition worsened, they talked with him and their mother and decided to call in home hospice care. But when their other siblings, who hadn't been very involved in their parents' care, found out, a battle ensued. "Our siblings were furious and flew in to talk Dad out of a decision he had made," says Dennis. "We thought we were doing the right thing, but our siblings were shocked and disagreed. We don't regret our decision, but we would have prevented a lot of family conflict if we'd communicated differently. Our mistake was not calling for a family meeting to discuss the decision to start hospice care."

When Teamwork Doesn't Go Smoothly

Keep in mind that your caregiving team is made up of people who have different relationships with the people you care for, with history and possibly lots of baggage. Two siblings may have had very different relationships with a parent. A wife may have years of resentment built up against a husband who needs care, but their children have no problem with their father and can't understand why their mother isn't caring better for him. Family history can't be erased, and, although it's best to live in the here and now and let go of old views that are no longer serving us, relationships or perspectives are difficult to change. Caregiving can often cause flare-ups of old resentments and hurtful feelings. We can all fall back into old patterns of communication and family roles, no matter our age.

When you face difficult relationships among caregiving team members, keep these tips in mind:

- **Accept differences:** Caregiving takes a lot of emotional energy. Don't waste your energy being angry and trying to change people. In the long run, it's best for *you* when you can accept differences and stay focused on the tasks at hand. Think about your own choices and conscience—that's all you can control.
- **Evaluate communication barriers:** When trouble crops up, the first thing to do is to evaluate communication. Was every team member on the same page? Was key information communicated *and* received?
- **Adjust roles and responsibilities**: If the team isn't functioning smoothly, think about changing a team member's role or tasks. Stay focused on what needs to get done, and if a role isn't working, ask a team member why. Team members could feel uncomfortable or inadequate or lack the resources, or their life circumstances may have changed.
- **Get help:** Sometimes aid from an objective third party is helpful—or even necessary—to get through a rough spot or a full-on roadblock. You might talk with a geriatric care manager, social worker, counselor, or therapist, or seek mediation from a trained family or eldercare mediator. Work on making compromises, negotiating, and staying focused

on the loved ones who need help, not on trying to solve deep-seated family issues, unless all parties are willing to do the work to do so.

Reinforcing, Recognizing, and Appreciating Your Team

Caregiving can be emotionally and physically draining, and many of us are making difficult sacrifices. Everyone on your team needs some positive feedback, even if they're driven by love and altruistic motivations. Even if team members aren't doing as much as you'd like, it's a good idea to reinforce what they are doing, if only because they'll be likely to contribute more if they feel appreciated. For some, appreciation from the people you're caring for means the most. Others want the primary caregiver, team leader, or fellow team members to recognize their contributions great and small. Some certainly will need more acknowledgment than others, and some will seem uncomfortable with recognition, but deep inside they'll no doubt appreciate it.

All team members, not just the primary caregiver or team leader, have a responsibility to reinforce one another. Find out what means the most to your fellow team members. Here are some suggestions for recognizing contributions.

- A simple, in-person "thank you" from you or your loved ones.
- A sincere thank-you note, phone call, text message, or email from you or your loved ones.
- A picture of the team member with your loved ones.
- A small gift card for a cup of coffee or ice cream, a bouquet of flowers, or edible treats.

Your Job Description: Team Builder

Congratulations! Working in teams isn't always easy, but you've become a key player of your loved ones' caregiving team and, perhaps, ringleader for the team. You've earned a new component of your caregiving job description:

> Participates as part of or as leader of a team that works to provide care for designated loved ones. Possesses excellent communication skills and facilitates ongoing information sharing among team members. Negotiates and designates team roles and responsibilities or accepts them graciously from team leader. Manages team reports and updates or provides input to team leader. Energizes and reinforces team spirit and drives team to achieve goals.

CHAPTER 4

THE ORGANIZED CAREGIVER: TIPS FOR STAYING SANE

As a working caregiver, I'm incredibly busy. I'm often asked how I do it all and stay sane. I can say from experience that the only way to be successful is to get organized.

I started my caregiving journey with a thick three-ring binder with pockets and a ream of lined paper for notes, but since then I've come a long way, baby!

When I first went to Arizona and began more intense caregiving for my parents, I found stacks of medical history in files and a fat Rolodex with doctors' contact information. Dad's system may have worked for him, but I was totally lost. I'd come home from their doctor appointments loaded down with receipts, instructions, booklets, and prescriptions. And I'd invariably lose something along the way.

That initial binder had organized sections for Mom and Dad. But all too soon it was overflowing, sloppy, and cumbersome to carry around. Then one day when I was in a work meeting rummaging for a pen and some paper to take notes, I noticed Patti, a co-worker, coolly pulling out her iPad and opening a note-taking website application (app) to write a summary of the meeting. I realized I could use that approach in my caregiving role too. She encouraged me to toss the pen and paper and embrace technology. I never looked back! Technology is one of the many ways I got—and stay—organized. I can't imagine caregiving without it.

Introduction

As a caregiver, you, like me, probably have an overwhelming number of tasks to do, documents to find, and details to track. You may be managing legal, financial, and medical plans and records; doctors, therapists, medical equipment, medical tests, and appointments; household matters, milestones, and memories; personal belongings and activities; and your caregiving team. If you are also working at a paid job, you have myriad things to keep track of at work as well. Your personal life may include care for children or other family members, your spouse or partner, volunteer work or hobbies, maintaining a home, and more. It boggles the mind.

Never fear! Many tips and tools—both traditional and high-tech—are at your disposal to make the job easier. There are only so many hours in the day, so being organized and efficient are key caregiver survival skills. And you probably use organizational skills in other areas of your life, or at a paid job, that you take for granted. Think about how you can apply those skills to your caregiving role. Spending a little time now to get organized and put simple systems in place can save a lot of time, effort, and frustration later. Disorganization is probably one of the top causes of stress in my life.

In this chapter you'll learn about:
- Managing your time and creating systems.
- Gathering, storing, and updating key documents and information.
- Using technology to get organized and to access and share information.

Managing Your Time

Sometimes good old-fashioned time-management skills can make the biggest difference in your day-to-day life as a working caregiver. Try using these approaches at work, with your caregiving role, and in all aspects of your life.

- **Nix procrastination.** It just makes you feel worse. Just do the next thing, even if it's small. You'll feel better, which will probably motivate you to do more.
- **Make a list.** If it helps, dump everything in all areas of your life into the list, but organize it, perhaps by categories: home, work, caregiving, family, shopping—whatever suits your lifestyle.
- **Prioritize.** List what you need to do in order of importance, according to your personal, family, work, and loved ones' needs.
- **Focus on one priority.** For that hour, day, month, or project, choose one top priority that, when completed, will make you feel like you've accomplished something important. Then pick two more priorities lower on the list. If you get one done, you'll feel really good; get the other one done and you're flying high; get more done and you'll feel like a superstar!
- **Manage your expectations.** Know that your to-do list will never, ever be totally completed, so stop making that your goal. There are always new things added to your list.
- **Work on your task for a short time.** If a task seems undoable, just start with a short time frame—5 minutes, 20 minutes, whatever you can do—and give it all you've got. You could stop there, but you may feel better about jumping back in after a short break.
- **Be mindful.** When your mind is scattered, you rob yourself of the ability to focus and accomplish anything. It's just not efficient, and you probably won't commit things to memory, which causes problems and wastes time later. Recently, I helped Mom out of the car and into her wheelchair and whisked her away to her doctor's office, all the time thinking about a pending work assignment. When we returned to the car I saw I had left the trunk wide open! We had a good laugh, but I was lucky nothing was stolen. Still, it was a reminder to tune into the present moment.
- **Touch it once.** Any efficiency expert will tell you to touch a piece of paper only once. In other words, read, do, follow up, and file at

one time, whether it's paper or digital. The more we start a task, set it down, pick it up again, stop, start, etc., the more time we waste. I'm the queen of multitasking, but I have also learned that I get more completed in the long run when I finish one task before beginning another.

- **Set up systems.** You'll want simple systems in place for organizing, updating, and sharing information. This will prevent you from wasting time and help with consistency among caregivers. For example, my sister and I both take our parents to doctor appointments, so we set up a system for sharing notes. I have a smartphone and take notes on the spot using an app called Evernote. As I close out the notes, I quickly email them to my sisters and our professional caregivers. My sister takes notes on paper and later either gives them to me or enters them into a shared Evernote folder on her computer. I've also created an appointment/emergency paper folder for each of my parents, which is easy to grab to take with us, as well as digital versions accessible from my smartphone and iPad. It includes medication lists, medical histories, copies of insurance cards, an emergency-contact list, copies of living wills, do not resuscitate (DNR) orders and powers of attorney, and blank paper for notes.
- **Define roles and responsibilities.** Clear roles are key. Even if they change over time, establish them and adjust as needed, but make sure everyone understands their responsibilities. This is a huge time-saver and prevents duplication. Decide, for instance, which member of the caregiving team updates the records and shares the information. When a medication for one of my parents changes, for example, the person who first learns of the change notes it on the printed medication list we keep near their medications, and then it's my responsibility to periodically update the copies I keep in my computer (you can use a shared storage system—see below), copy them into my note-taking app, and email them to my caregiving team. Our paid caregiver is responsible for letting me know when supplies are getting low; I then put them on my shopping list.
- **Plan ahead.** You'll always save time in an emergency or crisis if you've thought through and prepared the tools you'll need. See Chapter 11 for details about this topic.

Christie set up an efficient system when caregiving for her mom, who had dementia. Christie had her siblings send emails with updates so she could save their reports in Outlook folders. She created a Word document on her computer to track her mother's symptoms. She also went low-tech. "I used a spiral notebook in which I noted all doctors' contact information, listed meds and dosages, made notes during doctor/attorney/accountant,etc., appointments, tucked away information given to me by doctors and others," Christie says. She divided the notebook into medical, legal, and house information. This organization, she says, "gave me great peace of mind and helped keep me sane, because any time I needed a specific piece of information, I knew just where to go. [My] prior system of tracking down random notes I had written just didn't work!"

Information at Your Fingertips

Most of us have experienced the frantic search for a critical legal, health or financial document—often under heavy pressure due to a crisis or time crunch. Stop, catch your breath, and do yourself a favor: Start now to gather the information and documents I recommend later in this chapter and organize them for easy access. It may take you some time to find everything, so be patient with yourself. You may find them neatly labeled in a file cabinet, in a safe deposit box, or at the lawyer's office. On the other hand, they may be in a scrapbook or stashed away in a shoebox in the closet. Some items may be lost. Make it a treasure hunt and celebrate each time you find something—and you will likely also come across other precious family items in the process. Recently, while looking for a financial document, I came across my parents' tax returns dating back to the 1950s. They were full of family history, including locations of all their houses and how much they paid for their first house (less than $10,000)!

Then the next time you need one of these items, whether planned or unexpectedly, you'll be so relieved to have what you need. You can't control a lot of what happens to your loved ones in the course of caregiving, but this is one place where you can be proactive, and that's worth the effort, believe me.

Organizing the Information

You may want to leave documents where the people you care for had them, but make copies for yourself for easier tracking and access. If you're taking over management of your loved ones' affairs completely, you may want to move all these items and set up your own storage system. I recommend you keep your own personal documents separate from your loved ones' systems, either in separate cabinet drawers or separate cabinets. Here are a few organizing options to consider for paper or "hard" copies (more about how to organize digital copies using technology below).

- **Paper filing systems:** I purchased a filing system with preprinted file folder labels. These systems—some that offer guidance about what to file in each category and tips about what to keep and what to toss—are available at stores that sell office and organizational supplies.
- **Attorneys and financial managers:** Your loved ones' attorney should keep files for all key legal documents, such as advance directives (living wills and powers of attorney) and estate-planning documents (wills and living trusts). Financial managers should keep copies of everything they manage as well.
- **Safe deposit box:** Many people keep copies of important documents in safe deposit boxes at a bank. Your loved ones may already have a safe deposit box, and it might be a good idea to find out what's in it.
- **Multiple copies:** Don't hesitate to make copies of key documents and store them in more than one place. You'll need to be prepared in case of a natural disaster, fire, or flood or if you are several states away when a crisis occurs. I keep paper copies in a filing system as well as digital copies on my computer and in my apps for easy access.
- **Professional organizers:** If you can afford it, you might want to hire a professional organizer to sort documents and set up a filing system. I hired one just for a brief consultation, and then I implemented the plan myself. That approach cost less than if the organizer had implemented it.

Keep Records Up to Date

Equally important to gathering information is updating records. Information related to health, finances, and legal issues can change *often*, so keep everything current as changes happen. You never know when you'll need the information quickly, and too often I realize the information may be at my fingertips—but it's outdated. I find it more efficient to change things quickly as they happen than to take the time to go back later.

Technology

It seems like every day I hear about another website or app that can be helpful to caregivers. Some target caregivers specifically; others are good for many uses, including caregiving. Try out several in every category, and if the program doesn't make sense to you in the first 10 minutes, go on to the next one. I usually start with free apps or websites and try several to determine which features I like and how easy they are to use. I value recommendations from experts and friends, but app use is an individual thing—what is intuitive for me may not be for you. Here are some basic ways that technology can be help you get organized.

Your Computer

I have created a "Mom and Dad" folder on my computer, where I organize my parents' information in subfolders: legal, Mom health, Dad health, finances, caregiving, military service, family information, moving, etc. I keep Word and Excel documents for lists of medication and doctors, medical history, and financial information. This is personal and sensitive information, so be sure your computer is protected with a firewall and virus protection.

Emails

With emails, you can keep an organized record of vital information around your loved ones' care. You can create digital folders in your email program to categorize information. Some programs let you create rules to automatically file incoming emails in certain folders, which can save you time when you need to find that specific correspondence later. To keep a record of emails you send, you can cc (copy) yourself so you won't have to search through your "sent" box. Before I got app-savvy, I emailed myself notes and task lists that I could access later on my computer.

Online Storage, Backup, and File Sharing

You have many options to digitally store almost anything on your computer, including Cobalt, Dropbox, Google Drive, iCloud, and Mozy. Most options for storing in "the cloud" (that is, on the Internet) offer a limited amount of free space, with prices increasing as you add storage space. By allowing file sharing with others, you can give your family access to important documents from their own computers as well. The ability to access documents from any computer or mobile device can be invaluable to working caregivers. It also can give you the peace of mind that if the computer crashes, or you don't have your computer with you, your documents are safely stored. Many a time I have needed to access a Word document while on a business trip or in a doctor's office and have easily pulled it from the cloud to my phone.

Comprehensive Family Organizing

Websites and apps geared to family organizing can centralize your and your loved ones' lives with digital copies of documents and photos as well as coordinated calendars and task lists. These sites and apps differ from basic online storage or backup services because they organize everything for you and let you keep information in one location. Some options include AboutOne, Cozi, Doxo, and Famjama. These have a system to organize pictures and health, education, legal, and volunteering information as well as features that document family milestones and memories and inventory possessions and household information. You can put in a home address, for instance, and an app could provide its current estimated value.

Scans

The ability to scan documents into your computer via your printer, copier, or scanner can reduce clutter. Once you scan a document and store it safely online, you may not need to keep a paper filing system at all. (Be sure to ask your financial manager, accountant, and/or lawyer which documents you need to save hard copies of and for how long.) Scanning helped me out when I applied for veterans' benefits for Dad. I scanned in his military papers so that later I could just email them for the application or access them from my mobile device or computer.

Caregiving Team Coordination

Many websites and apps can help you communicate with family members, friends, and paid caregivers. You can coordinate your loved ones' needs, progress, and symptoms; share task lists; organize volunteer support; and ask paid caregivers to provide updates so you can monitor their activities. Some caregiving apps include Carezone, CaringBridge, Lotsa Helping Hands, and MobiCare Health. You can also create your own family website or shared calendar using tools such as www.myfamily.com, www.familylobby.com, and www.mygreatbigfamily.com.

Note-Taking

Do you find yourself with sticky notes everywhere? Jotting down notes at a doctor's appointment or family meeting and then searching for them in vain later? I used to stick notes all over my front door so I'd see them as walked out; I'd find doctor appointment notes on the back of work documents. No more! I use a note-taking app (there are many, including Evernote, Google Keep, OneNote, and SkyNote) that synchronizes automatically between my smartphone, tablet, and computer. Anywhere I go I can find notes and history organized by work, personal, and Mom and Dad. Frequently, Mom's doctors would ask me how long she'd been on a medication. I would pull up my notes, search by the doctor's name, and find all notes from visits with him. Voilá—I often found the date he had changed her medication faster than he could find it in his system! I also clip web pages that help me research medical conditions and send copies to my sisters and paid caregivers. When doctors give me brochures, I check to see if they are available online and simply save the links in easy-to-find folders. I also store key documents, recipes my parents like, and notes about their personal care or changes in their abilities.

Task Lists

Juggling life, work, and caregiving, my to-do lists are endless. But I no longer waste time and mental energy trying to remember what needs to be done. I have used several task-list apps; pick one that fits your needs. Apps include Astrid, Errands, Producteev, Remember the Milk, reQall, Todoist, Toodledo, Workflowy, and Wunderlist. I look for a few features: automatic synchronization, so when I create or check off a task, the update is made on all my devices; organization by categories (such as work, home, Mom and Dad); and a function to share certain lists with our team so I can assign tasks and we can work together to accomplish ongoing and special projects.

Shopping Lists

Shopping for yourself and your loved ones? Each shopping list app is unique, but in most you can separate items by stores or by your and your loved ones' lists. Some also synchronize and have a "history" feature so you can see and choose items you've bought previously. And the lists are sharable, so paid caregivers or other family members can add items for you to pick up—or you can add to their lists. Shopping list apps include Cozi, Green Grocer, Grocery Gadgets, Grocery IQ, Shopper, Shopping List, and Ziplist.

Bill Paying and Financial Tracking

Track money you spend on caregiving, pay your loved ones' bills, and track their finances using financial apps and software. Quicken is a popular personal finance software, and many apps, such as Check, Manilla, and Mint can help manage money.

Medical Alerts and GPS

Medical alert systems that allow your loved ones to push a button and get help (or that check in with them daily) have long been available for use at home; they're now available for use outside of the home, using GPS technology. And if the people you care for have dementia, you may be concerned about them getting lost. The latest technology enables GPS tracking via a cell phone your loved ones carry, a pendant, or even shoes they wear. You can see where they are and where they have been via your computer or mobile device. Some to consider are the Alzheimer's Association Comfort Zone, eCare+Voice, Lifeline, and the Mobile Alert System from Medical Guardian. Your local warehouse store (such as BJ's, Costco, or Sam's Club) may sell medical alert systems, and you can check with your local area agency on aging (www.eldercare.gov) about local companies.

Medical Records

Numerous websites and apps can help you keep track of medical information and history; some are geared toward specific conditions or diseases. The trick is finding those that work for you. One I like is iBlueButton because it transforms Medicare information into useful medical history, medication, and doctor lists. Others include Blood Pressure Monitor—Family Lite, Capzule PHR, Glucose Buddy, and WebMD. AARP offers an online Health Record tool (free for members at www.aarp.org/healthrecord), where all doctors, medical appointments, procedures, medications and more can be recorded in one place. Caregivers can also be given access to records to help keep track of things.

Electronic health records (EHR) are now available in most hospital systems and some doctors' offices, providing health records that are shared among multiple facilities and agencies. They usually include information about doctor visits, allergies, medications, insurance, family history, immunizations, diseases and conditions, hospitalizations and surgeries. Some doctors now have websites where patients can access appointment notes, prescriptions, X-ray reports, and more.

Bill Carter thought it would be a comfort to his mother if he helped her inventory her important personal possessions of both financial and sentimental value. "I wanted to give my mother peace of mind, and I wanted to do it efficiently in a way all family members could access in the future," says Bill. He started by taking pictures of family heirlooms and using Evernote to store the pictures, along with descriptions and stories his mother shared about each heirloom. When he's done, he'll have his siblings go through and discuss what they'd like to have.

Documents and Information to Gather

Depending on the amount of support you currently provide, you may not need all the documents and information I list below. But keep in mind that your caregiving role may increase over time, so you might need access in the future. Talk with the people you care for about gathering these items strictly for informational purposes for potential use in the future.

The Basics
- Address and phone numbers
- Driver's license
- State identification card, if your loved ones don't drive (available through the bureau of motor vehicles)
- Social Security number
- Military records
- Organ donor cards
- Burial and funeral instructions
- Cemetery deed
- At least three emergency contacts (including yourself), with full names, phone numbers, addresses, and emails
- Other family and friends in the order they should be called in case of emergency, again, with all contact information
- Passwords and personal identification numbers (PIN) for all accounts, including retail, banks, social media, and email
- Faith community (such as church, temple, synagogue, pastor, priest, or rabbi) with contact information
- Neighbors or friends who might be helpful, with contact information
- House cleaners, yard or pool caretakers, and handyman, with contact information
- Names and contact information for agencies and individuals serving your loved ones, such as home care, transportation, housing, adult day services, counseling, therapies, emergency response services (medical alert), volunteers, and telephone reassurance

- Other personal care service providers, such as manicurist, hair stylist, and massage therapist
- Veterinarian, pet sitter, dog walker, and groomer.

Legal (for details, see Chapter 6)

- Estate-planning documents (including wills and living trusts)
- Powers of attorney (can include finance, health care, mental health care, digital [for access to digital devices and assets such as phones, laptops, computers, websites]); consult an attorney regarding necessary powers of attorney in your situation.
- Citizenship or naturalization papers
- Passports, green cards, and visas
- Marriage certificates
- Divorce/separation decrees
- Adoption papers
- Automobile titles
- Deeds to house or other property
- Rental agreements or contracts.

Financial (for details, see Chapter 7)

- Name and contact information for financial managers, stockbrokers, investment advisers, and accountants
- Bank and investment accounts, including the name of institution, state where the account was opened, account numbers, names on each account, value, and associated debit cards
- Records for and amounts of income such as from insurance payments, Social Security, retirement, pensions, public benefits, veterans' benefits, real estate income and support from family members
- Number and location of safe deposit boxes and keys
- Credit card companies along with account numbers, expiration, websites, payment due date, passwords, and whether the accounts are on autopay
- Mortgage and home equity line of credit documents
- Expenses (such as utilities, care, medical, and rent), and whether they are on autopay

- Insurance policies (such as life, disability, long-term care, home, rental, and automobile)
- Inventory of valuable belongings (such as jewelry, art, silver, antiques, vehicles, boats, and real estate), and current value
- Recent tax documents, current receipts, and records for deductions.

Health/Medical (for details, see Chapter 8)
- Names and contact information for all doctors, with what condition they treat
- Names and contact information for local and mail-order pharmacies
- A list of medications and supplements, including the purpose, dosage, schedule, prescribing doctor, pharmacy where it is filled, and side effects
- Medical history, with past and present conditions, blood type, drug allergies, surgeries, and hospitalizations
- Health insurance coverage, with copies of all insurance cards, including Medicare or Medicaid and private insurance
- Advance directives, including a living will, health-care and mental health care power of attorney, do not resuscitate orders (DNR), and Physicians Orders for Life Sustaining Treatment (POLST) (Check with an attorney and/or the local area agency on aging to find out if there are additional advance directives forms or orders available in your loved ones' state.)
- Long-term care insurance documents.

Your Job Description: Efficiency Expert

Congratulations! You have tackled the mounds of paper and spent hours on the phone and computer. You have earned a new component of your job description:

Gathers documents and information pertinent to caregiving. Creates and implements filing systems and environmental changes to maximize productivity. Evaluates processes, routine activities, and tasks, designs streamlined procedures for maximum efficiency and achievement. Gains competency in using technology.

CHAPTER 5

WORKING CAREGIVERS

*O*n a recent morning, I helped Dad and Mom get out of bed and assisted them with toileting, brushing their teeth, and dressing. I fed their service dog, Jackson. I brought Mom the newspaper and cleaned her glasses, and I got Dad settled with music and coffee on the back porch. I administered medications for all three of them, fixed their breakfasts, cleaned up the kitchen, rescheduled Mom's doctor appointment because it conflicted with my paid job, sang and danced with Dad and reassured him repeatedly that everyone was OK and there was nothing he needed to be doing, and put something for dinner in the crockpot. That was interspersed with work for my paid job: reading and writing emails, sending out tweets and Facebook posts, preparing for a radio interview later that day, participating in a conference call, and researching an upcoming blog post.*

Just another crazy day in my life of juggling my life and two jobs: caregiving and my paid work.

Not every morning is quite so frenetic, though the juggling is typical. Somehow, like so many other working caregivers, I manage to get it all done. I go from sleeping in hospitals to being on the "Today" show to getting urine samples to deciphering insurance claims. Depending on the day, or the minute, you'll find me wearing designer dresses and make-up, or sweat pants and a ponytail.

Sometimes my life seems surreal. Most of the time, I'm grateful . . . but exhausted.

Introduction

The majority—nearly three-quarters—of the more than 42 million caregivers in the United States have also worked at paid jobs at some point during their caregiving journey. Those of us who juggle life, work, and caregiving may feel, or indeed may be, very alone in this important endeavor. As you read this chapter, you may see yourself in the working caregivers described. Whatever our circumstances, we all have challenges, and we all struggle to balance work and caregiving along with our other relationships and personal lives.

We really have at least two jobs: The work we get paid for and our caregiving job, because make no mistake: Caregiving at *any* level is hard, but rewarding, work. We may feel we don't have enough hours in the day to work and manage our own lives, much less support our loved ones. Often we don't know how long we will play this role, but we do know that the needs of the people we care for and the demands on our time and energy will more than likely increase over time.

In this chapter you'll learn about:
- Who working caregivers are and the roles we play.
- The special challenges working caregivers face.
- Ways to talk with your employer about your caregiving role.
- How to adapt your work schedule, location, or position.
- What kinds of employer leave policies and other benefits can support you and your loved ones.
- What to do if caregiving causes problems at work.
- When to consider a job change.
- How to get paid for caregiving.

Barbara, an executive in a large technology company, is the primary caregiver for her husband, who is older. Her work requires her to be in an office 300 miles away from her husband four days a week, so he has a part-time professional caregiver. Barbara is in meetings all day long and struggles with constant phone calls from her husband. "Sometimes he calls just to ask what I'm doing!"

Barbara says. "I don't want to be short with him, but what am I supposed to do when he's calling me all day at work?" Barbara says she prioritizes work and caring for her husband, but she misses having personal time. "I'd just love to have time to go out for dinner with friends, see a play, or even get my watch battery replaced!" she says.

The Lowdown on Working Caregivers

Who Are Working Caregivers?

If you are a working caregiver, you are not alone. As I mentioned, out of the 42 million people who are caregiving, 74 percent have worked at a paying job at some point during their caregiving experience. Many of us have our own spouses and children to care for. Some care for multiple family members or friends. In addition, according to an AARP Public Policy Institute study of caregivers in the United States:

- 61 percent of caregivers age 50+ work: 50 percent work full-time, 11 percent work part-time.
- 42 percent of U.S. employees have cared for an older relative or friend in the last five years, and 49 percent of the workforce expects to provide care in the next five years.
- 20 percent of all female workers and 16 percent of all male workers in the United States are family caregivers.
- 22 percent—almost a quarter—of caregivers in the workplace are 45 to 64 years old.

Working caregivers are employed in every industry and at every level. We are self-employed and work for a wide variety of companies, from small local businesses to large global conglomerates. We work as CEOs, teachers, and receptionists. We work on Wall Street, in restaurants, and on construction sites. We work from home, offices, stores, and factories. We interact with people on the phone; we use computers and videoconferencing; and we serve customers face-to-face. We work full-time, part-time, flextime, night shifts, day shifts, and every combination in between. Some of us travel for our jobs.

Working caregivers are everywhere, though you may not know it. Some of us are open at work about our caregiving roles, but others keep it to themselves. Those who don't disclose their caregiving situations may do so for personal reasons, but many keep quiet because they are concerned about repercussions at work.

Challenges Specific to Working Caregivers

Working caregivers are in the position of keeping (or finding) work while meeting the constantly changing needs of the people we care for. We never know when a crisis is around the corner that will disrupt our work schedule. Some of us have employers who are generally supportive of our caregiving roles, seeing the value of keeping good employees; other caregivers struggle to work in inflexible situations. Most of us have an excellent work history and ethic, and we worry about keeping up our standards at work while also being the best possible caregivers.

You may worry about making work deadlines because you have to take your loved ones to an appointment or deal with an emergency or another unexpected caregiving issue. You may use your lunchtime, breaks, and vacations to care for your loved ones, adjust your work habits and hours to meet their needs, and talk to your employer about your situation. You may feel guilty when you are working because you aren't with your loved ones—and vice versa. You may even feel forced to choose between the people you care for and your work, and in reality there will be times when you have to do that. If the situation becomes too stressful, you may refuse paid work because you don't have the time; you may look for a less demanding job or change your career goals. In the extreme, you may quit your job altogether because you just can't juggle all your responsibilities.

At one point, Charlie was caring for not one, not two, but three fam-
ily members—his mother (who has Parkinson's disease), his father
(who had dementia and was living in a facility), and his younger

brother (who suffered brain damage and paralysis from an acci-
dent)—each of whom lived in a different location scattered across
the city. At the same time, Charlie was working a demanding job
as a Senate investigator. "I often felt that I was not giving any of
them enough time and attention. If any of them had an emergency,
I couldn't spend time with the others, and frequently more than one
of them needed urgent care," he says. "I am glad I was able to be
there for all of them, but it was a real struggle."

According to the AARP Public Policy Institute, working caregivers often
have to alter their working situation, to the detriment of long-term career
advancement and financial security:

- 68 percent of caregivers have had to make work accommodations,
  such as taking time off, coming in late, leaving early, refusing a promotion, reducing work hours, changing jobs, or quitting. Low-income
  employees, minorities, and women are most likely to make work
  accommodations to care for older relatives. Cutting back on hours or
  quitting can hurt earnings as well as health insurance, Social Security
  benefits, and contributions to retirement plans.
- 19 percent of retirees stopped working earlier than planned because
  of caregiving, with significant loss of income: Female caregivers age
  50+ who stop working to care for a parent lose an average of $324,044
  in wages and benefits over the course of their lives; male caregivers
  age 50+ lose an average of $283,716.
- Caregivers who work are more likely than their non-caregiving colleagues to have health challenges and report fair or poor health in
  general.

Let's face it: Caring for our loved ones can be very demanding and requires
sacrifice. Working caregivers have an additional layer of burden. Studies
have shown how taxed we are. Compared to our non-caregiving colleagues,
we are less rested, have elevated daily and chronic pain, and have more
health issues, such as high blood pressure. We generally have more to
deal with in terms of emotional health. Guilt, frustration, anger, despair,

sadness, grief, and fear may be our constant companions. We often sacrifice financially and struggle with our loved ones' legal issues, such as advance directives or estate planning. Our careers may be short-circuited. Relationships with partners, spouses, children, siblings, and friends may suffer. Finding balance can be tough.

How Working Can Help Us

Some of us keep working to earn a living, support our own families, prepare for retirement, and perhaps also support our loved ones. But besides bringing in vital income, working can help us in other ways with our caregiving duties. Some of us love our work and have a strong desire to continue working; work is an important part of our identity. Or we find work to be a respite, a break from caregiving.

Our work experiences can also help us in our roles as caregivers. Some of us are managers, coordinators, customer-service experts, organizers, and planners. Or we know how to use technology, ask questions, and research solutions. We can advocate and prioritize. We know how to manage budgets and monitor investments. We have lots of experience at building relationships. We are resourceful and have the ability to juggle several issues and projects at once. All of these skills are needed for caregiving.

Communicating with Your Employer

Employees been long been coached to leave our personal lives at home. Not surprisingly, then, many working caregivers are afraid to let their employers or colleagues know they are caregiving. We fear we will be seen as distracted, uncommitted, or unreliable; discriminated against; passed over for promotion opportunities; or, worst of all, lose our jobs. We worry that if we share all the ups and downs—and we encounter crises almost daily, it seems—our bosses will see us as whiners.

Our fears aren't always unfounded. Some employers don't understand the important connection between employees' personal lives and their work—or they just don't seem to care. And not all working caregivers are treated equally: Many have told me they feel that colleagues who care for children are treated very differently from those who care for older family members. Some male caregivers have shared their frustration that they are not treated the same as female caregivers.

While every job is unique, keeping your employer apprised of your situation is usually a good idea. If you're missing deadlines, coming in late, or using a lot of leave, your supervisor may wonder why or simply assume you are not focused or committed. It's better for your employer to know the challenges you are facing and understand that you are, and want to continue to be, a valued employee. Here are some tips for approaching your employer.

- Consider talking with your human resources or personnel manager about any company benefits and policies that might help you as a caregiver (see below).
- Schedule a face-to-face meeting, if possible, with your immediate supervisor to explain your caregiving situation.
    - Be professional, sincere, calm, and confident.
    - Affirm your commitment to your job.
    - Explain the basic facts about your role as a caregiver, including the unpredictability of your situation. You probably won't want to go into all the details; you just want to convey the gist of your responsibilities.
    - Agree on how you will communicate changes in the future.
    - If you are experiencing a specific challenge, suggest solutions, such as a flexible work schedule or leave of absence, and ask for suggestions as well.
    - Work out an agreement with the understanding that the situation could change. Put your arrangement in writing and make sure your human resources or personnel office has a copy or knows about it.
- Keep your employer apprised of changes as they occur, and update your agreement as needed so everyone is clear about roles and expectations.

Employer Support for Caregivers

Many employers offer support for working caregivers. Some reasons are altruistic: Caregivers provide a crucial part of support for our loved ones, including the growing number of older adults who need care. Without our help, our loved ones might need to depend on public or private services—or go without. But the primary driver is probably the company's bottom line. We caregivers are often experienced workers who have a great deal to contribute in the workplace. If we stop working, our employers can lose our talents and experience. That's why many employers offer policies, benefits, and services that have been shown to increase productivity, lower employee stress, reduce company health-care costs, reduce absenteeism, increase employee retention, improve health of current workers, increase company loyalty, and attract new employees. It's a win-win situation. With these supports, many caregivers can more easily accomplish their work and caregiving responsibilities. Caregivers also say they are happier about their work and feel an increased sense of loyalty and commitment to their employers.

Workplace policies that help caregivers can be as simple as providing a private place to make a caregiving-related phone call at work or allowing employees to have access to their mobile phones so they can be reached in case they are needed in an emergency or have to arrange backup care or handle other caregiving issues. Many employers now offer flexible work schedules and locations, thanks to advances in technology. The largest employers are more likely to offer specific services to help you juggle work and caregiving, although the supports may not be exclusively for caregivers. Sometimes they'll fall under the category of work-life programs, benefits, or policies.

Check with the human resources department, personnel manager, or your union. If you work for a smaller company that doesn't have those, talk with your supervisor or the company owner.

Laurette Bennhold-Samaan was a caregiver for her father, her mother, and her husband for more than 20 years. She worked that entire time, sometimes for companies that required her to work in an office,

sometimes for those that allowed her to telecommute. "Some super-
visors were more understanding than others about taking time off,
and some organizations didn't care at all how I managed my time, as
long as I got my work done," she says. "The virtual jobs have been
less stressful and more flexible so I could get both my caregiving
tasks and my work done." Despite many years of balancing work
and caregiving, her career advanced well: She is now chief operat-
ing officer of a global company and continues to work from home.

Work Hours
Changing Work Hours
You might consider requesting a permanent change to your work hours.
If people you care for primarily need help in the mornings, perhaps you
could work in the afternoons and evenings. Or if the people you care for
mostly have medical appointments in the afternoon, perhaps you could
work a split shift—mornings and evenings. For some caregivers, simply
starting their workday an hour or two later and working into the evenings
can make life more manageable.

Requesting a Predictable Hourly Schedule
It can be difficult for hourly workers with erratic schedules to help loved
ones. If you are able to request set hours, you may be better able to arrange
your loved ones' care needs around your work schedule.

Asking for Flexible Hours
Some employers want employees to have a fixed schedule, but others are
flexible as long as employees work a specified number of hours per day.
A flexible schedule can be ideal for a working caregiver, since it's hard
to predict when your loved ones will need your help. One day you may
work 9 a.m. to 5 p.m.; the next you may take your loved one to an appointment in the morning and work 12 p.m. to 8 p.m. I've found that flexible
hours are one of the greatest benefits of being an independent contractor
or consultant. According to AARP and National Alliance for Caregiving
studies of caregivers in the United States, more workers (65 percent) in

2009 than in 2004 (57 percent) reported shifting their arrival or departure times or taking time off to provide care.

Working Compressed Weeks

Does your company offer the opportunity to work longer hours for fewer days? Some employers offer a one-week compressed schedule (work four longer days and take the fifth day off, for example) or a two-week compressed schedule (work nine longer days and get one day off). Before telecommuting full time, I worked a compressed schedule for many years, and that extra day was a lifesaver, allowing me to get my caregiving duties done.

Working Part-Time, Sharing Jobs, Cross-Training, and Phasing in Retirement

If you can't work full time but want to keep doing your job, you might propose scaling back to a part-time position with your current employer or finding part-time employment with another company. Another option you could propose is job-sharing—keep your current job but share it with another person, splitting the work and the pay. Some employers cross-train employees so one can easily step in when another needs time off. Your employer may provide opportunities for a "phased retirement," in which you'd work part-time for a period of time before full retirement. With these options, you'll want to make sure you adjust your budget if you'll have a reduced income.

I was living and working in the Washington, D.C. area when the call came: Dad needed a hip replacement. Mom had suffered a stroke, so I knew she couldn't care for him and their home. So I went to Arizona for a month to help, taking a bit of vacation leave and the rest of the time tele-commuting 2,000 miles from my workplace. I met my work goals, helped Dad through his recovery, and took care of Mom. Technology, along with an employer who knew I worked hard, trusted me, and offered flexible work options, made it possible.

Work Location
Telecommuting
Sometimes called "remote work" or "telework," telecommuting is an option that allows you to work from home or some other location, such as your loved ones' home or another office. Some employers offer full-time telecommuting jobs. Others allow some telecommuting time every week, or short-term telecommuting during an emergency or acute caregiving time. Caregivers often cite telecommuting as the most helpful flexible work option, because it allows them to help the people they care for with personal care or transportation to doctor appointments and then get right to work wherever they are located, rather than wasting time traveling to work or taking more time off. Some companies will support telecommuting with computers and other equipment; others will require you to supply your own equipment.

Transferring Locations
If you're caregiving long distance or even across town and your company has a work site closer to your loved ones' location, you might consider a permanent or temporary transfer.

Paid and Unpaid Leave
Employers offer different paid and unpaid options for taking time off. Because these policies vary widely, it is important that you understand your employer's policies. Not all employers offer all of these options.

Caregiving Leave
While it is rare, some employers have a policy for taking time off specifically for caregiving, either paid or unpaid.

Paid Vacation Leave
Many caregivers devote their vacation time to caregiving. For many years before I was self-employed, I used the majority of my vacation time to help with my grandparents and parents.

Paid Sick Leave

Some employers allow employees to use sick time for caring for sick family members; in fact, this is required or mandated in some states and jurisdictions.

Paid or Unpaid Bereavement Leave

Some companies allow time off when an immediate family member dies. Find out what relatives this policy covers. Does it include your grandmother, aunt or uncle, partner or close friend? Find out how much time you'll be allowed.

Paid Personal Leave

You may have paid time off for unspecified "personal" use (in addition to sick or vacation time off). Usually personal days can be used for whatever purpose you need.

Donated Leave

Some companies allow employees to donate their unused vacation, sick and/or personal time to other employees who are experiencing a hardship and need more paid time off.

Paid or Unpaid Leave of Absence

If you need to take an extended period of time off work, your employer may offer several options. *Most extended leave will be unpaid.* Keep in mind that your job may be protected for a period of time but perhaps not indefinitely. Contact the U.S. Department of Labor or talk with your employer to find out if you are eligible for any of these forms of leave.

- **Family and Medical Leave Act (FMLA):** The federal FMLA entitles eligible employees of all public agencies, all public and private elementary and secondary schools, and companies with 50 or more employees who work within a 75-mile radius to up to 12 weeks a year of unpaid leave as well as job protection. One caveat: You must have worked there for a full year prior to requesting leave and have worked at least 1,250 hours in the past 12 months. Under the FMLA, employers must continue to provide group health insurance coverage during your time off and protect your job; in other words, your job (or a job that is equal in pay, benefits, and responsibility) will still be there when you return. Intermittent leave is also a protected right under the FMLA; you do not have to take all of the time off at once. You can take FMLA leave for specified family and medical reasons, including caring for a spouse, child, or parent with a serious health condition. Some states also have paid family and medical leave, so be sure to find out about state laws and policies.

- **Military caregiver leave:** Military caregiver leave provisions of the FMLA provide specifically for those who are caring for a covered service member—your spouse, child, parent, or next of kin—with a serious injury or illness. You can get up to 26 weeks of unpaid leave during a single 12-month period, although there are some restrictions.
- **Smaller employers' leave policy:** If your employer has fewer than 50 employees, find out if your state has additional laws requiring certain unpaid family and medical leave policies. Even without state laws, some employers will offer unpaid leave for family and medical care.

Services and Support for Working Caregivers and Their Loved Ones

While not every employer will provide these services, the following is an overview of the types of services that some employers offer.

For Working Caregivers
- **Employee Assistance Program (EAP):** Some employers offer employee assistance programs to help employees with personal issues that might otherwise affect their work. Services might include short-term counseling and referrals to services.
- **Caregiver support groups:** Some employers offer caregiver support groups that meet on-site during lunch or after working hours. They may provide a trained facilitator, speakers, a place to meet, and refreshments.

- **Counseling benefits:** Does your health insurance include mental health support, therapy, or counseling? These may give you valuable support and guidance to navigate the caregiving journey.
- **Information and referral/assistance:** These services might include caregiving fairs with a variety of local eldercare and other types of services, lunchtime seminars, printed materials, access to websites with targeted information, and a call center.
- **Legal assistance:** If your employer offers discounted legal services as part of its employee benefits package, you might get help with powers of attorney or other legal issues related to caring for your loved ones.
- **Health and wellness:** Some employers offer on-site exercise facilities and activities. I once worked for an organization that offered weight-loss groups and yoga and meditation classes. We know that taking care of ourselves as caregivers is vitally important, but finding the time to do so is a major challenge. The ability to work these activities into a lunch hour or immediately before or after work can make it possible. Some companies offer fitness club memberships at reduced costs, which can motivate us to take care of ourselves and make it affordable.
- **Volunteer programs:** If your employer isn't able to provide paid professional services or discounts, perhaps employees could volunteer their time to help each other, arranging for knowledgeable speakers on caregiving topics, bringing in brochures from local agencies, sponsoring workshops, or running support groups. Some employers may provide limited financial support for such efforts.
- **Child or adult care:** If you're sandwiched between caring for children or grandchildren and caring for an older loved one, employer assistance with child care may be helpful. Some employers offer on-site child care, discounted child care services, or information and referrals to child care. A few employers have tried on-site eldercare services, such as adult day services.
- **Concierge services:** Some companies offer concierge services that help employees with errands so they can spend more time—and be more focused—at work.

For Your Loved Ones

- **Needs assessment:** Employers may offer the free or discounted services of an individual or agency trained to assess your loved ones' situation and home environment and to make recommendations.
- **Geriatric care management:** Some employers offer the free or discounted services of a geriatric care manager for a one-time consultation, on-call advice and support, emergency intervention, or ongoing services. A geriatric care manager can assess your loved ones' needs and your family resources, help you create a caregiving plan, and monitor your loved ones' care.
- **Backup care:** Some employers offer discounted backup care for employees who have a temporary breakdown in their normal care arrangement so they can still go to work.
- **Help with insurance paperwork:** Some employers have staff that understand insurance, Medicaid, and Medicare and will help guide employees and their families through the complicated maze of paperwork.
- **Discounted professional care services:** Some companies provide vouchers, subsidies, or discounted services for the people their employees are caring for, such as for adult day services, professional caregivers, or respite services.

Workplace Discrimination Toward Caregivers

Unfortunately, you may find yourself being treated differently than other employees. There are a growing number of lawsuits alleging stereotyping of and discrimination toward caregivers, known as "family responsibilities discrimination" or "caregiver discrimination." I've heard of caregivers who are denied time off to care for chronically ill family members because their supervisors judge the care as not necessary. I've heard of caregivers who, when they return to work after attending their loved ones' funerals and dealing with end-of-life issues, are told their jobs have been filled. I've heard of supervisors discriminating against a male caregiver because they don't see caregiving as a "man's job" and won't support flexibility. Even if you are keeping up with your work and performing your duties perfectly, the perception may be that you are not as serious about your career or as competent or committed because you are dealing with caregiving issues.

Caregivers are not a protected group under the federal Equal Employment Opportunity statutes; in fact, no laws specifically protect working caregivers. There are very limited federal protections from the Family and Medical Leave Act, the Americans with Disabilities Act of 1990, the Rehabilitation Act of 1973, Title VII of the Civil Rights Act of 1964, the Age Discrimination in Employment Act of 1967 and the Employee Retirement Income Security Act of 1974, all of which were enacted to protect against other forms of discrimination. Some state and local laws also provide protections. You may also have other protections based on your employer's policies or, if you are a member of a union, your collective-bargaining agreements.

If you feel you are a victim of family responsibilities discrimination, you can consider taking these actions:

- Maintain written records of all conversations and incidents related to your situation (including date, time, people involved, and what was said) as well as relevant emails and letters. Be sure to write this outside of work time, and keep your documentation at home.
- Keep track of the time passing from the first incident, because state and federal laws may have time limitations for filing claims.
- Ask your employer about any policies that may protect you. Ask your union about benefits or protections you are entitled to as well as union advocates or legal support to help you.
- Check your human resources or personnel manual for specific procedures to follow when filing a claim of discrimination, and follow the steps precisely.
- Explain your situation to your manager or your human resources or personnel department and see if you can negotiate an agreeable solution.
- If you are unable to resolve the situation, you can contact an attorney who specializes in employment law, your local legal aid or legal services office, your city or state human rights commission, the U.S.

Department of Labor, or, to file a complaint, the local Equal Opportunity Office or the U.S. Equal Employment Opportunity Commission (EEOC). Explain your situation to find out about your rights.

When You Need to Make a Job Change

Knowing When It's Time

If your health is suffering, if your stress levels are off the charts, if your friends and family are concerned, and if you've exhausted your options for getting help to care for your loved ones, perhaps you'll have to change your paid job. It's hard to know when you reach that point, primarily because you're probably caregiving at such an intense level that you're in "keep moving" mode. Hopefully you do stop and consider your options, though, before you crash. You'll want to consider ways to replace lost income as well—such as a different type of job or public benefits, if you qualify.

Your Options

When "something's gotta give," check out these opportunities. Be sure to consider the financial consequences as well as the changes in lifestyle and the repercussions on your career and retirement goals. Meeting with a career counselor and a financial planner to discuss options is a good idea.

- You could take a less demanding job for now that either keeps you on your career path or takes you in another direction that you're interested in.
- You could transition from full-time to part-time work, or job-share, freeing up your time for caregiving but continuing to bring in income.
- You could try a less stressful position, either with a new employer or in your current company. Staying with your current employer where people know you might afford you an opportunity to return in the future to a full-time job or a position with higher responsibility.
- You could try to fashion a consulting or contracting position where you arrange more flexible hours for yourself.

- You could retire. Some caregivers who have reached their retirement savings goals or receive an early retirement package from their employers retire so they can focus more energy on caring for loved ones.

Your Caregiving Experience Can Be a Plus

Remember that the experience you are gaining as a caregiver may open doors for you to develop a new career path. Check out the "job descriptions" at the end of each chapter in this guide to catalogue the skills you are building.

Finding the Best New Employer for You

When you assess a prospective employer, find out about their policies and benefits that might be helpful to you. Look at the list above: Do they offer flexible work options? Supports for caregivers?

Being Paid to Care for Loved Ones

For some people, caring for loved ones is so consuming that they need to stop their other paid work. In some cases, the people we care for can pay us to be their caregiver.

Income Sources to Pay Caregivers

Anyone can pay a family member, just as they would a professional caregiver, to provide care. Some families may have enough money in their budgets. Others rely on special income sources like these:

- **Veterans' benefits:** Veterans who were in active duty during wartime and meet other asset and expense requirements may be able to receive Veterans Aid and Attendance and Housebound benefits to help with long-term care. These funds can be used to pay for caregiving services. Vets may also receive health care as well as special funds to pay for a limited amount of respite care. (See the Resources section for more information.)

- **Long-term care insurance:** If your loved ones have long-term care insurance that covers home care, those funds might be used to pay you as their caregiver.
- **Medicaid:** In some states, Medicaid funds can be used to pay family caregivers to provide care at home.

The Nitty-Gritty of Working for Loved Ones

If you are paid to provide care for your loved ones, be sure to take these steps:

- **Create a family caregiving agreement:** A written caregiving contract or agreement should outline your full duties and responsibilities, schedule (including time off), and payment amount. The more detail the better. You and the people you care for should sign and date the agreement. It's a good idea to have a witness also sign.
- **Pay your taxes and Social Security:** As a self-employed worker, you will have to declare the income from your loved ones and may have to pay estimated quarterly taxes. Consult a tax professional.
- **Have loved ones count your payment as a medical expense for tax purposes:** The people you care for may be able to include your pay in their total medical expenses when they submit their taxes. Consult a tax professional about how to handle these expenses.
- **Be professional:** You'll likely feel better about providing care for your loved ones compared to someone else doing so, but you need to keep in mind that it is a job, and it may be stressful. Get feedback from your loved ones and other team members to ensure you are meeting their expectations.

Your Job Description: Work-Life Coordinator

Researches work/life benefits and policies. Requests flexible work arrangements necessary to maintain work while caregiving and communicates with employer about caregiving roles. Relies on extensive experience and judgment to plan and accomplish work goals while living up to caregiving responsibilities. Employs creativity in balancing work, caregiving, and personal life. Adjusts career goals as appropriate while maintaining professional identity and bringing in necessary income.

CHAPTER 6
LEGAL MATTERS

*O*ur family has wonderful memories of our farm in the rolling hills of southeastern Ohio. We rode our horses, grew gardens, and explored every inch of the 75 acres, with Dad walking stick in hand and leading the way with enthusiastic descriptions of the plants and wildlife we discovered around every corner. When my parents moved to Arizona in 1981, they rented out the property. Recently, though, the family farm became a financial drain, so we had to put it up for sale. It was a difficult and emotional decision, because the farm meant so much to us and because my sister and her family had been living there for many years.

The farm was in my parents' living trust, and I was empowered—through the trust and a legal document known as a durable power of attorney for finances—to handle their business. With the help of our attorneys, I was able to facilitate the sale.

But then complications arose after the sale was final. I was unable to deposit the check in my parents' checking account. The bank required a new account in the name of their living trust. In addition, the bank would not allow me to open the new account for my parents, although they had designated me as their agent in their power of attorney and I am a trustee in their living trust. It turned out, according to our attorneys, that the bank should, but did not have to, honor the power of attorney. So my parents had to complete the bank's forms requiring more than 10 signatures each—a difficult and discouraging process for them because of their disabilities.

I had thought we were prepared for any legal issue that might arise, but now I know that banks and other financial institutions as well as the Social Security Administration can require completion of their own powers of attorney and other authorization forms.

Introduction

Legal challenges inevitably arise when we care for our loved ones. They may suffer health problems and become unable to make medical decisions for themselves or manage the never-ending insurance issues that arise. You may need to make those decisions and take over dealing with the insurance. You might need to pay bills, sign papers, and make financial decisions for them. When they pass on, you may need to manage their estate. You're likely dealing with a job as well as a roller coaster of energy and emotions when you're caregiving. That's why it's so important to make sure that legal issues are taken care of before a crisis occurs. Equally important, you don't want to worry your loved ones with legal matters when they can't understand or when they need their strength to fight illness.

If the people you care for haven't already taken the steps to get their legal affairs in order, encourage or help them to do so now. You might check with your employer to find out if any legal services are offered to you as an employee benefit that might be helpful.

In this chapter you'll learn how to:
- Communicate with your loved ones around delicate legal issues and planning.
- Determine what legal documents you might need, such as these:
  - Powers of attorney for health care
  - Do not resuscitate (DNR) orders
  - Physician Orders for Life Sustaining Treatment (POLST)
  - Living wills
  - Powers of attorney for finances
  - Wills and trusts
- Handle a determination of incapacity.

- Organize legal documents.
- Find the right professionals to help with legal matters.

Talking with Your Loved Ones About Plans and Wishes

As you care for and support your loved ones, talking about their plans and wishes for their future—and making sure the legal documents to carry out those plans and wishes are in place—can be difficult. Most of us don't want to think about, much less talk about, a time when the people we care for won't be able to make decisions or what will happen after they pass on. I've experienced this myself. When my sister suddenly became gravely ill after cardiac arrest, I thought I had electronic copies of her legal documents. I discovered that I didn't, and I had to search her house for the most recent copy of her advance directives. When she died and I became the executor of her estate (or her "personal representative"), I realized I didn't have a witnessed original of her most recent will. I had to search through stacks of papers for information about her house, mortgage, utilities, and other financial matters. It was incredibly stressful on top of the shock and deep grief. Perhaps I'd been so focused on caregiving for my parents that I neglected these details for my sister. I was reminded that even when we don't think death is imminent, we should all have the basic legal documents and contact information for attorneys and other key professionals in place and readily accessible to our loved ones who will carry on.

The reality is that it's much better to talk about these matters early and often, before a crisis occurs. If they haven't taken the steps outlined in this chapter, you'll need to help your loved ones do so. Here are some topics you'll want to address with them.

- What plans and legal documents they already have in place and how to access them.
- Who they want to make financial and medical decisions on their behalf.

- Whether they would want life-sustaining treatments if they have a terminal condition.
- How they would like the end of their lives to be handled.
- What their preferences are for funeral, burial, and/or memorial service arrangements.
- Whether they want donations in their name in lieu of flowers, and if so, to what organizations.
- What they want done with their property after their death.

Sometimes, even when approached with sensitivity and respect, loved ones resist discussing such personal matters and plans. Know that you can only do your best to help them. If they refuse to accept assistance or share information, but can still make their own decisions, you may not be able to do anything. In that case, be there for whatever help they allow you to provide and choose to act differently in terms of your own long-term planning. Often it helps to bring in an objective third party, such as a counselor, doctor, lawyer, or mediator. For more help, take a look at Tips for Challenging Conversations in the appendix.

Chrissy says her mom sees any advance preparation as an infringement on her independence and privacy. "She needs help from my sibling and me, but only on her terms," says Chrissy. "It's difficult for us to help or to make good decisions about her health or finances because we have so very little information, and she tells us it's none of our business, even when asking for help. It's extremely difficult to deal with this while working, particularly when it affects where I live, which jobs I can take, etc. I completely understand not wanting to lose independence and privacy, but my advice is to also put yourself in your kids' shoes when you need them to help. And be prepared; don't wait until something traumatic happens to put a plan in place."

Legal Documents

Power of Attorney

A power of attorney allows people you care for to appoint someone—known as an "agent," "attorney-in-fact" or "proxy"—to act for them to make decisions, manage their affairs, and access important records or documents. There are several types of power of attorney, and some can be combined:

- A "conventional" power of attorney begins when your loved ones sign it and ends when they become mentally incapacitated.
- A "durable" power of attorney begins when it's signed and remains in effect throughout your loved ones' lifetime, unless they cancel it. Your loved ones can continue to manage their finances even after signing a power of attorney. But if they become incapacitated, the agent will have the authority to step in.
- A "springing" power of attorney begins only when a specified event occurs, such as when the principal becomes incapacitated. A springing power of attorney must be carefully drafted to prevent any difficulty in determining exactly when a triggering event has happened to make it "spring" into place.
- A "limited" power of attorney is created for a limited time or for specifically outlined circumstances. Your loved ones might create a limited power of attorney when they leave the country temporarily or undergo surgery or treatment for a specific illness. It can also be limited to certain financial matters or funds, such as a bank account, retirement fund, or investment portfolio.

Your loved ones may appoint more than one power of attorney or stipulate in what order people should serve in that capacity if the first person appointed is unable to do so. As my parents' current primary caregiver, I generally make most of their health and financial decisions, but I share power of attorney with my sisters in some cases; it is a comfort to know that if anything happened to me, they would be able to step in. Keep these things in mind about powers of attorney:

- All powers of attorney will expire when your loved ones die. After that, the agent no longer has the authority to make any decisions. (See Financial and Estate Planning Documents, below.)
- Power of attorney laws vary from state to state, so if your loved ones reside in more than one state, be sure to set up a power of attorney in each state and understand the differences in each document.
- When you need to sign documents as an agent or attorney-in-fact, always clarify that you are signing *on behalf of* your loved ones. Sign your name and follow it with the phrase, "as agent for _____" or "as attorney-in-fact for _____" (complete the phrase with the name of your relative). If you sign correctly, you will avoid personal liability.
- If your loved ones ask you to serve as their agent, discuss exactly what your responsibilities are or will be in the future. Understand their plans and wishes before you have to take any actions.

In the sections below, I go into more detail on health-care and financial powers of attorney.

The first time we took Mom to the emergency room, the hospital wanted her health-care power of attorney and living will documents. My parents' attorneys had created a 6-inch binder—not easy to lug around with me. I called the attorney, who faxed copies to the hospital, which kept them on file in Mom's medical records. But the hospital insisted on a new "do not resuscitate" form in the meantime, so we had to explain all the choices and make sure Mom understood what she was signing—an arduous process when she was very sick. Now the hospital has copies with her medical records, and I keep copies in cloud-based apps and websites (see Chapter 4) so I can easily access them from my computer, tablet, and smartphone. I've got all the bases covered now!

Medical Documents
Power of Attorney for Health Care (an Advance Directive)
With the power of attorney for health care, also known as a medical power of attorney, your loved ones appoint a health-care agent. That person carries out directions about only health care and medical decisions, regardless of his or her own personal or religious feelings or influence from family and friends.

Power of Attorney for Mental Health Care (an Advance Directive)

This type of power of attorney designates an agent who will carry out your wishes specific to mental health care, treatment, services, and procedures, including medication and therapy. Most mental health power of attorney documents will outline specific wishes around consent for electroconvulsive therapy and laboratory trials, as well as specific issues that are not included in the document's definition of mental health care. Ask your attorney if mental health is included specifically in a health or medical power of attorney or if a separate document is needed in your state.

Living Will (an Advance Directive, also known as Health-Care Instructions)

A living will is a legal document that informs physicians, family, and all others of your loved ones' wishes regarding their medical treatment if and when they become incapacitated and unable to make their wishes known. A living will can stipulate, for example, when medical attempts to prolong life should be started *and* stopped. Your loved ones can specify life-sustaining treatments they do or do not want administered, such as feeding tubes, intubation, or mechanical ventilation (breathing machines). They can state their wishes about the circumstances in which they would or wouldn't want kidney dialysis, intravenous (IV) fluids, food, liquids, and comfort care (such as pain or nausea medicine). Organ or tissue donation instructions can also be included here (and are often also on a driver's license or state-issued ID card). Some living-will forms are fairly general but can be supplemented with written explanation of more specific wishes. A living will, for instance, can describe the atmosphere that your loved ones desire at the end of life. Many people choose music they want to hear, flowers they love, books or poetry they'd like to have read to them, who they'd like to have in the room and where they want to be. This level of detail can be vitally important to many people.

The Five Wishes living will template created by Aging with Dignity (www.agingwithdignity.org), a nonprofit organization whose mission is to promote better care for people as they age and at the end of life, is easy to fill out and includes more nuanced questions about wishes for the end of life. It meets legal requirements in many states, and people in other states often attach it to their state forms.

By thinking ahead and communicating treatment preferences early on, the people you care for can help prevent arguments and spare those close to them the anxiety of having to guess what decision should be made about end-of-life treatments. Most important, your loved ones can make very personal health-care decisions for themselves. Encourage them to talk with their doctors if they need help understanding the options and making these decisions.

It's important to have *both* a living will and a power of attorney for health care (and possibly a separate power of attorney for mental health care). Many states combine them into one advance directives document that can be used to record one's treatment preferences and name a health-care advocate. The Five Wishes document mentioned above includes both. Each state has specific formats and rules for living wills and other advance directives. For your state's free advance directives forms, visit www.aarp.org/advancedirectives. Your loved ones don't necessarily need to work with an attorney to create advance directives. But state law may require that the documents be signed in the presence of one or more witnesses.

Feelings about advance directives may change depending on life stage and health conditions, so be sure that your loved ones' directives are up to date and you are aware of their most current thoughts about end-of-life issues.

(This is a good time to get *your own* advance directives in place as well, no matter your age or life circumstances. When I began more intensive caregiving for my parents, I didn't have my own advance directives. After going through several health crises with them, I created mine. I don't want anyone in my life to have to worry about how I'm cared for if something should happen to me. I think of it as a gift to my loved ones.)

Without advance directives, a court may need to appoint a guardian to make medical and mental health decisions for your loved ones. The court-appointed guardian might not be their first choice to oversee care and might not make decisions based on your loved ones' values and wishes.

Do Not Resuscitate Orders

A do not resuscitate order (DNR) is sometimes referred to as a "no code" or "allow natural death" order. It can only be created by a doctor in consultation with the patient, or with a health-care agent if the patient cannot make his or her wishes known. A DNR generally directs medical staff not to attempt cardiopulmonary resuscitation (CPR) or intubation if the patient stops breathing or the heart stops beating. A DNR does not affect other treatments such as chemotherapy, antibiotics, pain control, comfort care, or dialysis. If patients cannot produce their own advance directives, in some cases hospitals will require newly admitted patients, especially older patients, to complete a DNR form.

Be sure the hospital has current DNR on file *every time* your loved ones are admitted to the hospital. When Mom "coded" in our local hospital, I was with her but they whisked her away to ICU and inserted a breathing tube without my knowledge. She had a DNR created by her attorney, and she also had one that the hospital had her complete a few years before. I assumed it was still on record there, but apparently they didn't find it and did not ask me about it when she was admitted with a simple urinary tract infection. Had I known what they were doing, I would have adhered to her wishes not to have a breathing tube. Instead, we had to make the difficult decision to remove her breathing tube a few days later. She died within minutes. It was terribly heartbreaking to lose her, and having to make the decision to remove the breathing tube just made it harder. While it did provide the time for Dad to see her again and two of my sisters and my boyfriend to travel to be there, I wish I'd checked about the DNR when she was admitted.

Bill Carter served as a firefighter, paramedic, and captain in the fire department for 33 years. On numerous occasions, his squad was called to nursing homes or the private homes of older patients. When there was no DNR or living will, the squad had to administer CPR and other measures to revive patients who were, for example, in cardiac arrest. "It was often frustrating knowing that most likely the patient wouldn't do well if revived and could very well have had advance directives in place to make their wishes known," he says, "but family just couldn't find them or medical staff didn't have them on record." Instead of creating unnecessary trauma, he advises, make sure your loved ones' wishes are clear, in writing, and easy to access quickly in case of an emergency.

Physician Orders for Life Sustaining Treatment (POLST)

The national Physician Orders for Life Sustaining Treatment paradigm is an approach to end-of-life planning. The POLST is a standing medical order intended for people of any age with serious, progressive, advanced chronic illnesses. Created by a health-care professional after conversations with your loved ones and other health-care providers, it provides specific medical orders and offers some detail on the course of treatment to be administered.

The POLST is a form you can fill out for a *current* illness, complementing advance directives that have been created in the past with *future* treatments in mind. POLST forms should be filed in medical records with health-care providers such as hospitals and nursing homes. A copy should be kept with your loved ones, whether at home or in a facility. Patients receiving palliative or hospice care often create POLST forms. Many but not all states have POLST programs. They may be identified with different names other than POLST in some states (such as Physician Orders for Scope of Treatment (POST) or Medical Orders for Life Sustaining Treatment (MOLST). Check www.polst.org to find out if there is a program in your state.

Financial and Estate-Planning Documents

Power of Attorney for Finances

A power of attorney for finances authorizes an agent or attorney-in-fact who your loved ones select to handle business, financial, property, and legal transactions on their behalf. This legal document is tailored to each individual's situation. The more detailed it is, the more helpful it will be, but generally it includes the ability to pay bills; manage or sell property; apply for public benefits; deal with insurance companies, investments, and banks; and handle other financial issues.

A financial power of attorney can specify a wide range of powers—the ability to access bank accounts, sign income tax returns, sell stocks and manage real estate, for instance—or give authority for a short-term or single transaction. It's a good idea for your loved ones to have a power of attorney for finances set up to cover long-term needs, including if they become incapacitated. Remember that the person designated doesn't own any of the principal's property. The agent has the authority to make decisions regarding property only when your loved ones cannot.

If your loved ones designate you as their agent, it's a good idea to discuss exactly what your responsibilities will be and understand their wishes before you take on the responsibilities. Get a handle on your loved ones' current financial situation, including bank accounts, loans, credit card accounts, investments, properties, and other assets. Who is listed as beneficiary on their insurance policies, pensions, or retirement accounts?

Try to project into the future how their finances will best be handled if the people you care for become incapacitated and need long-term care or other assistance. Will there be enough funds? Will they want you to sell assets to pay their expenses? What source of funds should be used or sold first to cover expenses? To prevent confusion or resentments in the future, I recommend that all family members be aware of your loved ones' plans.

As I discovered when handling the sale of my parents' property, even when a financial power of attorney is in place, banks, insurance companies, and stockbrokers sometimes insist that you use *their* power of attorney forms. You may need to become a joint owner of the bank account to ease accessing funds and paying bills. The Social Security Administration (SSA) does not recognize powers of attorney. If the people you care for cannot manage their Social Security or SSI payments, Social Security's Representative Payment Program provides financial management for them. You'll need to be appointed by the SSA as a "representative payee" to deal with your loved ones' Social Security issues. This is because institutions want to protect themselves from liability if people (even family members) try to take over another person's finances for their own good to the detriment of that person. Protections are a good thing—elder abuse is a real problem. But for well-meaning caregivers, this can pose an obstacle that is time-consuming and sometimes difficult to resolve. If at all possible, find out what forms these institutions require and have your loved ones sign these forms while they are still able to. You'll save yourself a world of trouble in the future.

Digital Power of Attorney

Digital assets may be specifically covered in a durable power of attorney for finances to specify the ability to access, manage, transfer, or change financial digital or online assets, such as electronic statements for bank accounts (including paying bills online), investment or brokerage accounts, and credit cards. But a separate digital power of attorney document may be necessary, depending on the state where those you care for reside. A digital power of attorney might address computers and other digital devices; email accounts; digital music, photos, and videos; websites, blogs, and domain names; digital file storage; social media accounts, such as Facebook, Instagram, LinkedIn, Twitter, and YouTube; and passwords associated with these accounts.

Wills and Living Trusts

Even if your loved ones have only a small estate, they may want to create a will to ensure that their money and property are distributed according to their wishes. If they have a sizable estate, they may also want to consider a living trust. Otherwise, if they die without a valid will or trust, the state will distribute any probate assets in accordance with local laws. This can take years to resolve and may not end up the way your loved ones would have wanted. The probate process differs by state.

Regardless of whether your loved ones have a will or a living trust, any property that's jointly owned with someone else, such as real estate or a bank account, will go to the joint owner upon your loved one's death. Any asset with a designated beneficiary, such as an individual retirement account or insurance policy, will go to that beneficiary. Property in the trust will also be distributed according to the terms of the trust, not the will.

Will: Sometimes called a "last will and testament," a will is a legal document that details how a person's assets will be distributed after death. Your loved ones can divide assets in whatever way they choose. For instance, the entire estate may be left to a spouse, or it may be divided equally among children and grandchildren. Specific items may be left to friends, family members, or charities. A will may even specify how a beloved pet will be cared for.

Your loved ones should appoint an executor for the estate (sometimes called a personal representative or agent) who will carry out wishes after death. The executor will pay taxes, pay money due to creditors, and distribute or manage the assets. Digital assets are increasingly becoming an issue in estate planning and should be addressed if needed. If your loved ones don't appoint an executor, the state will do so.

Your loved ones can change or revoke their will at any time as long as they're not mentally incapacitated. In fact, they should review the will periodically to make sure that it still reflects their wishes. Be sure you have access to the most recent version of the will as well as the contact information for the attorney who prepared it. An attorney may need to help file the will upon death and deal with the legal aspects of managing the estate. If your loved ones create their own will, be sure it has been witnessed and is legal in their state. Ask them to provide the name of a local attorney you can work with upon their death.

Living trust: Like a will, a living trust details how a person's assets will be managed and distributed upon death. Unlike a will, though, a trust also enables your loved ones to designate someone to manage assets *during* their lifetime should they become incapacitated. A trust is usually more expensive to set up and maintain than a will. It may be a better option for someone with a larger estate. Also, a trust is totally private in most states while a will is a public document, open to anyone once it is submitted for probate.

Your loved one who creates the living trust is called the "grantor" of the trust. A living trust can be either "revocable"—that is, it can be changed or cancelled at any time as long as the grantor has the capacity to do so, or "irrevocable"—that is, it cannot be changed.

For a living trust, your loved ones transfer ownership of selected property to the trust and name a trustee to manage the trust for the benefit of the beneficiaries. The grantor can appoint himself as the initial trustee so that he can manage the trust property himself; if he names himself as trustee, then he also must appoint a successor. My parents originally had me and my sisters listed as successor trustees after their death, but several years ago made me a trustee as they wanted me to manage their assets while they were living.

Note that a living trust differs from a "testamentary trust" that may be outlined in a will but only goes into effect after death. Testamentary trusts are often referred to as "trust funds" and sometimes skip generations.

Comparing Wills and Living Trusts

A Last Will

- Usually easier and less expensive to set up and maintain than a trust.
- Goes into effect only upon death.
- Appoints a legal representative (executor) to carry out wishes.
  Distributes probate property to beneficiaries.
- Appoints a guardian for minor children.
- Subject to probate court proceedings upon death. Under court supervision, legal representative settles debts, finishes legal matters, and oversees distribution of assets to beneficiaries.
- Becomes part of public court records.

A Living Trust

- Can be more costly up front than a will.
- May require a minimum amount of assets to create.
- Goes into effect when created or "funded."
- Allows grantor to designate someone to manage assets while the grantor is living or becomes incapacitated.
- Distributes trust property to beneficiaries.
- Can provide for the long-term support and maintenance of a child or grandchild with extraordinary needs.
- Legal representative not subject to court supervision of management or distribution of assets.
- Appoints a trustee and successor trustee to carry out wishes.
- Covers only the property and other assets such as insurance policies that have been legally put in the name of the trust.

Incapacity

If your loved ones don't create advance directives or plan for who will manage their finances if they become incapacitated while they're still able to make decisions, you may find yourself in a difficult position. How do you know if someone is incapacitated? There's no cut-and-dried definition. It's one of those words that people use all the time, but it has layers of meaning. A person might have the capacity to do some things but not others. For example, she may have lost the ability to drive, but she may be capable of writing a will or deciding where to live. Further complicating the issue is that a person's capacity to do any one thing can fluctuate over time and even day to day.

Various formal and informal assessments can be done to evaluate capacity. A driving examiner may determine that your father no longer has the capacity to drive. A lawyer may determine that your aunt doesn't have sufficient capacity to sign a contract but does have capacity to write a will. A doctor might determine that your mother doesn't have the capacity to make a medical decision; after some treatment, however, her capacity to make the next medical decision may return.

The only way to determine if someone is legally incapacitated is through a guardianship proceeding. In such proceedings, the court determines if an individual has lost some or all of the ability to make decisions about personal or financial matters. Incapacity laws vary from state to state, but most require two physicians to certify someone as incapacitated.

If your loved ones haven't planned for incapacity or are unwilling to allow someone to help, and you feel that they can no longer safely manage their health and finances or care for their property, you'll need to file a petition with the court explaining why a guardian is needed and who is qualified to be appointed. Your loved ones will need to be examined by experts who can determine the extent of any incapacity, and you and they will have to appear in court. Before considering filing for guardianship, consult with an attorney about state requirements.

The court will also decide how much authority to give that person. A guardian might have the authority to make decisions about finances and real estate only. Or the guardian might be responsible for making all

decisions, including those having to do with health care, living arrangements, and personal needs.

The guardianship process can be emotionally and financially draining.
It also can take away a person's rights to make decisions about his or her
life. That's why you'll want to make sure the proper legal documents are
in order.

Keeping Track of Legal Documents

While it's critical that your loved ones have the documents I've mentioned,
you also need to be able to find them. Some people keep them at home,
in a safe deposit box or online. Know where originals and duplicates are
kept. And give copies to all the key players. Nursing homes, hospitals,
doctors, spiritual advisers, family, and friends may need copies of both
the power of attorney for health care as well as the living will. Banks or
other mortgage holders, insurance companies, and credit card companies,
for example, should have copies of the power of attorney for finances.
Attorneys, estate executors, and successor trustees should have a copy of
the will or living trust. If your loved ones wish, family members could
also have copies of these documents, although some people prefer not to
make their estate planning known until after they die.

You can't always anticipate when you'll need copies of the documents,
so be prepared for emergencies. Several websites and apps can help you to
ensure quick access on the go. Your loved ones' attorney may also be able
to email you or fax the documents when needed. See Chapter 4 for more
tips on staying organized and using technology to make your life easier.

*Maureen Statland's father had a liver condition that created high
levels of ammonia in his system, causing a change in his cognitive
abilities—"squirrelly" she says, and unable to make decisions for
himself. He became so ill one night that she called the emergency
squad to take him to the hospital. When paramedics arrived, her
father refused to go! The paramedics had no context for his cognitive
status, so Maureen rushed down to the basement to find his power*

of attorney for health care assigning her the ability to make medi-
cal decisions for him. Once they were assured of her legal power,
they agreed to transport him to the hospital. Much to her relief, her
dad regained clearer thinking after treatment in the hospital, but
she would have been in a real fix if he hadn't had the advance direc-
tive—and she hadn't been able to locate it.

Finding Professional Help for Legal Issues

For advance directives such as a living will and power of attorney for
health care, as well as a power of attorney for finances or digital assets,
consult with a licensed attorney who specializes in elder law, estate planning or perhaps family law in the state where your loved ones reside,
since laws vary from state to state. When one creates a will or living trust,
an estate-planning attorney is crucial. Many firms specialize in estate
planning. My parents' attorneys have both estate-planning and elder-law
specialists, so I trust them to be up on any changes in the laws. They have
also helped us with the application process for Dad's veterans' benefits.
The attorneys contact me when any changes need to be made to the trust
in accordance with changes in the laws. My parents paid them an upfront
fee, and they rarely charge for any additional consultations unless consid-
erable changes need to be made.

When you evaluate potential law firms or individual attorneys, ask if
an initial free one-hour consultation is possible. Get a firm estimate of
the *total* costs. Do they charge one up-front fee only, or will your loved
ones be charged every time a consultation or update to legal documents is
needed? Get references and find out who in the firm will actually work on
the documents. An attorney may oversee the process and have a qualified
paralegal create the documents and meet with you and your loved ones.

To find professionals, ask friends and family members if they have
attorneys they trust, but be sure the attorneys recommended specialize in
the specific legal issues for which you are seeking legal advice. A divorce
attorney probably isn't the best expert to help you with estate planning.
Attorneys who specialize in elder law can generally address most issues

related to caregiving, including powers of attorney, estate planning, and veterans' and other public benefits.

You may be able to find a referral for legal advice or even free or reduced-cost legal help through a local legal services agency, the AARP Legal Services Network (www.aarplsn.com), a bar association, or other organizations focused on legal assistance for older adults (see the Resources).

While some of these legal documents can be created without the help of an attorney, it's critical to ensure that such documents are legal in the state where your loved ones reside. Some states, for instance, require that certain documents be witnessed. My sister created her own will and advance directives, but I found a more recent version of her will that had not been witnessed, so I was told by an attorney that it was not legally viable in her state. Because I live 2,000 miles away and she did not use an attorney, I had to search for one in her area who could help me with filing the will and taking other legal steps.

Your Job Description: Legal Manager

Congratulations! Legal matters are an essential element of caregiving, and you have embraced the steep learning curve. Here's your "official" new job description.

> Hires and evaluates legal consultants as needed. Has working knowledge of various advance directives, as well as estate-planning and other legal documents. Understands legal ability to manage affairs and make decisions for loved ones. Excellent written and verbal communication skills. Strong organizational skills.

CHAPTER 7

MANAGING FINANCES

I remember an afternoon about six years ago, when I was visiting Mom and Dad in Phoenix. Dad went to his study, saying he'd better work on the bills. Two hours later, I checked on him. Despite lovely classical music playing in the background, he was visibly stressed out and frustrated. Usually upbeat, optimistic, and capable of handling anything, Dad's shoulders sagged. Defeat was written all over his face. There were piles of paper stacked up all over his desk, covered with sticky notes with questions for my sister and me. It broke my heart as he sadly admitted he would appreciate some help managing all that paperwork. Here was my hero—my very intelligent, highly educated dad, a university professor and decorated World War II veteran—and he could no longer manage his bills and other paperwork by himself.

We were starting to be concerned about possible dementia, so I wanted to lessen his stress—I'd recently noticed that increased stress hurt his cognitive abilities. At the same time, I wanted to make sure he still had enough mental challenge in his life to keep his brain stimulated—a difficult balance to achieve.

My sister Susie and I had already been helping Dad with some complicated financial matters, but this called for increased support. Intervention started slowly. I opened a second checking account so he could withdraw spending money from the ATM and write certain checks if needed without having to worry about balancing the accounts or making sure the bills got paid on time. My sister and I were added to checking accounts, and

111

I transferred money online to the second account every month. I had his bills sent to my home and, during my lunch hour or in the evening, paid them online from his checking account.

Sure, taking on this financial responsibility added to my own stress, but I could handle it better than he could—and watching Dad's stress drop immediately made me feel better.

Introduction

Many caregivers help their loved ones with finances. Some slowly increase support over time; others are suddenly thrust into the role after a health or financial crisis. Either way, money is inherently a tricky subject, so tread lightly, and the earlier you can discuss current finances and long-term financial plans with your loved ones the better.

Finances are often handled by caregivers who work or live at a distance, leaving the more hands-on support with activities of daily living like personal care, cooking, or housekeeping to those who live closer. The challenge is that many calls and meetings with financial advisers, banks, and credit card or insurance companies need to take place during your workday. Be careful about how you use time at work to handle these matters. Try using your lunch hour and breaks to make phone calls or pay bills, but be sure to protect confidential information. Talk with your employer about making up time that has to be taken during the workday for calls or appointments. Do as much as you can in the evening or weekends, and use online options to manage bill paying, credit cards, and insurance. If you have trouble keeping up with your busy work schedule and your loved ones' financial matters, consider hiring an assistant to sort, prioritize, and prepare the mail and paperwork for you. If the budget is tight, perhaps other family members can help pay for this or other professionals to help with financial matters. That way your time is focused on the things *only you* can do, such as actually paying the bills or making important phone calls.

In this chapter you'll learn how to:

- Spot the red flags indicating your loved ones need help managing finances and determine how to help.
- Evaluate assets, create a budget, streamline bill paying, and find ways to save money and increase income.
- Deal with insurance and taxes.
- Ensure that the people you care for receive the public benefits they're eligible for.
- Find the right professionals to help you with finances.

Signs Your Loved Ones Might Need Help with Finances

I could see Dad struggling, so I asked and he finally accepted help with tasks such as sorting mail, paying bills, managing properties, and tracking insurance claims. If your loved ones' needs aren't so clear, look for these signs:

- Unopened mail stacking up, or opened mail found in odd places around the house.
- Late payments and unpaid or overpaid bills.
- Confusion about how to interpret an invoice, statement, or letter.
- Misfiled documentation or statements.
- Inability to write a check or balance the checking account.
- An unusual amount of telemarketing calls, sweepstakes mail, or trinkets or "prizes," which could indicate your loved ones may be vulnerable to scams.
- General disorganization of paperwork.
- Loss of the capacity to use a computer to manage finances as they have in the past.
- Inability to get taxes organized and completed.
- Unusual spending patterns, such as denying themselves the basics or splurging on unusually big items.
- Mounting credit card debt.
- High levels of stress and confusion about finances or other paperwork.

The wake-up call for Robin Hungerford Burgess came when she noticed her mom was falling prey to telemarketers. On one occasion, her mom bought an extended warranty service for appliances she no longer owned. "Mom could not say no to a sob story from unscrupulous fake charities," says Robin. Then a few times her mother paid her credit card bill twice, misreading the "payment" line as the "amount due" line. Robin began following up on her mom's behalf, getting a refund from the credit card company. Later, Robin's mother designated her as power of attorney for finances and—much to her mom's relief—Robin gradually took over managing the finances.

Increasing Help . . . Gradually

Unless the people you care for suffer a sudden catastrophic injury or illness, you will likely not be thrust suddenly into managing their finances. For most families it will be a process, not an overnight takeover. The idea of having someone take over all business and financial matters may be understandably frightening or overwhelming for those you are caring for. Communicating regularly, clarifying wishes, and increasing support *gradually,* if possible, are the keys to success.

An informal arrangement may work for a while, with your loved ones retaining the ability to sign checks or documents and make final decisions. You may just need to help interpret complicated matters, make phone calls, and help them stay organized. At some point your loved ones may, like Robin's mother and my dad, gladly turn things over to you, relieved to have help. On the other hand, you may have a fight on your hands if your loved ones believe themselves to still be capable when in fact they are making risky decisions and becoming vulnerable. That, however, can be very difficult to prove. Are you simply disagreeing, or are they, in fact, jeopardizing their own financial security?

If the people you are caring for have planned ahead, they may have a power of attorney set up designating you or someone else as the "agent" or "attorney-in-fact" who can begin handling their financial matters. If not, you may even need to go to court to get a ruling on incapacity. (See Chapter 6 for more on legal affairs.)

Helping your loved ones with finances is a big responsibility. Remember, your goal is to help them remain as independent as possible for as long as possible and retain some sense of control in their lives. Whether you act under a power of attorney or not, here are some things to consider as you get started.

- Be sensitive. The inability to manage one's own finances can be a major blow. Your loved ones have led interesting and complex lives, surviving many challenges. Now they may feel they've failed because they just can't keep up with the mail, property, or finances. Reassure them that they have earned the support and you are happy to help— just as they helped you and others in the past.
- Keep the people you care for informed and involved so they don't feel powerless. This is not only the right thing to do, but it's crucial for their peace of mind—unless they are unable to understand or they just don't want to know.
- Know where to find all their personal and financial documents.
- Keep their assets separate from yours.
- Maintain good records of all their resources and your actions on their behalf.
- Avoid misunderstandings by sharing information with other family members about how you are managing the affairs. Open communication can help prevent resentments and problems down the line.
- Consider hiring a professional accountant, financial adviser or planner, money manager, insurance broker/agent, or other professional to help (see the section below). Even if you can't afford ongoing help, an occasional consultation can be valuable, saving money and agony in the long run.

The most important thing you can do is to simplify. When I took over my parents' finances, I was stunned at how complicated it all was. No wonder Dad was struggling. They had properties in two states, two mortgages, multiple insurance policies, multiple credit cards, numerous medical bills, and mounting debt—it was overwhelming for me, much less Dad! I have had to sell a property and find other ways to simplify their finances and save money.

Evaluating Assets

Get a clear picture of your loved ones' assets, including from online accounts. Make sure you (or the person they specify as their agent) know where the records are for all assets and the value of each, including these:

- Vehicles
- Property (their current home, vacation homes, rental properties)
- Checking and savings accounts, including online accounts
- Retirement income (Social Security, IRAs, 401(k)s, pensions) and other investment accounts, including stocks, bonds, money market, and mutual funds
- Valuable personal property (jewelry, antiques, collections etc.)
- Other items in the safe-deposit box.

Creating a Budget

If your loved ones had a budget to plan and track all income and spending, take a look at it to see everything going in and out of their checking accounts and how bills are being paid. If no budget exists, I highly recommend you create one. Once you have everything down in print, evaluate. Do any changes need to be made? For example, I noticed Dad had been paying some bills with his credit card because he was having trouble balancing his checking account, but because he wasn't paying off his credit cards every month, he was paying interest. So I put most of his bills on autopay (automatic bill payments) and started paying off credit cards every month.

A few tips for creating a budget:

- Include all sources of income such as wages; unemployment; Social Security, 401(k)s, IRAs, pensions, and other retirement income; veterans' benefits; rental income; interest; dividends; and disability benefits.
- List all monthly expenses. This can be a moving target, with unexpected costs popping up all the time for health care, medications, and more. Try to estimate an average monthly amount by looking at spending over the last 12 months. You can do this by reviewing bank and credit card statements as well as recent purchases and receipts. Include these expenses:
  - Mortgage or rent and property tax
  - Home repairs, housekeeping, and yard care
  - Utilities: gas, electric, water, sewer, phone (land lines and mobile), computer, TV
  - Household items (cleaning and paper products, etc.)
  - Health care, medications, and paid caregivers
  - Security or medical alert
  - Taxes
  - Loans, bank charges, and credit card debt
  - Automobile: loan payments, insurance, repair, annual registration, parking, and gas
  - Insurance: homeowners/renters, life, auto, health, long-term care
  - Groceries and dining out
  - Self-care: toiletries, haircuts, massages, trainer, manicures
  - Entertainment and travel
  - Pet care
  - Monthly memberships, magazines
- Subtract the expenses from the income. Is there anything left? If so, determine how you will save or invest it every month. If the balance is negative, you'll need to make some changes, such as cutting expenses or increasing income.
- Try to look ahead and anticipate possible future expenses, adjusting the budget as needed. Many budget items can change, including the cost of care. AARP's Long-Term Care Calculator (www.aarp.org/relationships/caregiving-resource-center/LTCC.html) can help you estimate the cost of care over time, including expenses for care in

a nursing home, assisted living facility, or adult day care, and home health aides or homemaker services.

Paying the Bills

If a person you are caring for is ready for you to pay the bills, you can have them sent directly to your home address or arrange for "paperless" or online delivery. You can save a lot of time and stress by setting up online or automatic bill payments directly with the service provider or from a checking account. Just be sure the checking account always has adequate funds. The great thing about this approach is that you can manage payments from your computer or mobile device anywhere, any time of day.

You can also switch to direct deposit for all benefit checks (as of March 1, 2013, all Social Security benefit payments were required to be direct-deposited into a checking account or to a Direct Express debit card); it's safer and alleviates worries about having lost or stolen checks or forgetting to deposit them in time for bills to be paid. If your loved ones are still paying the bills, ask if they want companies to notify *you* when payments are due or if a payment is missed so you can help them stay on track.

My parents receive a huge amount of mail every week, so sorting out the junk from the bills takes time, and envelopes pile up. I now have a system in place: I have my assistant, Debbie, sort, prioritize, and organize the mail into five folders: urgent, bills to pay, follow up, read, and miscellaneous. I can pick up the "bills" folder and take it with me anywhere—even when I travel for business—and easily pay bills whenever I can grab free moments in my schedule.

Finding Ways to Save

A wide range of books and websites can help you find ways to save money, but I'm going to give you just a few tips that can help you as a working caregiver.

When money becomes an issue, we all get creative. Cutting coupons, shopping during sales, shopping online, and dining out less are some good old standbys, but there are also other strategies to consider when you're caregiving.

Medications

Medications can be a huge expense. If your loved ones have Medicare Part D coverage, you can help save money on medications, and maybe even avoid falling into the coverage gap or "doughnut hole" by using AARP's Doughnut Hole Calculator (www.aarp.org/donuthole).

AARP also offers an online Drug Savings Tool, at http://drugsavings .aarp.org, to help you find out if the medication is really the best one for the given condition, as well as whether there is a less expensive but equally effective medication. Bring the list and any suggested changes to your doctor.

You can also save by using the mail-order services that most prescription drug plans offer. You can order a three-month supply, which also saves you time on ordering. My parents didn't understand how to use their mail-order plan, so I set it up for them many years before they needed help managing other financial matters; it saved a bundle.

Switching to generic can save a great deal on medication costs. Generic versions aren't always available or appropriate, so ask your loved ones' doctors or pharmacists.

Utilities

Utilities may also offer opportunities to save. You can arrange or help to install programmable thermostats and make sure your loved ones use appliances like the washer and dryer during low-use (lower-cost) hours. Ask service providers about the pros and cons of paying utilities on a "budget" plan that balances payments over the year to an equal amount every month. See AARP's Benefits QuickLINK (www.aarp.org/quicklink) to find out if your loved ones qualify for the federal Low Income Home Energy Assistance Program (LIHEAP).

You can also evaluate phone plans for both landlines and mobile phones. Perhaps your loved one isn't making phone calls like in the past. You might combine cable, phone, and Internet services for a package deal, first making sure that they really need all those cable channels. I know that my parents would be lost without certain movie channels, but they would never watch others. You can help them set up a DVR. Dad mainly enjoys old movies and music these days—so we record a lot of musicals and the "Lawrence Welk Show" and watch them over and over. It saves money we might be spending on movie rentals and DVDs. We also use Netflix, Amazon Prime, and other subscription services to watch favorite programs.

Income from Home Ownership

If the people you care for own a home and need increased cash flow to pay for expenses, there are a few options to consider. But they all have risks and could affect income, taxes, and eligibility for public benefits, so take that into account when you make decisions. Be sure to consult with your banker, attorney, and accountant to determine if the benefits outweigh the risks. Here are some options:

- Taking in renters.
- Sharing the home with someone who helps care for your loved ones in exchange for rent or reduced payment.
- Borrowing money, using the home as collateral by refinancing, taking out a home-equity line of credit or a second mortgage.
- Taking out a reverse mortgage, which provides some cash now based on equity in the home. The loan doesn't require repayment until the house is sold or your loved ones move or die. But beware: You'll pay hefty fees at the beginning, such as mortgage insurance premiums, loan origination fees, and closing costs, as well as ongoing fees like homeowner's insurance and property taxes, additional mortgage insurance premiums, interest, and servicing fees. This option is available to homeowners age 62 and older.

Income from Benefits Programs

Money becomes an important issue for many people as they grow older. How to pay for necessities can pose real challenges. Thankfully, state, federal, and private programs can help save money and even create income.

Find out what public benefits your loved ones are already receiving and what others they may qualify for. Make a list of these benefits and add to it as needed so there's always an up-to-date record. These programs can be quite complicated and confusing—don't hesitate to call and ask for clarification. If you're not sure your loved ones are currently receiving benefits they have earned or are entitled to, or to find out what else they may qualify for and learn about other programs unique to their state, use AARP Benefits QuickLINK at www.aarp.org/quicklink. Then be sure to monitor your loved ones' mail for important notices about changes in their public benefits. Here are some of the public benefits available:

Social Security

A federal program, Social Security provides monthly income to people starting at age 62 or those who become disabled and meet strict disability and work eligibility requirements. Social Security also pays survivors' benefits. To receive retirement benefits, you must have paid Social Security taxes for a set amount of time. The amount of your benefit depends on earnings on which you paid Social Security taxes and the age at which you start receiving benefits. The program also provides benefits to family members under certain conditions. To apply, visit your loved ones' local Social Security office, call 800-772-1213, or visit www.ssa.gov. Another good resource is AARP's *Social Security for Dummies,* www.aarp.org/ss4dummies.

Medicare

Medicare is a federal health-care program that helps pay for a wide range of (but not all) health services, such as certain doctors' visits, hospital stays, lab tests, medical equipment, and prescription drugs for people 65 and older, and some younger people with disabilities. Medicare has monthly premiums, deductibles, and co-pays. There are Medicare savings programs that help pay for Medicare premiums and, in some cases, deductibles and co-pays. For more about Medicare, visit www.medicare.gov or call 800-633-4227, or see AARP's *Medicare for Dummies,* available at bookstores nationwide. Your State Health Insurance Assistance Program (SHIP) can help with applications or questions. Go to www.shiptalk.org to find a SHIP counselor near you. For programs to help pay for Medicare costs, visit the local Social Security office, which you can find by calling 800-772-1213, or log on to www.ssa.gov. For help understanding your Medicare statement, visit www.aarp.org/decoders.

Medicare Part D Extra Help Program

The Medicare Part D (prescription drug coverage) Extra Help program assists people with Medicare who have limited incomes and assets. The program can pay for most Medicare Part D premiums, deductibles, and co-pays. If your loved ones are enrolled in Medicaid, Supplemental Security Income (SSI), or a Medicare Savings program, they will automatically get Extra Help with paying for Part D. Otherwise, they will need to first apply for Extra Help. Apply online through AARP's Benefits QuickLINK (www.aarp.org/quicklink) tool or by using Social Security's online application at www.ssa.gov/prescriptionhelp.

Medicaid

A federal and state health-care program, Medicaid assists people with limited resources. Each state designs and runs its own program, so eligibility criteria and covered services vary. Medicaid may cover costs not covered by Medicare, such as long-term nursing home care and, depending on the state, personal or other home-care services, eye exams, eyeglasses, and transportation to medical care. For information, call the local department of social or human services or visit www.healthcare.gov/using-insurance /low-cost-care/medicaid/.

Food Benefits Program

Now referred to as the Supplemental Nutrition Assistance Program, or SNAP, this program can help people with limited resources buy food. SNAP is free, and benefits come in the form of coupons or an electronic benefit card that looks like a credit card. The amount depends on assets, expenses, and number of people living in the household. To apply, see AARP's Benefits QuickLINK at www.aarp.org/quicklink, call the local department of social or human services, or visit www.fns.usda.gov/snap.

Supplemental Security Income
SSI pays monthly income benefits to people who are 65 and over, blind, or disabled if they have limited resources. People may receive both Social Security and SSI payments if they meet the requirements. Visit the Social Security Administration's website at www.ssa.gov to learn more or to apply.

Veterans Aid and Attendance and Housebound
An additional or special monthly pension (cash assistance) program, Veterans Aid and Attendance and Housebound benefits are for certain veterans and their spouses who require care. To qualify, the veteran must have been in active duty during one of these wartime periods: World War I, World War II, the Korean conflict, the Vietnam era, or the Gulf War. Find out about qualifications and how to apply at www.benefits.va.gov/PENSIONANDFIDUCIARY/pension/aid_attendance_housebound.asp or contact the nonprofit organization www.veteranaid.org or your elder-law attorney. The application process is lengthy and complicated, so help is a good idea, but a word of caution: Some organizations that offer help take a cut of the monthly pension payments.

Getting Out of Debt

Unfortunately, when a person starts to have difficulty managing finances, debt often gets out of control, so you may have a real challenge digging out. Many companies advertise ways to settle debt and repair credit fast. Beware: Many could actually cost you money, and others are fraudulent scams. The best option is a consumer credit counseling organization, where you can get free or low-cost advice on money management and personalized debt repayment and consolidation. Even with credit counseling, you'll need to be careful about whom you trust. Contact the National

Foundation for Credit Counseling (www.nfcc.org) at 800-388-2227 for a referral to a reputable credit counselor.

Dealing with Insurance

When managing a loved one's finances, insurance can be one of the most complicated and confusing issues. There are so many different types of insurance, including health, dental, vision, long-term care, disability, life, homeowners, and automobile. You may discover policies that have been purchased long ago but can't find good records. It can be difficult to understand how claims are processed, and benefit statements certainly don't seem designed for us to grasp. Dealing with insurance can be intimidating. But take heart— approach it systematically and you'll manage.

- List all insurance policies your loved ones own.
- Make notes about each policy: company, policy number, basic benefits, value, monthly premiums, how to file claims, websites, personal identification number (PIN), where to find forms, and contact numbers. Keep this list handy—you'll need it frequently.
- Try to get a copy of the actual policy. Talk with insurance agents if possible and ask them to explain the policy in simple, everyday terms.
- Identify any policies that cover the same things. If you find duplicate policies, evaluate them thoroughly to determine which policy best meets the needs of those you care for and cancel the other policy.
- Monitor statements of benefits against bills received and actual benefits. Mistakes do happen, so contact the insurance company right away if you find any discrepancies.
- If you suspect insurance fraud or scams, visit www.insurancefraud .org/report-fraud.htm to find out how to report your concerns.

Long-Term Care Insurance
Understand the specifics of the policy if your loved ones have long-term care insurance; it can be a critical resource. Your loved ones may have

had a policy for many years and forgotten about it. Discovering it should be high on your priority list. These policies vary greatly.

- Some have stringent requirements or "triggers" to begin claiming benefits (in terms of cognitive impairment or inability to perform a specified number of activities of daily living), while others are more flexible. Most require a health-care practitioner's plan of care, evidence from doctors, etc.
- Policies may include home health, assisted living, and/or skilled nursing.
- Many policies have a waiting period after a policyholder qualifies before they will begin paying benefits, so start the process as soon as you believe they might qualify. For example, your loved ones might have to wait 90 days after they are deemed eligible for benefits.
- Long-term care insurance will not pay out benefits for care that Medicare or another form of insurance is already paying—for example, if your loved ones are in a nursing facility and Medicare is paying for the first 90 days.
- Most policies will pay out benefits for only a limited number of days or years, so be strategic about when your loved ones start collecting. My parents' policy helps pay for home care, but I know we only have a few more years before it runs out, so I'm planning ahead.
- Policies are either "tax-qualified" or "non-tax-qualified," which will determine several issues, including triggers to begin collecting benefits and whether or not payments are tax-deductible and benefits are considered taxable income.

Paying Taxes

Caregivers often have extra stress around tax time. Even a simple tax situation can be daunting, especially as many of us are simultaneously organizing our own and our loved ones' taxes and juggling our other personal life and family responsibilities. The good news is there may be some ways to ease the burden for the people you care for.

If you're helping loved ones with their taxes, make sure they are taking *all* their possible deductions, including medical expenses and long-term care nonmedical expenses, which could include paid caregivers, assisted living, and other services, such as help with bathing and dressing.

As a family caregiver, *you* may be able to take some deductions. If you are paying more than half of your family members' expenses and their income meets IRS requirements, you may be able to declare them as dependents on your tax return. Another option is the Child and Dependent Care Credit.

Tax laws change from year to year, so be sure to consult a tax professional. Contact the Internal Revenue Service at www.irs.gov for tax information. AARP's Tax Aide program at www.aarp.org/money/taxes/aarp_taxaide provides free tax assistance for those with low to moderate incomes.

Getting Professional Help

You're not alone if you feel like you're in over your head when it comes to managing a loved one's finances. Financial matters directly affect both your loved one *and* you as a caregiver. These issues are complicated and unique to every individual's intricate life and financial picture. The financial and tax laws, rules, and policies may vary a great deal from state to state and year to year. That's why it's a good idea to make informed decisions. Consult with an experienced and qualified professional to understand investments, insurance policies, budgeting, saving strategies, and debt management. In the long run, it will give you peace of mind and may also save you time and money.

Regardless of the type of professional you are considering, I recommend asking friends and family for recommendations. Ask who helps them with finances and taxes and if they are pleased with the services. Check credentials carefully. You may want to consider working with financial planners who hold the certified financial planner (CFP) or personal financial specialist (PFS) certification, which means they have met education, examination, experience, and ethics requirements. Or you may choose financial managers or accountants who specialize in elder care. Check with the Better Business Bureau to see if there are any complaints registered for the professionals or companies you are considering. Call and ask about qualifications, experience, organization, and fees. You can often schedule a free, one-hour initial consultation to see if it's a good match.

Some caregivers hire a professional to manage the entire financial picture. Individuals and companies can do everything from sorting the mail to paying bills to managing insurance claims and filing taxes. As with any situation where you turn things over, there is always the risk of mismanagement, so screen companies very carefully. Look for experienced professionals, get references, and monitor their work regularly.

To find a local personal financial adviser who charges on a fee-only basis, contact the National Association of Personal Financial Advisors (www .napfa.org) or the Garrett Planning Network (www.garrettplanningnetwork .com). For Certified Financial Planners™, visit www.cfp.net.

Your Job Description: Financial Manager

Congratulations! As a result of dealing with finances as you dive into your caregiving job, you have developed your skills and abilities. Here's your "official" new job description. You've earned it!

Tracks assets. Prepares, reviews, and manages short- and long-term budgets. Supervises and participates in the preparation and review of various financial payments, statements, and reports, including tax preparation. Supervises or submits insurance claims and monitors statements of benefits. Evaluates and applies for public benefits and monitors benefit requirements and policy changes. Creates and implements financial crisis management plans as needed.

CHAPTER 8
HEALTH AND HEALING

I woke suddenly—startled by an all-too-familiar sound—rolled off my makeshift bed on the couch and ran to Mom's bathroom. Too late: She lay on the floor, unable to get up.

She'd just been released from the hospital for a fall and diarrhea, which turned out to be from colitis. We'd done our best to prevent another fall. That day, I'd bought a baby monitor so I'd be sure to hear her get out of bed. It didn't work, but it was too late to go to the store for an exchange, so I'd given her a bell to ring if she had to get up during the night; she didn't ring it. Dad usually woke up when she got out of bed; he didn't this time. So despite our efforts, there she was on the floor. Panic, fear, and guilt overwhelmed me as I tried to help her up. Her legs were like spaghetti and she couldn't stand at all. Back to the hospital.

After hours of waiting, I learned she'd fractured her spine and urgently needed surgery at another hospital. The doctor must have sensed my shock and had to repeat several times, "Without surgery, she will never walk again." That finally snapped me out of my daze. The nurse at the desk looked up and, seeing the emotions flooding through me, put her arm around me.

Mom survived a risky seven-hour surgery as well as a second surgery for spinal stenosis. But it didn't end there, as I discussed in Chapter 2. She developed multiple conditions that presented a vicious cycle. We treated the colitis with steroids, for example, but the steroids caused bone and joint degeneration and so much pain she refused to walk. They also caused thinning skin and susceptibility to infections, so she ended up with skin tears and chronic urinary tract infections, which eventually, heartbreakingly, caused her death. Dad, too, has had complicated health issues. Managing my parents' health care is like a leaky hose—we plug one hole and another one develops.

Introduction

Helping loved ones manage their health care can be the most time-consuming aspect of caregiving. It is a high-pressure role with a steep learning curve. In addition to ongoing basic and preventive care, such as getting immunizations and regular checkups and encouraging healthy eating and exercise, you may be dealing with a complicated mix of concurrent diseases or conditions and their treatments. For working caregivers, dealing with loved ones' health can have additional challenges: Most doctors see patients only during daytime working hours, and health crises and hospitalizations can come up without warning, requiring caregivers to leave work.

In this chapter you will learn about:
- Advocating for your loved ones' best health care.
- Promoting wellness.
- Identifying changes in your loved ones' physical and mental health.
- Managing medications.
- Interacting with doctors and specialists.
- Finding professionals who make house calls.
- Handling the sensitive issues of toileting and incontinence.

Your Role as Health-Care Advocate

At a doctor appointment with Mom before she passed on, I pulled out my phone, opened my notes app, and began rattling off questions I had prepared for the doctor. At first, he looked surprised, perhaps impatient with my questions, but by the end of the appointment he was complimenting me. "I have hundreds of patients, many of them older," he said, "and you are one of very few family members who brings them to appointments, asks questions, and looks out for them." He said many patients come from health-care facilities either with no one to help them or with someone who is only able to help them in and out of the car—totally unequipped to ask questions, share information, act on their client's behalf, or even take notes to share with family members. A friend recently told me of an older woman she came across at a medical complex who had been dropped off—she couldn't remember the name of her doctor or how to find out where she should be; she was lucky my friend was there to help. These patients are adrift in the sea of health care. Mom's doctor said my parents were lucky to have me to help them navigate the health-care system, advocate for good care, and communicate with medical practitioners.

When it comes to health care, patients do need to advocate for themselves or, if they are ill or suffering from cognitive impairment, have someone advocate on their behalf. That's where you come in. Here are some tips to help you refine this role while building good relationships with health-care practitioners.

- **Know your top priority:** Keep your goal—the best possible care and treatment for your loved ones—always at top of your mind.
- **Do your research:** As time-consuming as it can be, learning about their conditions and possible treatments is the patients' or their advocates' role. It's not realistic to fully count on the health-care system to cover all the bases. When the people you care for are acutely or chronically ill, they may not have the ability to do this research themselves, so step in where you can to help. I've found most doctors open to sharing information and answering questions about possible causes or treatments; more than once my research has resulted in trying new medications or approaches that have improved my loved ones' conditions. Many caregivers identify tests, experts, and new or experimental treatments that their loved ones' doctors would never have taken the time to locate.
- **Get clear on roles:** Health-care practitioners are responsible for giving your loved ones the best possible and most thorough care. Your job is

to be an advocate. While it's important to develop good relationships with health-care practitioners, your priority is not to be best friends with them or even to get them to like you. If they seem impatient, so be it. It is your right and responsibility to ask questions, get information, and communicate complaints.

- **Exchange respect:** Treat health practitioners with respect—they work hard, have a great deal of training, and often work under tough conditions dealing with people all day. At the same time, gain their respect. Be pleasant, model respectful behavior in the way you interact with those you care for, be prepared for appointments with a list of problems, ask questions concisely to minimize appointment time, and be firm about your thoroughness.
- **Know who really runs the office:** I've saved time and gotten better results by building relationships with receptionists, billing staff, assistants, and others who know how to get things done.
- **Make their job easier:** Provide copies of any research you've done, have referring doctors provide their notes and test results prior to appointments, and, when possible, cancel appointments ahead of time.
- **Appreciate good service and care:** When a practitioner or support staff does a good job, be sure to thank them. I've even brought thank-you notes, flowers, and cookies to affirm our gratitude, and they really appreciate this. They hear a lot of complaints, but compliments? Not so much.

Helping Loved Ones Stay Well

As caregivers, we deal with so many health crises and urgent matters that we sometimes forget about basic wellness. For working caregivers, it may be even harder to fit this in. But I find that taking preventive measures can help avoid more acute health issues in the long run. I make it a priority to keep up with the following important matters.

Health Screenings

Depending on their age, gender, and health status, your loved ones may be due for certain health screenings, such as for diabetes; hepatitis C; depression; alcohol and tobacco use; obesity; breast, cervical, colorectal, and prostate cancer; cholesterol; blood pressure; osteoporosis; and abdominal aortic aneurysm. Visit eye doctors, dentists, and podiatrists as needed. Ask their doctors for a list of health screenings they recommend, and take a look at the health-screening information (broken down by age and gender) at www.aarp.org/healthscreenings.

Immunizations

Vaccinations, some depending upon age, may be recommended for your loved ones. See www.aarp.org/vaccines, and ask their doctors about immunizations for influenza, pneumonia, Td (tetanus, diphtheria), and Tdap (tetanus, diphtheria, and pertussis), herpes zoster (shingles), MMR (measles, mumps, and rubella), hepatitis A and B, and meningococcal meningitis.

Nutrition

Your loved ones' nutrition supports (or undermines) their general health. Changes in health may be related to eating habits. If you have concerns, you might consult with a nutritionist or dietician; ask their doctor if their health profile might support insurance paying for a consultation. Here are some suggestions to help you monitor and evaluate their eating habits:

- **Regular meals:** Are they eating meals regularly or skipping meals? Why?
- **Healthy meals:** What are they eating? Do they have a well-balanced diet? Or are they eating a lot of processed, fatty, or sugary foods?
- **Special diets:** Do they have special restrictions, such as a diabetic diet? Is salt restricted? Do they have food sensitivities or allergies? Are they able to manage these diets by themselves? If they are in a facility, are they getting the right foods?
- **Hydration:** Are they drinking plenty of fluids? How many caffeinated and sugary drinks do they drink per day?

- **Weight:** Are they overweight or underweight? Are they eating too much, not enough, or unhealthy foods? Do they dislike the food available to them? Has there been a marked weight loss or gain recently? What is the reason? Rapid weight loss could signal illness, so get to the bottom of it quickly. Rapid weight gain could alert you to water retention, congestive heart failure, or other health conditions.
- **Help with meals:** Are they able to make their own meals? Could you or someone make meals for them or cook ahead and freeze meals they can heat up? Would having meals delivered or going to a community meal site be helpful? (Contact your local area agency on aging at www .eldercare.gov for information on these options.)
- **Cost of food:** Do they have enough money to pay for food? If not, look into SNAP, the Supplemental Nutrition Assistance Program (formerly Food Stamps). For more information, see Chapter 7.

Sleep

Caregivers rarely underestimate the importance of a good night's sleep—for themselves and those they are caring for. For your loved ones, be on the lookout for insomnia, sleep apnea, restless legs syndrome, and narcolepsy, which in turn can cause or intensify many health conditions. If you notice the people you care for are consistently snoring, waking up frequently, sleeping throughout the day and staying awake at night, or experiencing other sleep disturbances, consult with their doctors. Dad's cardiologist ordered a sleep study when his heart monitor indicated an unsteady heart rate during the night. Diagnosis: intermittent sleep apnea. His doctors prescribed a pacemaker to address the slow heart rate and a continuous positive airway pressure (CPAP) machine to address the apnea. Unfortunately, Dad couldn't tolerate the CPAP and, because of his dementia, we couldn't convince him to get used to it. It's frustrating because I'm sure his sleep disorder impairs his cognitive functioning and causes him to sleep longer and nap during the day. Those with Alzheimer's disease often get their days and nights mixed up, and his sleep disorder makes it even harder to manage.

Natural and Alternative Approaches

I've always been inspired by my parents' openness to new and alternative approaches to their health and well-being. They learned about many new approaches at the stroke support group they attended, and Mom tried biofeedback and acupuncture to address her chronic pain. They both have seen chiropractors and naturopaths, and herbal remedies and supplements have been a part of their daily regimen. I've seen many of these approaches make a real difference in their mental and physical health. Even in an advanced stage of Alzheimer's, I take Dad to a Chinese medicine doctor for special massage and acupuncture. You might find out if the people you care for are interested in alternative approaches; if so, help them research options and access treatments.

Physical Activity

Your loved ones' physical strength, abilities, and goals will vary according to their health conditions, and their activities may range from stretching while seated to riding a bike or swimming. Regardless of their physical health, it's important to encourage a level of regular, appropriate physical activity to help maintain mobility, flexibility, balance, strength, energy, stamina, and brain health. Studies show that physical activity helps prevent falls, improves self-esteem, increases independence, strengthens bones and joints, relieves pain, improves bowel function, and reduces the risk of or improves conditions such as heart disease, cancer, osteoporosis, and diabetes. It's amazing how quickly our loved ones' abilities can decline without regular physical activity.

My parents' abilities have been very different. Dad has Alzheimer's disease, but he has been physically strong and has enjoyed being active. As his cognitive abilities and visual processing decline, physical activity has been one of the few things he still fully enjoys—walking, lifting weights, or using stretchy resistance exercise bands; bouncing on a trampoline; dancing; and, until just recently, swimming. I'm frustrated when I find physical therapists or assistants who automatically treat him as if he is frail or don't challenge him enough because he has Alzheimer's disease. Mom, on the other hand, had chronic pain and has never really enjoyed exercise, so it was difficult to get her to do minimal exercises to stay strong enough to be able to maintain balance, get in and out of a chair, get settled in bed and walk. But it's been equally important that they both do something every day. For Dad, we aim for a minimum of a half-hour walk a day; for Mom, it was walking back and forth to the bathroom. But my emphasis on keeping her moving meant that up until the last few days of her life, we were able to care for her at home, and she was able to walk and use the bathroom. The night before she got sick, we were able to go out for dinner to celebrate Dad's 90th birthday, and I feel really good about the fact that she remained active all her life.

Incorporate movement and challenge into the activities your loved ones enjoy. Dad has been highly motivated to be doing something and loves his dog, so walking Jackson has been a wonderful way to work in his physical activity; he also loves to dance, so we do that together. As Alzheimer's progresses and his vision worsens, he's less excited about taking walks, so they are shorter, but instead sometimes we just walk inside the house with him (which he used to do on his own before Mom died). Mom loved to play cards, so I used to move the deck a little farther away so she had to stretch when she drew a card. She was also more motivated to walk around the house if I had something to show her, such as a decoration. They were both interested in doing seated yoga and tai chi with me if I played music or used DVDs to guide us. Open your thinking to creative ways to keep the people you care for active, such as these:

- Taking walks—even very short ones. For some, a few steps are better than none.
- Dancing
- Exercising to music, which can be done seated
- Doing regular or seated yoga and tai chi
- Swimming
- Bouncing on a mini-trampoline (but be careful, using a handrail and mats and keeping the area around the trampoline clear to prevent tripping)
- Riding a recumbent stationary bike or other appropriate, safe exercise equipment
- Playing games
- Using elastic exercise bands.

If your loved ones aren't willing or safely able to get moving by themselves, you might talk to their doctors about physical therapy, or find a qualified trainer or exercise assistant to help them with physical activity. My parents have both been in physical therapy many times, but when they aren't, I have also employed people to exercise with them several times a week. Keep safety foremost in any physical activity, and be sure to check with your loved ones' doctors, physical therapists, or other experts before starting any new activity or resuming activity after a health crisis.

Socialization, Entertainment, and Reminiscing

Is having fun and talking with friends part of health care? You bet. Research has shown that social interaction and having fun are crucial to being happy and living a long life. They can improve overall health, motivate us to be physically active, spur brain activity, and produce endorphins that block pain and give us joy. Studies show that isolation impairs health and well-being. Social connectedness can increase resiliency and change attitudes; some studies indicate that social relationships are even more important than genetic factors in preventing illnesses. Are your loved ones isolated and bored? Help them find ways to interact with people, have new experiences, bring up old memories, and simply have fun. Consider talking to them about attending their local faith community, joining a club or senior center, taking a class (exercise, arts and crafts, cooking or other interest), going to family gatherings, seeing friends, shopping, gardening, enjoying nature, making arts and crafts, scrapbooking, seeing a movie or play, attending musical performances, making music themselves, or attending community events. Volunteering—giving and providing service for others—can provide a major lift and change your loved ones' focus from internal to external. Intergenerational relationships are especially important to nurture as they are a normal part of life—I don't believe we are meant to be age-segregated.

Animals

A relationship with a dog, cat, bird, fish, or even a lizard can boost your loved ones' health. Research has found that animals can boost our immune systems, lower blood pressure and anxiety, and, among those who have dementia, lessen anxious outbursts.

Jackson, Dad's service dog, not only provides crucial services for him, but he is also vital to his overall health picture. For many years, feeding and caring for Jackson helped Dad use cognitive skills. In the past, when Dad, who is hearing-impaired, didn't hear Mom fall, Jackson did and alerted Dad. Jackson also alerted Mom and Dad when there was someone at the door or in the yard. Now Jackson helps Dad stay safe when he is out in the community. Dad is also more focused and secure with Jackson when facing the uncertainties of leaving the house. As a bonus, Jackson has kept my parents laughing and loving; for improving and maintaining their mental and physical health, he's proven invaluable.

If the people you care for had a pet in the past or have one now but are no longer able to care for it on their own, they have a few options. You might want to look into one of the organizations that help with care and costs to keep people and their pets together (see the Resources section for more information or contact a local veterinarian). Or consider pet sitters who walk and feed pets. You can also bring your own pets or ask neighbors or friends to bring theirs for regular visits. Another option is animal-assisted therapy and service animals, which I discuss below.

Religion and Spirituality

Research indicates that religion and spirituality have positive effects on physical and mental health. People who have religious or spiritual beliefs have stronger immune systems and are more likely to stay well; they tend to be more resilient; and they have an increased ability to deal with physical pain and illness. They are also more motivated, report higher levels of happiness and lower levels of depression, and remain more hopeful. If your loved ones are able and want to participate in a religious or spiritual community, help them attend local services or bring services to them at home; many faith communities have volunteers who will visit those who are homebound. You can also help them find books to read or meaningful television shows to watch.

Brain Health

Taking care of our brains is an important part of health care, and researchers are learning more about what is good for them. A healthy brain is essential for independence, and you'll find that cognitive abilities affect every other aspect of life. Keep up with the latest research on what stimulates the brain and keeps it healthy, such as nutrition, medications, supplements, physical activity, socialization, and games. If your loved ones have a disease that affects their brains, such as dementia, you'll want to talk to their doctors and other health-care practitioners about how to best care for their brain health. I have several game apps on my iPad that Mom's speech therapist recommended, and I could see her brain functioning improve when she played them. Before his vision worsened, Dad liked playing simple card games such as Uno, which stimulated his brain; we helped him, but he could identify the numbers and colors and enjoyed the socialization. It was something Mom and Dad could both enjoy (Mom was very competitive!). You can find information on brain fitness at www.aarp.org/brain.

Changes in Health

If you see a sudden or marked change in your loved one, never assume it's just old age or the natural progression of a disease. Always check their health status first, because it could be a symptom of an illness or condition that should be addressed and treated. It may even be an emergency situation, such as a stroke or heart attack. All too often, people assume that nothing can be done, and with lack of treatment, the people they care for get worse or go downhill fast. As a working caregiver, you may also want to enlist others on your team to be on alert for changes. Here are three steps to guide you in this area.

Step 1: Look for These Red Flags If Your Loved Ones Seem Different

- **Affect and mood:** Do your loved ones look flat, lacking expression? Are they withdrawn, anxious, or upset? Are they smiling normally?

- **Cognitive status:** Are they thinking clearly? Do they seem confused or lost? Do they seem "out of it"? Is there a change in their personality?
- **Fatigue and sleeping patterns:** Are they groggy and sleepy during the day? Are they up at night?
- **Weakness:** Are they unable to get in and out of a chair and bed? Is one side of their body weaker than the other side? Are they unable to do physical activities they could previously do?
- **Daily routine:** Are they refusing to engage in their regular routine, such as reading the paper, watching TV, or going to events or classes? Are they suddenly unable to handle their usual activities of daily living, such as getting dressed, toileting, grooming, or bathing?
- **Eating:** Are they eating their meals? Are they leaving more food on the plate than normal? Are they suffering from digestive problems?
- **Strange or unusual behavior:** Are they shaking, repeating themselves, vomiting, having diarrhea, feeling dizzy, having pain, or falling? Are parts of their body painful or swollen? Can they hear and see well?

Step 2: Investigate Possible Causes

When you notice changes in your loved ones' health or behavior status, look for these common causes, and don't hesitate to get a doctor's opinion.

- **Medications:** Have your loved ones started a new medication recently? Or could they be experiencing a negative side effect of a drug they are taking? Many of my parents' apparent serious illnesses have ultimately turned out to be reactions to medications. One night, Dad suddenly became violently ill; he was vomiting, having diarrhea, acting very confused, and appearing practically catatonic. I called the emergency squad and we took him to the hospital. I reported that Dad had, on his primary care doctor's orders, just restarted a medication for dementia he'd been off of for more than a month, and now he was taking a higher dose. The neurologist said Dad had a classic overdose reaction to the medication, and I learned that the drug should never be started at that high dose. Yes, I was furious at the (now former) primary care doctor, but I was also relieved to know that Dad would recover. I'm glad I knew to tell the hospital about the new medication.

- **Infection:** Urinary tract and other types of infections can cause significant changes that are often fully reversible once the infection has been treated. At another time, Dad became very confused over the course of a weekend. He went from independently going to the bathroom to being unable to find the bathroom much less the toilet in it. Sure enough, he had constipation, a urinary tract infection, and prostate inflammation. The doctor in the emergency room told me urinary tract infections are the first things to look for in older patients who are admitted because they are confused or fell.

- **Pain:** Your loved ones may not tell you they are feeling more pain, or they may be screaming about it constantly—either way, pain can cause other major changes in their status. Ask if they are in pain, and get a physical exam to find the source. If your loved ones have severe dementia and you notice drastic behavior or mood swings, look for pain as a possible cause. If they can't express their pain verbally or do anything about it, it has to come out in other ways.

- **Change in routine:** If your loved ones are used to a certain routine, it may be very difficult for them to deal with changes that may seem simple to you. Everything may be magnified for them. Stop to consider if any changes to their daily routine have taken place recently.

- **Dehydration and nutrition:** While changes in eating or drinking habits may be a symptom of another problem, the changes themselves could also be the cause of other changes in their health status. Did they start eating new foods recently? Have they started skipping meals or eating too much? Did they start or stop using caffeine or alcohol? Have they been drinking enough liquids? Dehydration can lead to many health problems (such as blood pressure fluctuations, constipation, urinary tract infections, fatigue and weakness, pneumonia, and bed sores) and can be caused by medications, a dulled sense of thirst (common as we age), vomiting, diarrhea, and reduced kidney functioning.

- **Emotions and mental health:** Have the people you care for suffered a loss or another important change in their lives recently? Are they worried about something? Do they have mental health issues, such as depression, anxiety, or bipolar disorder, that need treatment? Or is this a situational issue? Are they feeling isolated or out of control of their lives?

Step 3: Call for Help

If you are concerned about your loved ones' immediate health and safety, call the emergency squad. If you are having trouble determining the cause of a change in their health status, help them see their primary care doctor, mental health professional, or a specialist.

Mental Health

Your loved ones may have dealt with mental health issues for many years, or they may be dealing with new issues as a result of their physical health conditions, medication side effects, changing life circumstances, or alterations in their body chemistry. Mental health issues may include anxiety, depression, obsessive-compulsive disorder, bipolar disorder, alcoholism or drug addiction, grief and loss. Mental health problems, in turn, can trigger challenges in other areas of your loved ones' lives. They may isolate themselves, lose cognitive abilities and independence, and experience changes in their relationships. Keep in mind that accurate diagnosis is key, and mental health issues can be complicated, with more than one diagnosis in some cases. Have a trained specialist, a primary care doctor, and, especially if medications are indicated, a psychiatrist work with the people you care for. If your loved ones are older, a geriatric psychiatrist may have the best knowledge of medications and how they work best for older people.

Dementia

Dementia is not a specific disease. Rather it is a broad term for symptoms that are so serious they cause problems with daily living. Symptoms may include memory loss, cognitive impairment, trouble with thinking or intellectual abilities, difficulty communicating, impaired visual perception, impaired judgment, and loss of ability to focus. Dementia is *not* a normal part of aging; it indicates a disease process somewhere in the body that is affecting the brain.

Some causes of dementia—thyroid disorders, vitamin deficiencies, infections, excessive use of alcohol, depression, or medication reactions—can be treated, sometimes reversing the dementia. Other causes are diseases that progressively damage the brain and cannot be reversed.

Alzheimer's disease is the most common cause of dementia—about 60 to 80 percent of all cases. The Alzheimer's Association also lists these types of dementia:

- Vascular dementia
- Dementia with Lewy Bodies (DLB)
- Parkinson's disease
- Frontotemporal dementia
- Creutzsfeldt-Jakob disease
- Normal pressure hydrocephalus
- Huntington's disease
- Wernicke-Korsakoff disease
- Mixed dementia (multiple causes)

If you suspect that your loved ones have dementia, never assume it's Alzheimer's disease. It is important to get them a thorough evaluation to determine the cause, and to start treatment as early as possible. Knowing the cause of dementia may also help you plan for care over the long term and understand what to expect, as all causes of dementia have different paths.

If you are caring for someone who has a progressive form of dementia, such as Alzheimer's disease, you will need increased support over time. Caring for someone with dementia is extremely demanding; it's one of the most intensive types of caregiving. My Dad has been battling Alzheimer's for more than ten years and I anticipate we have more years ahead. As his abilities have gradually diminished over time, the care he needs has increased. He is in advanced stages of the disease now and requires 24-hour care. But he is still mobile, able to dress himself and do some other activities of daily living with direction and some hands-on assistance. Alzheimer's has now affected his language skills, his sleep, his emotions, and his visual perception. I know it may eventually affect his motor skills. I have found that both traditional western medicine and complimentary treatments have been helpful in addressing the symptoms of his disease, such as acupuncture, Chinese herbs, massage therapy, physical and occupational therapy, aqua therapy, use of supplements, and nutritional support. Always consult with your loved ones' doctors before adding any new treatments to their care plans.

You'll want your loved ones showing signs of dementia to be evaluated by a neurologist, geriatric psychiatrist, or other physician who specializes in diagnosis and treatment of dementia. See the Resources section for contact information for the Alzheimer's Association (www.alz.org) and other organizations that provide information, services, and support for those with dementia and their caregivers.

Managing Medications

If you are caregiving, you are likely helping your loved ones with their medications. Between them, at one time, my parents took 22 prescriptions that I managed, including topical creams and salves, eye drops, nasal sprays, and pills. As a working caregiver, I try to be as efficient as possible, because dealing with refills and new prescriptions via their mail order and local pharmacies is a time-consuming and complicated ordeal, as is staying on top of—and watching out for—drug interactions and side effects. I also try to ensure they are taking the right medications and that they aren't taking medications simply because "they have been for years" (as one doctor told me). Here are my tips for keeping up with your loved ones' medication needs.

- **Your local pharmacist is your new best friend.** Get to know your local pharmacists, even if most medications are delivered by mail. The pharmacists at the local grocery store where we get short-term prescriptions filled are very helpful, answering my questions about drug interactions, side effects, and when to take medications—even if the original prescription is mail order. Local pharmacists have a great deal of information about medications, so don't hesitate to ask. They are also very accommodating when we need medications quickly because they know my parents and my caregiving situation.

- **Watch for drug interactions and side effects.** Do read the information that comes with a prescription. The elderly and sick may be more vulnerable to negative side effects and drug interactions. Many websites and apps also provide drug information quickly and easily.

- **Medications list.** As mentioned in Chapter 4, you'll want to keep a current list of all medications and supplements, with the name of medication or supplement, strength, prescribing doctor and phone number, purpose, dosage, whether it's on auto-refill or the date to call for a refill, and any other comments.

- **Pill organizers.** Medication boxes or organizers can ensure that the correct pills are taken at the right times, no matter what you're doing or where you are. In the past, I helped Dad learn how to use the pill organizers, and he filled them. Then, once a month, I filled four pill organizers for both Mom and Dad with all their medications and supplements. Now I fill organizers for Dad once every two months. This saves me time in the long run, and the organizers serve as reminders to me or, when I'm not there, other caregivers. The organizers come in all sizes and configurations. For instance, Mom took pills three times a day and more of them, so her organizer was bigger than the box we use for Dad, who takes pills twice a day. You can find pill organizers at your local pharmacy or buy them online. There are also "smart" pill organizers that feature timers with alarms or recorded announcements that go off at specified times to remind users. Some have functions so that while you're at your paid job, you can check online to see if your loved ones have taken their pills.

Find more on organizing and medications in Chapters 4 and 7, and go to www.aarp.org/healthtools for AARP Health Tools, including a drug encyclopedia and pill identifier.

So Many Health Practitioners, So Little Time

If you're like me, your loved ones see many doctors and specialists. The list of all my parents' health practitioners is four pages long and growing. I spend a lot of time finding the best experts for my parents' various conditions and diseases, taking them to appointments and managing communications. Whether your loved ones see practitioners in their offices or at home (read about mobile health services below), here are some tips that could help to make your life as a working caregiver more efficient.

Finding Practitioners

Your loved ones' doctors and other practitioners may be well established, having treated them for years. Or they may be assigned doctors during a hospitalization whom they continue to see afterward. If you're looking for a doctor, it's a good idea to start with their insurance company to find out what doctors participate in their insurance plans and if a written referral from a primary care doctor is needed. Many primary care doctors have referral lists of doctors they respect and recommend. Personal recommendations from friends and family are also helpful if you can get them. If your loved one is older, you might consider a geriatrician who is trained in working with older adults (although geriatricians may be hard to find in some areas).

Keep a Current List of Practitioners

My list includes the names, specialties, phone numbers, fax numbers, emails, and street addresses as well as the distance round-trip to their offices (I use that information for taxes at the end of each year). I also note the names and direct extensions of their assistants or office managers. I use the list during emergencies and for sharing with family, other caregivers, and other doctors. I also create a contact in my electronic address book for each doctor, which I can easily access on my phone or computer.

Appointments

You probably feel like you spend half your life going to medical appointments. At one time in a typical week I might take Mom to four doctor appointments and Dad to one. And that's not counting Jackson's veterinarian appointment! Each appointment takes about half a day. Medical appointments are one of the primary reasons I wind up working late into the night, making up for lost time. Keep in mind that mobile health-care services (house calls) are another way to deal with appointments, which might be a time-saver for you and easier for your loved ones.

Accompanying Your Loved Ones

If at all possible, go to appointments with your loved ones. If they are struggling to keep up with the details of their conditions, it may be a great comfort to have another listening ear at the appointment. You can take notes, help answer questions about medical history or symptoms, and ask pertinent questions as well. But if possible, let your loved ones take the lead in the appointment so the practitioner treats them as the VIP in the room. If your loved ones can't communicate well, you'll have to take a more prominent role. One of my pet peeves is a practitioner who talks only to me, ignoring my parents. My mom had aphasia—problems with communicating—so I always explained that I would be doing most of the talking because it was difficult for Mom. But I asked her questions and had the practitioners explain things to her, ensuring she was the focus of the appointment. Dad's dementia and hearing loss make it hard for him to process, but I still draw him into the conversation and urge doctors to talk to him. It's a matter of giving them respect and helping them feel they have some control over their health care.

When You Can't Be There in Person

If work, distance, or other responsibilities make it impossible for you to accompany your loved ones to appointments, here are some alternatives:

- **Calling in:** Have your practitioners call from an office phone, or have your loved ones call from a cell phone. Clear it with the office beforehand so there are no surprises and the logistics are clear.
- **Video chat:** With tablets and smartphones, it's easier than ever to "virtually" attend a medical appointment! Ask your loved ones or

their caregiver to Skype or Facetime you so you can see and talk with the practitioner.

- **Have someone else go:** Make sure it is a relative or caregiver who can advocate for your loved ones, take notes, and report back.
- **Follow up afterward:** Ask your loved ones to give permission for you to call the practitioner later and follow up as needed.

Keeping Records

I've found taking notes during appointments to be a crucial part of my parents' care. (See more about how I use technology to take notes and keep track of health records in Chapter 4.) In my experience, practitioners don't always look at their notes before they see a patient. Most now have computers or tablets so they can look up notes if they need them, but quite frequently I'm the one telling them what they said or prescribed at my parents' last appointment. Notes don't have to be complicated; a few simple bullet points describing what you and the practitioner said as well as any medication prescribed will probably be enough.

Therapeutic Services

The people you care for may benefit from therapeutic services to treat, prevent, and improve a wide range of disabilities, conditions, and challenges—from physical to cognitive deficits. Never hesitate to ask if there is a therapy that might be helpful as your loved ones' symptoms and abilities change. I've found that doctors don't always automatically suggest these therapies but are open when I inquire. Some therapies are covered by insurance and, if so, require a doctor's prescription. You may find a therapist via a doctor's recommendation, home health agency, or online search of related professional associations. (See more information in the Resources section.)

Physical Therapy

Physical therapists are licensed professionals who work to improve mobility, reduce pain, improve strength and balance, restore functioning, and prevent disabilities. Physical therapy can be offered in a private home, hospital, rehab center, nursing facility, adult day services center, or outpatient clinic. In some cases, a physical therapy technician may implement the plan a physical therapist makes for your loved ones. Physical therapy techs are often less costly for ongoing exercise assistance.

Occupational Therapy

Occupational therapists, also licensed, assist patients with life skills and tend to approach treatment of the whole person, rather than a specific injury or deficit of functioning. These professionals often evaluate patients' home or workplace to help them safely adapt their basic activities, such as working, bathing, dressing, cooking, and getting in and out of the car and bed. These therapists may recommend and help patients adjust to special equipment, such as canes, walkers, wheelchairs, special toilet seats, and special eating utensils.

Speech Therapy

Speech therapists, also known as speech pathologists, evaluate, diagnose, and treat speech and communication problems, including language, voice, and fluency. They often work with clients who have cognitive disabilities like dementia or who have suffered from a stroke or other condition that affects their ability to speak or understand others. Speech pathologists can also diagnose and treat swallowing disorders.

Creative Arts, Recreational and Pet (Animal-Assisted) Therapies

These therapeutic interventions use the arts (such as art, dance and movement, drama, music, poetry or psychodrama), recreation (sports, games, outdoor activities or hobbies) and animals (domesticated pets such as dogs and cats, farm animals such as horses, or marine animals such as dolphins) to address physical, emotional, social, or cognitive needs. Therapists who use these approaches (and the animals involved) are highly trained and registered or certified. Therapists evaluate a patient's needs and design and implement individualized, goal-oriented treatment plans. These therapies—administered in hospitals or facilities or at home—can be quite effective, because many patients find them nonthreatening and are therefore more open than they might be to more traditional therapies.

I started out my career as a music therapist, so I have used music therapeutically a great deal with my parents.

Barbara became a caregiver at age 36 when her husband, Greg, suffered a stroke after routine surgery at the age of 37. "Greg was a very verbal sales-oriented investment banker, but the stroke left him with a communication disorder (aphasia) and paralysis on the right side of his body," says Barbara. The first speech therapist he had didn't connect with her husband's personality and used boring topics in therapy sessions. "Greg felt that if he was going to work hard to find words to communicate, he wanted to communicate something interesting to him, like current events or sports," says Barbara. She requested a different therapist. Over the years, Greg has had a number of speech therapists, but the best were those who took the time to learn about his life and interests. Barbara says a sense of humor also helps to lighten the situation and may help Greg find the words he wants to say.

Assistance or Service Dogs

As I've mentioned, Dad's service dog, Jackson, makes a big difference in his life. Jackson is a special and vital member of our caregiving team. Specially trained dogs may help your loved ones if they have limited vision, hearing, or mobility as well as other disabilities.

- **Guide dogs** assist people who are blind and visually impaired in a variety of ways, including going around obstacles and stopping for traffic or at curbs or stairs.
- **Hearing dogs** assist people who are deaf or hard of hearing by letting them know when they hear sounds such as alarm clocks, timers, smoke alarms, telephones, knocks on doors, or a doorbell.
- **Seizure-alert dogs** are trained to alert a person when a seizure is about to happen.
- **Mobility dogs** help those with limited mobility do a wide range of tasks, such as managing doors, picking up items, and providing stability for walking or standing.

- **Dementia or Alzheimer's dogs** provide support for those with cognitive and memory impairments.

See the Resources section for organizations and practitioners who provide and train assistance or service dogs.

Home or Mobile Health Care

When Mom came home from a rehabilitation facility, she was told to follow up with a home care agency, which told me about "mobile doctors." We have used them ever since to treat both of my parents. As a working caregiver, I was thrilled to learn about doctors and other specialists and services that come to us.

Home Care Physicians

You may think doctors who make house calls are a thing of the past, or only a part of hospice or palliative care, but there seems to be a trend toward treating people at home. Home care doctors and nurse practitioners can also see those you care for at independent, assisted living, and skilled nursing facilities, although some skilled nursing facilities only allow their own doctors to see patients on-site. The health-care practitioners' visits are usually covered by insurance, but check to make sure. According to the American Academy of Home Care Medicine, Medicare accepts qualifying home care visits for various reasons, including being homebound, low mobility, lack of transportation, the need to assess the home situation, the need to involve home-based caregivers, and cognitive, psychiatric, or emotional inability to get to an office visit.

To find a physician or nurse practitioner who makes house calls, visit the American Academy of Home Care Medicine locator at www.aahcm .org/?Locate_A_Provider.

Nursing, Home Health, and Home Care Services

Home health care includes a wide variety of services, including therapies, skilled nursing, and help with activities of daily living (ADLs), such as managing medications, grooming, bathing, dressing, and eating. It can also cover so-called instrumental activities of daily living (IADLs), which include cooking, cleaning, housekeeping, or doing chores. The people you care for may qualify for these services when recovering from an illness or after a fall or another health-care crisis. My parents have both been referred for home health services by a discharging physician in a hospital, their regular practitioners, and mobile doctors. When Dad had a feeding tube, I requested a home health nurse to visit and help us when the tube was clogged and then regularly to ensure that we were cleaning and using it properly. Home health nurses have helped us manage Mom's many wounds from skin tears and falls. In the past, Medicare paid only when a patient was showing progress, but a recent Medicare ruling allows for maintenance as a viable goal for certain therapies and services, so be sure to investigate your loved ones' eligibility and question any rulings that they don't qualify for therapy. Ask the insurance company which providers they contract with, or contact the local area agency on aging (www.eldercare.gov).

Medical Tests and Services

You may be surprised by how many technical medical tests can be done in a home setting. Mom had many X-rays and an ultrasound done in the comfort of her bed or chair at home. Once she had a swallow test performed in a van parked outside; it was done exactly like a previous test she had in a hospital. You can also get mobile EKGs, bone-density scans, echocardiograms, mammograms, and sleep studies. If it's difficult for your loved ones to get out, always ask their doctor if a mobile test is possible. Many doctors don't know about these mobile options, so you might also check with a physician who does home care or search online for providers in your area.

Palliative Care

Palliative care is aimed at providing patients who have been diagnosed with a serious illness—whether potentially curable, chronic, or terminal—with relief from symptoms, pain, and stress. Palliative care can be provided at home or in hospitals or facilities and includes pain and symptom control, emotional support, and care-team coordination. Many palliative care programs have volunteers and support for caregivers. Palliative care usually includes regular visits from doctors, nurse practitioners, nurses, and other trained health-care professionals. There is usually a focus on treating the whole person, providing the best quality of life, and avoiding hospitalizations. (The people you care for can receive curative treatments at the same time they are involved in palliative care, unlike hospice care.)

Hospice Care

Hospice care provides a palliative care protocol to those who have a prognosis of six months or less to live. Those in hospice care no longer receive curative treatments but may receive treatments, such as infection and pain control, to keep them comfortable. (If your loved ones in hospice care decide to seek curative treatment, they can leave hospice care and return if they decide to stop curative treatments.) Hospice care is a benefit of Medicare and is primarily provided at home, though it can be provided in a hospital, hospice, or other facility when needed.

Sensitive Issues: Toileting and Incontinence

You may find yourself involved in very private aspects of personal care if the people you care for are experiencing difficulties with the logistics of using the toilet; if they are unable to control their urinary or bowel functions; or if they have diarrhea, constipation, or hemorrhoids. This is uncomfortable and even unpleasant for many of us. I always say if it's tough for you, put yourself in their place and imagine how much more difficult it must be for them to need help with these basic bodily functions. It can be an even trickier situation for caregivers of the opposite sex than those they are caring for, and especially if you're caring for your parents. I have helped both of my parents with every aspect of these issues, and it has become just a routine task of caregiving. A few tips to help you with this delicate issue:

- **Observe:** Your loved ones may not want to tell you they are having trouble in this area, so be on the lookout for stains on clothing or sheets, frequency of using the toilet, stress around the subject and, of course, odors. On a visit to my grandparents' home, I noticed a bad odor in their bedroom. Upon investigation, I noticed my grandfather had been cutting up trash bags to lie on the bed where my grandmother, who had dementia, slept. I realized she was incontinent and got him briefs and bed pads for her. He would never have known such supplies existed, nor would he have asked me what to do about it—he was doing the best he could on his own.

- **Be matter of fact:** Toileting is simply a fact of life, and it's one that I don't want my parents to worry about. I approach these matters very matter-of-factly, so they tend to respond the same way. Dad used to be very private, and it was sometimes difficult to find out if he needed help. As his dementia has progressed, he has grown more comfortable, and even grateful, for assistance. I respect his boundaries when he lays them down as long as his safety and hygiene aren't compromised.

- **Look for the causes:** If difficulties exist around logistics such as finding bathrooms, getting clothes on and off, or navigating different types of toilets or sink faucets and soap dispensers, the problem may be visual or cognitive impairment. Make sure the bathroom and hallway are lit at night. Buy clothing that is easy to manipulate, perhaps with elastic or Velcro. If mobility issues make it difficult for them to get to the toilet in time, perhaps helping them develop a regular toileting schedule would help.

- **Get medical help:** If your loved ones can deal with the practicalities of toileting but are still having trouble, the problem may be a medical issue, and they might need to see a urologist for urinary problems or gastroenterologist for bowel problems. Medications or procedures may help with incontinence, prostate inflammation, constipation, or diarrhea. An infection may be at the root of incontinence. Work with your loved ones' doctors to ensure that you're using the best supplies and over-the-counter remedies; you don't want to do more damage than good.

- **Encourage independence:** This is one area that we all want to be in control of all of our lives, so it's a top priority for independence. Whenever possible and safe, help your loved ones work out routines and use supplies that they can more easily manage themselves.

- **Get practical help:** If the people you care for won't allow you to help them with toileting, perhaps it's time to bring in a paid caregiver or an occupational therapist to help adapt logistics. Sometimes it's less embarrassing to have a professional help and give recommendations to adapt the environment, personal care, or routines.

Your Job Description: Health-Care Advocate

Bravo! You have worked on one of the most difficult tasks of caregiving and earned another component of your caregiving job description.

Works on behalf of loved ones to manage high-quality physical and mental health care. Promotes health and wellness activities. Navigates the complex health-care system and gains appropriate evaluation, diagnosis, and treatment for loved ones. Develops working knowledge of a wide range of medications and in-depth knowledge of medications loved ones are taking. Requests appropriate therapeutic interventions to ensure loved ones' resiliency, independence, and optimal recovery from illness.

CHAPTER 9
WHEN YOUR LOVED ONES LIVE AT HOME

When my parents moved to Arizona in 1981, they bought a single-story house, knowing the floor plan would be ideal as they aged. They chose well; even after Mom had a stroke in 1989, she managed admirably, with loving help from Dad, for the next 15 years.

After Mom broke her hip in 2004, my brother-in-law creatively modified the sunken bathtub, installing, on top of it, a walk-in shower with grab bars, and we purchased a portable bedside commode that could easily be converted to a toilet frame with arm handles or a raised toilet seat. Mom and Dad did well in the home for another five years, at which time they moved to a senior-living community.

When they moved back home with me in 2012, I called in a certified aging-in-place specialist to help assess the house. With some inexpensive and relatively easy changes—including offset door hinges to widen doorways for Mom's walker or wheelchair; grab bars in both bathrooms; furniture arranged to block a sunken living room as well as Dad's access to the pool area of the backyard; and a stool with adjustable legs and arms for Mom to use in the bathroom as she brushed her teeth—voilà! The house was ready.

Introduction

The vast majority of people want to stay in their own homes as they age; chances are your loved ones are no different. Like many of us, you'll likely begin supporting them while they are living in their own homes. In fact, your entire caregiving experience may be home-based. As your loved ones' needs and abilities change, you'll want to continuously assess the situation to ensure that living at home is the optimal situation for them. (See Chapter 10 for information about living in a facility.)

If they live in their or your home, some modifications for safety and livability may be required. And as a working caregiver, you may not be able to handle the amount of care your loved ones may require, so you may need to coordinate and pay for additional help from in-home professional caregivers. Also, if you're living together and you work from home as well, you'll likely need additional adaptations—a discrete area for your work, for instance, or rental office space outside the home to get your work done. While living at home poses some challenges, there are also many advantages. This chapter addresses the issues you'll face as their needs increase.

In this chapter you'll learn about:
- Helping loved ones assess their needs and their home environment.
- Making home modifications for safety, accessibility, and livability.
- Finding home-based services to help your loved ones stay at home.
- Living with your loved ones.

The Decision to Live at Home

Whether your loved ones live in a house in the country, a bungalow in the suburbs, or a studio apartment in the city, their homes mean more to them than four walls and a place to hang their hats. Most people value their homes as a place of personal security, continuity, and, if they own, a long-term investment that will always be there for them. It makes sense that, despite illness, disability, or changes in skills, your loved ones probably want to remain in their home as the years go by. There are advantages to doing so. It may cost less than living in a facility. For some, since dramatic changes can worsen dementia symptoms, the familiarity of living at home and keeping up routines can be helpful. Additionally, since most people want to remain in their homes as they age, being able to do so may keep them happier. On the other hand, depending on your loved ones' level of activity, living in their homes can be isolating, and home maintenance can be a challenge. You'll want a living situation that makes sense for all of you.

For some people and their caregivers, joining households works best. You may want to move in with your loved ones, or have them move in with you, so you can more easily provide care and oversee others who are caring for them. The cost of their care may be more than their budgets can handle, so you may decide to cut costs by moving in together. Perhaps your loved ones can't manage the upkeep of their home anymore, even though they are still fairly independent.

If it makes sense for them to stay in their home or yours, eventually your loved ones may need help modifying their environment, getting assistance and care in the home, and identifying community resources and modes of transportation.

The Home Environment

Who Can Help You Assess Needs and the Home Environment

If you and your loved ones have evaluated their needs and the livability of their current home, and they've decided to remain there, you'll need to determine what modifications need to be made for both safety and lifestyle. Your 360-degree assessment in Chapter 1 will come in handy with this process. These professionals can help you.

- **Occupational therapists:** Occupational therapists who are familiar with your loved ones can assess their health conditions, routines, activities, and abilities; see how they fit with the home environment;

and suggest modifications. Find an occupational therapist through the American Occupational Therapy Association at www.aota.org or through a local home health or occupational therapy agency.

- **Certified aging-in-place specialists:** The National Association of Home Builders, in collaboration with AARP and others, developed the certified aging-in-place specialist (CAPS) program to help people who want to make their house a home for a lifetime. A specialist will come to the home and advise you about modifications—from inexpensive changes to more elaborate remodeling projects—that can make the home safer and more accessible now and in the future as your loved ones age. CAPS professionals may be contractors, remodelers, builders, interior designers, architects, occupational therapists, or other health professionals. If you need help making home modifications or remodeling and your CAPS is not a contractor, he or she may be able to point you to a reputable contractor who has special training in home modification and aging in place. Find a CAPS through the National Association of Home Builders at www.nahb.org/capsdirectory or www.aarp.org/caps.
- **Geriatric care managers:** A care manager may help assess the home and refer you to local occupational therapists or aging-in-place specialists. These professionals can provide one-time assessments and consultations, or ongoing help managing care and the environment as your loved ones' abilities change. Find a geriatric care manager through the National Association of Professional Geriatric Care Managers at http://memberfinder.caremanager.org.

Home Modifications and Smart Home Design

As a working caregiver, you know you can't always be with your loved ones, so you'll want their home to be safe and accessible for people of all ages and abilities. A home with smart design—sometimes called universal design—is easily adaptable even as needs and abilities change. It includes features and products that make a home stylish, flexible, and comfortable for everyone who lives or visits there. You can find a complete guide for making your home fit in the *AARP Guide to Revitalizing Your Home: Beautiful Living for the Second Half of Life,* at aarp.org/Revitalizing

Your Home, or in the *AARP Home Fit Guide*, available at www.aarp.org /homefit. Here are a few simple and some more extensive modifications that can make your loved ones' home accessible and livable, enhancing both safety and quality of life.

- **Single-floor living:** Having a bedroom, kitchen, full bathroom, laundry area, and family or living room on the same floor can be safer and more convenient. All areas within that level should be accessible. If your loved ones live in a multifloor home, you might consider modifying the first floor so they can live on just one level.
- **Entryway:** A covered entrance can protect your loved ones and visitors from rain and snow, and keep the walkway safe and dry. Carrying groceries, managing a pet, or looking for house keys in the pouring rain or on an icy surface is a recipe for disaster. Make at least one entry into the home step-free so anyone can enter easily, whether with a baby stroller, walker, wheelchair, or arms full of groceries. This might not be the front door, but in some homes a garage entry or side door will work.
- **Wide doorways and hallways:** Ideally, doorways should be at least 36 inches wide to allow for moving furniture or appliances as well as walker and wheelchair accessibility. Hallways should be 42 inches wide and free of hazards or steps.
- **Bathrooms:** Install grab bars, a raised toilet seat with handrails, and nonslip strips in the tub. A low- or no-threshold shower entry is best, and a shower seat or built-in bench allows for seated bathing without climbing in and out of a tub. A handheld showerhead adds flexibility and ease for seated showering. Try a memory foam bathmat with a slip-resistant base.
- **Reachable controls and switches:** Anyone—even a person in a wheelchair—can reach light switches and thermostats that are from 42 to 48 inches above the floor and electrical outlets 18 to 24 inches off the floor. Remote controls are another option; I had them installed for all our overhead lights and ceiling fans.
- **Easy-to-use handles, door knobs, and switches:** Lever-style door handles and faucets, easy-to-grasp D-shaped cabinet pulls and

rocker-style light switches make opening doors and cabinets, turning on water, and lighting a room easier for people of every age and ability.

- **Kitchen cabinets and countertops:** Adjustable-height cupboards, lazy Susans and pull-down shelving systems can prevent the need for step stools for people who are short or have trouble reaching. Multilevel kitchen countertops with open space underneath make it easier to work while seated in a chair or wheelchair. Task lighting over countertop or work areas can prevent cuts when chopping or slicing food and also aid in cleaning. Lights in cabinets can help people find items.
- **Appliances:** Raised clothes washers, dryers, and dishwashers don't require bending over. Side-by-side upright refrigerators and freezers are easier to navigate than models with the freezer at the top or bottom, and an external water and ice dispenser provide easy accessibility.
- **Windows and window treatments:** Windows, curtains, and blinds that are easy to open and close can be a safety factor in an emergency, such as for a quick escape in case of a fire; they also aid in circulating air and cooling if the house does not have air conditioning.
- **Hot water:** To avoid burns and accidents, set the hot water heater to 120 degrees Fahrenheit.
- **Smoke detectors:** You'll want smoke detectors installed and checked monthly to ensure that they're working. Some people change the batteries annually on a set schedule. If your loved ones have a security or medical-monitoring system, find out if smoke detectors are included.
- **Use bright lighting:** Check lighting in and outside the home. Plug in motion-sensor nightlights along walkways—especially between the bathroom and bedroom. Use lampshades that reduce glare.
- **Stairs:** Install handrails on both sides of stairways inside and outside, and encourage loved ones to use them at all times, even when carrying items. Even one step can cause a fall. We have one step down to a sunken living room; my best friend's mother fell and cracked her ribs there because she didn't notice the step. Now I arrange furniture along that entire step so my parents won't fall.
- **Laundry:** In many homes, laundry facilities are in the basement. If that is the case, make sure your loved ones can navigate steps

while holding laundry; if they can't, move the laundry room or make arrangements for someone else to help.

If you decide to make more expansive changes to your loved ones' home, look for a contractor who is reputable and has experience with universal design or homes for people with disabilities or limited mobility. Meet with at least three contractors and get estimates from each, then consider which plan best meets your loved ones' needs as well as quality and price.

Laurette Bennhold-Samaan's husband, Cornelius, had cancer that eventually invaded his spine, and he could no longer walk. Their bedroom was up a long flight of stairs. "We considered setting up a bedroom on the first floor," Laurette said, "but there was no private room with a door." They decided on a chair lift: pricey, but more cost-effective than renovation. The chair lift worked perfectly, and after her husband had surgery and learned to walk and climb the stairs safely again, Laurette's aging mother was able to use the lift for many years. When she passed on, the lift was easily removed with no permanent damage to the staircase.

Fall Prevention

Every year, one in three adults age 65 or older falls. Among that age group, falls are the leading cause of injury or death and are the most common cause of hospitalizations for hip or spine fractures and brain injuries. In addition to the home modification suggestions listed above, consider these tips to prevent falls:

- **Exercise:** Establish an exercise regimen to maintain balance, a steady gait, and strength, especially leg strength.
- **Watch for health issues:** Be aware of medication side effects like dizziness, weakness, or drowsiness. Make sure your loved ones have their vision checked at least annually. Be aware of numbness. Be extra vigilant when loved ones are sick. See more about this in Chapter 8.
- **Eliminate trip hazards:** Remove clutter and debris, such as newspapers, extension cords, dog toys, and leaves. Remove area rugs unless

they're secured firmly with tacks, double-sided tape, or a nonslip gripper pad; even a thin rug can slide, catch a toe and cause a fall. Doormats, too, should be secure. Outside, trim overgrown shrubbery to allow clear pathways.

- **Chairs:** Use chairs with arms to make it easier to stand up. Replace wheeled casters with glides for tile or wood floors. I ordered online a set of glides for our kitchen chairs so Mom could more safely stand up and sit down. The caster wheels popped off easily with pliers.

- **Avoid the obvious:** Stay away from slick floor wax, step stools, shoes that don't fit, and pants or robes that are too long.

- **Use assistive devices:** A doctor, nurse practitioner, or physical therapist might recommend a cane, walker, wheelchair, stair-lift, or a grabber for out-of-reach items. Make sure your loved ones know how to use these devices properly, and monitor their use.

- **Monitors and alerts:** If you know your loved ones are at high risk for falling, make sure someone is always with them or create a system they can use to call for help before they fall. I could have prevented so many of Mom's falls had these been readily available in earlier years. Now they are easy to find online. I used an inexpensive wireless doorbell that Mom rang when she was ready to get out of bed as well as an audio and video monitor and two alarms that sounded an alert if she got up: one clipped to her sleeve, the other was a pad under the bed sheets or chair cushion. I added a floor-mat alarm for Dad so when he gets out of bed it sounds off as soon as he puts his feet down. I also have a motion-sensor alarm in the hallway. Many sensors are activated by movement that can set off alarms and/or send notifications to your smartphone, tablet, or computer. I recommend having several monitors in place as backups in case one fails—technology is so helpful, but you never know when a battery will die or a connection will fail!

Home- and Community-Based Services

Many services are available to help your loved ones stay at home for as long as possible. Here are some that might be helpful.

- **Medical alert:** This is a service in which your loved ones have a pendant with a button they can push to contact a call center or call 911 directly. Some medical alert systems operate only at home; others include a GPS function so your loved ones can have access to it anywhere they go. Some systems also link to smoke detectors or home security systems.
- **Friendly visitors:** Arranged through a companionship service or volunteer organization, these people will check in on, visit with, and reassure your loved ones, providing both socialization and a safety check.
- **Chore services:** You can get help around the home with changing lightbulbs, caring for the yard, taking things in and out of an attic or basement, putting up decorations, or doing other household chores. Some programs offer minor home repairs at reduced costs as well.
- **Home health aides, certified nursing assistants (CNAs), home care aides, personal care aides, and paid caregivers:** These professionals provide a wide range of help with personal care and grooming (toileting, bathing, and dressing), exercises, laundry, cooking, running errands, housekeeping, wound care, and medication management or reminders. Typical duties, as well as certification and training requirements and fees for these positions, vary from state to state, so find out about requirements and expectations in your loved ones' state.
- **Home-delivered and community meal programs:** Meals delivered or served at a community site can be free or at a low cost. Home delivery usually offers breakfast or lunch and a bagged meal to refrigerate for dinner. These meal programs also provide social interaction.
- **Community centers:** Local community centers may provide classes, entertainment, and exercise facilities for people of all ages that would be a good way for your loved ones to stay intellectually stimulated and interact with others.

- **Senior centers:** Most communities have a senior center that specializes in activities, education, and fitness for active older adults who are still fairly independent. These centers often have meal sites, entertainment, and group trips to museums, stores, cultural events, and historical sites.
- **Adult day services:** These centers are geared for adults with disabilities or older adults who need a more structured environment or can't be left alone during the day. Programs can include social activities; speech, occupational, and physical therapy; nursing and medication administration; and meals. (See the Resources section for a checklist to help you choose adult day-care services.)
- **Transportation:** Transportation services in a car or van, driven by volunteers or paid staff, can take your loved ones to doctor appointments, stores, and senior or community centers. Senior taxi services will usually take older adults wherever they need to go for a reduced fee. You might check with the local department of transportation to see if there is a "travel training" program that provides help to learn how to use public transportation. Some senior, community, or adult day services centers will provide their own transportation.

To find out about home- and community-based services or long-term services and supports available in your loved ones' area:

- Contact your local area agency on aging (AAA), which provides, funds, and monitors local services and may provide case management or information and referral to help you find local community resources. The AAA may also help you find out if your loved ones qualify for benefits and free or reduced-cost services. Find the local AAA via the Eldercare Locator at www.eldercare.gov.
- Visit Medicare's Home Health Compare website at www.medicare.gov /homehealthcompare for information about the quality of care provided by local "Medicare-certified" home health agencies (approved by Medicare and meeting certain federal health and safety requirements). This site provides information that may help you choose a provider.

- Contact a local Aging and Disability Resource Center (ADRC), a single point of entry center to help streamline access to long-term services and support options for older adults and individuals with disabilities. ADRCs provide information and one-on-one counseling on the full range of options. Sometimes the AAA and the ADRC are the same agency. Find a local ADRC at www.eldercare.gov.
- Dial 211 on your telephone for an information and referral service that can connect you with community services.
- Find out if your loved ones live in a "naturally occurring retirement community" (NORC). A NORC is a condo or apartment building or a neighborhood where the residents are mostly older adults who generally have aged in place or all moved to a certain area. NORCs are not purposefully created for older adults—they evolve naturally. Many NORCs have developed supportive services programs, usually in partnership with a housing or community group, offering case management, health, or personal care services; wellness programs; and lifelong learning and activities.
- Find out if there is a "village," part of the Village to Village Network (www.vtvnetwork.org), in the area. Its website describes these villages as "membership-driven, grassroots organizations that, through both volunteers and paid staff, coordinate access to affordable services including transportation, health and wellness programs, home repairs, social and educational activities, and other day-to-day needs, enabling individuals to remain connected to their community throughout the aging process."
- Find volunteers to help. There are some agencies that recruit and manage volunteers to provide companionship to older adults or those with disabilities. Conduct a thorough background check to ensure that your loved ones are safe with volunteers. You may find volunteers through a local faith-based community, the area agency on aging (www.eldercare.gov), the local Alzheimer's Association chapter (www.alz.org/apps/findus.asp), or a volunteer-matching organization. Get referrals from family and friends. Personal referrals from people who have used the services are often a good way to find quality local resources.

Tips for Evaluating Workers and Services

Be sure to ask the area agency, as well as the individuals or services you are considering, about these issues:

- **Fees:** Some services are provided by volunteer organizations or for minimal costs; others are provided by agencies that generally charge hourly, daily, or weekly rates. Some offer sliding-fee scales based on ability to pay. Be sure to find out if Medicare, Medicaid, or insurance covers the services and if so, time limits (some are covered only on a short-term basis).
- **Qualifications and monitoring:** Some services must be provided by certified, registered, or otherwise trained and qualified individuals or agencies, usually as determined by the state. Find out about these requirements as well as how providers are monitored, and ask to see the latest evaluations or complaints about their services.
- **Experience and references:** It's a good idea to get a detailed description of specific pertinent work experience as well as personal recommendations from at least three people who have used the services.

Hiring Home Care Workers

You can find home health aides, certified nursing assistants (CNAs), home care aides, personal care aides, and paid caregivers through agencies or you can hire them yourself. There are pros and cons to both approaches. On the one hand, agencies can handle insurance (if their services are covered), screening, hiring, scheduling, and other personnel issues. On the other hand, agencies may cost more and continuously switch out workers, and you'll still need to coordinate and monitor their work. If services aren't covered by insurance, you could hire workers directly yourself. The costs will be lower, but you'll have to find, screen, hire, and schedule each person. If you do take this on, keep in mind that your loved ones are very vulnerable, so it's vital that you screen potential home care workers and conduct background checks before arranging for anyone to come to their homes.

Finding Home Care Workers Through an Agency

You can find an agency through the area agency on aging, an online search, a geriatric care manager, or a local senior services directory. Be sure to do your research.

- Ask about fees.
- Get a description of experience as well as references for the agency *and* for individual workers they want to assign to your loved ones.
- Check the Better Business Bureau (www.bbb.org) and state monitoring agencies for complaints or pending lawsuits.
- Ask where the agency finds its workers; how it screens, selects, trains, and manages them; how much it pays the workers versus how much you pay for the services; and how complaints or poor service are handled.
- Be very clear about your expectations and the tasks involved.
- If you sign a contract or agreement with the agency, be sure you understand what you are signing. Some agencies will ask you to sign a form indicating that you will be responsible for fees if your loved ones can't pay.
- If the worker the agency sends isn't a good fit, don't hesitate to ask for another person. I've learned the hard way that keeping an under-performing home care worker past the time when I knew she wasn't doing a good job can cause problems, and even injuries to loved ones. Even if you have to go through several workers before you find a good fit, keep asking—and change agencies if necessary.

Finding Home Care Workers on Your Own

If you and the people you care for decide not to use an agency to find a home care worker, these are steps to take to hire workers yourself.

- Decide how much you're prepared to pay. If you hire workers directly, you need to advise them about paying their taxes and ensure that you are paying any necessary employer taxes. Check with an accountant or the Internal Revenue Service for proper tax forms and instructions. You can also find companies that manage payroll for you via online caregiver-matching services or other agencies that include this service when they help you find a paid caregiver.

- Write a job description and include the amount you are willing to pay (or, if you are undecided, say that the fee is negotiable). Write a detailed list of all the tasks you will require, the hours and days of the job, and personal preferences with regard to driving and other transportation options. Indicate time off and benefits, such as vacation or sick time. Include a phone number or email address, but don't give out your name or other personal information. (If your email is your name, you might want to set up another email account for this purpose.) Ask for a résumé or job history as well as names and telephone numbers for at least three people they've cared for in the past or the families of those they've cared for.

- Ask family, friends, neighbors, co-workers, or other caregivers for referrals.

- Use an online service or website, such as www.care.com, www.carelinx.com, www.caringly.com, and www.gonannies.com, where workers can list their availability and you can post a job listing to recruit workers. You can get background checks through most of these services. Find out if they tack on extra fees or require you to pay workers only through their online system. Some of these organizations include payroll services to make pay and tax issues easier for you.

- Post a flier on online or physical community bulletin boards at local places of worship, the library, community centers, senior centers, adult day centers, doctors' offices, hospitals, colleges and universities (try nursing, social work, physical, occupational, or speech therapy students), or through a jobs placement program.

- Post an ad in the local newspaper or on the community website or email list.

- Follow the tips for evaluating workers and services listed in this chapter.

Screening, Interviewing, and Selecting a Home Care Worker

- First, talk with candidates on the phone. Ask about work experience, hours of availability, driving experience, special training, and references. Get an initial feel for their personality to see if your loved ones' needs and their skills are a good match. Ask why they left their last job.

- If you like the candidate well enough, schedule an in-person meeting. Meet candidates at a neutral site—a coffee shop, restaurant, or other public place. Talk more about their experience, why they are interested in caring for your loved ones, what they like about their work, and anything they refuse to do. Answer any questions they have about the job.

- If, after a phone call and an in-person meeting, you still like the candidate for the job, arrange for a time for them to visit your loved ones' home for an opportunity to meet and have an interview. Observe their interaction. Are they respectful? Do they ignore your loved ones and talk only to you? Can they communicate well with your loved ones? Do their personalities blend well? How do your loved ones react to the candidate?

Checking References and Conducting a Background Check

- Call each of the three requested references. Some caregivers prefer to check references before they even meet a prospective worker. While references may not give you much negative information, they will either confirm your impressions or widen your perspective of the candidates. Ask specific questions about punctuality; attendance; how the candidates handled certain situations, such as emergencies or daily tasks; and why the candidates left the position.

- Perform a criminal background check. If you are hiring directly and found the candidate from a care-finder website, it may have the ability to get the background check done for you (usually a preliminary background check for free and a deeper check for a fee). Or check with your local law enforcement agency to find out how to do this.

Hiring and Transitioning a New Home Care Worker

- Be clear about the details of the job, including responsibilities and tasks. If you are hiring directly, discuss pay, time off, and benefits, such as vacation or sick time. The more detail, the better to ward off misunderstandings later.

- Once you've made a choice and the worker has accepted, write a care agreement that includes information about a trial period, job duties, salary, pay schedule, time off, start date, and termination policy. You and the worker (and your loved ones if possible) should sign and keep copies.

- Consider starting workers for a one-month trial period to see if it's a good fit before making it permanent.

- To train new care workers, spend 100 percent of the time with them for at least the first two days, showing them the tasks they are to perform and helping your loved ones acclimate. But be sure to let the workers do the job and allow them to build a relationship with your loved ones. After the first few days, drop back to part of the day and eventually let them take over the routine.

- Monitor their work frequently. Your loved ones are vulnerable, so you'll need to oversee the care the worker is providing. Drop in unexpectedly to get a clear picture of care that is provided. Be sure to get your loved ones' feedback about how the workers are doing, too. Provide feedback to the workers to encourage growth in the job and keep the work on track.

When You and Loved Ones Live Together

Living with people who need care and support can be a wonderful experience. As a multigenerational or extended family or as friends, you'll have the opportunity to spend precious time together. You'll be able to know about and have more control over the details of their living situation, including the food they're eating, the care they're receiving, the activities they're engaging in, and the general quality of life they're experiencing. It will be much easier to understand and track changes in their needs, health conditions, and cognitive abilities. You won't waste time constantly running back and forth between their home and yours. As a working caregiver, I've found it's actually *less* stressful living with my parents. And I have loved having meals with them and kissing them goodnight. It's much easier for me to enjoy quality time together and provide hands-on care in non-work hours while still taking care of my personal tasks, such as housecleaning, yard work, laundry, and bill paying.

Living together does require some sacrifices, of course. Freedom and personal space become more limited, and "alone time" may feel like a lost commodity. You'll no doubt have to adapt your daily routines, including your meal, TV, and bathroom time. If those you care for live with you, you may need to make modifications to your own home.

Tips for Living Together

Here are some of my tips for sharing a home with your loved ones.

- **Plan ahead:** Talk before you move in together about boundaries, use of space, and how you will communicate what's working and what's not working.
- **Prepare the home:** Look at the home modification and fall prevention tips listed above, and make sure your home is ready for sharing. Some families move to a home designed for sharing, while others modify an existing home.
- **Give everyone some privacy:** It's important that you each have a spot to call your own, such as a bedroom, sitting room, or even a corner of a room or place for a favorite chair for watching television. Your loved ones may be giving up a lot if they've moved out of their own home to live with you (and vice versa), so be responsive to needs for privacy and ownership.
- **Be sensitive to your kids:** If you have children as well as your loved ones living under one roof, be sensitive to the needs of your children. In addition to bearing up to the changes in their routine and living space, they may feel they've lost some of your time and attention.
- **Organize shared expenses:** Money can be a sticky subject. Create both individual and shared household budgets. Be clear about who is

paying for what and how bills will be paid. There are many ways to slice it. For example, you could create a shared checking account in which all members of the household deposit funds; you could collect from your loved ones and pay all the bills; or you each could pay different household bills. Those with fewer resources could contribute in other ways, such as housecleaning. Whatever you come up with, periodically reevaluate the plan to ensure that it's working.

- **Make time for fun:** You have a golden opportunity to spend quality time with your loved ones on a daily basis—take advantage of it! Don't make every moment about health care or the difficult aspects of caregiving. Make memories and create routine fun time together—sharing meals, playing games, watching movies, going on outings, enjoying your yard, making music, or telling stories. Take photos and make video and audio recordings to create keepsakes you'll always treasure.

- **Go with the flow:** There are bound to be conflicts, frustrations, and moments when you long for privacy and freedom. If you accept this as fact, it won't be so unexpected or catastrophic when it happens. Take a little time away, get clear on priorities, and go back with a loving approach. If feasible, set up regular times to talk about challenges rather than discussing them in the height of emotion and drama. If you can't reach a compromise, consider a professional family mediator to help iron out the nitty-gritty aspects of your living situation.

Working from Home

Living with my parents has, frankly, put a cramp in my work style. I have to constantly balance my work needs with my parents' needs. Here are some suggestions if you are a caregiver who works from home, based on what I've learned.

- **Work space:** If you're working from home as a telecommuter, consultant, or other arrangement, you'll need to make sure you have the space to get your paid job done. I worked from home for three years, until my parents moved back home and we had to convert my office into a bedroom. Now there are certain times of day I can still work from home, but the rest of the time I work from an office I rented a few miles away. My parents' housing expenses went down, but my business expenses went up.

- **Flexible scheduling:** Consider any work schedule changes that might be helpful, as discussed in Chapter 5. For example, if your loved ones need more help in the mornings, perhaps you could arrange with your employer to get your work done in the afternoons and evenings. Or maybe you could work weekends when another family member could come to be with your loved ones.
- **Other options for your loved ones during the day:** If you work during daytime hours, perhaps your loved ones could go to an adult day services center or have other activities away from home while you're working.

Your Job Description: Home-Based Care Coordinator

Helping loved ones remain in their own or your home can be a challenge, but you've learned a lot and now you've gained a new component to your job description:

Evaluates needs in home environment. Plans and coordinates targeted "universal design" home modifications as needed to adapt for safety and livability. Determines which supportive home-based services are needed, arranges for such services, and coordinates hiring and monitoring of home-based workers.

CHAPTER 10

WHEN YOUR LOVED ONES LIVE IN A FACILITY

When my parents decided to move out of their home of 28 years and into a senior community, I lived 2,000 miles away and had no idea what facilities were available in their area. With the help of an experienced professional who evaluated our needs and was familiar with the local options, I visited about a dozen facilities and took my sister to visit several, and then we narrowed it down to three for Mom and Dad to visit. We decided on independent living, supplemented with some additional services to help Mom with personal care. We also wanted a continuing-care retirement community (CCRC) so that as their needs changed, they would be able to move, either temporarily or permanently, to higher levels of care—assisted living and skilled nursing—on one campus. In the end, Mom chose the place that had the biggest apartment, the nicest grounds, and the ability to put up a fence for Jackson so he could have a doggy-door. Luckily, my sister and I liked the facility the best, too, and it was the closest to my parents' house, where I would be living.

For about two years, the independent living facility served them well. Then, after surgery and severe illness, Mom went to the CCRC's skilled nursing facility for rehab for three months, and Dad could walk over from their apartment to see her every day. It was only a five-minute drive for me, so I could easily visit daily to monitor Mom's care, and my sister came from Ohio when I was out of town. After Mom left rehab, and as

Dad's Alzheimer's progressed, we increased the supplemental services until they needed 24-hour care. We quickly found that the one-on-one attention they needed was too costly in that setting, so they moved back home with me. While it meant a lot of change for all of us, I don't regret their move to independent living. For those years, with meals and some transportation provided, they had more independence than if they'd been at home by themselves. Besides, the Goyers are always up for a new adventure!

Introduction

Living in facilities can offer multiple benefits, such as more socialization, less isolation, support services so residents can remain more independent longer, and on-site medical care. The assumption is that when your loved ones live in a facility—such as an independent living senior community, assisted living, a group home, or skilled nursing facility—you'll have more time and less involvement, because someone else is taking care of them. Right? Not necessarily. Your role may change, but it's far from over. While you may be doing less hands-on care, you'll have the important, often life-saving, task of overseeing the care that is provided by an ever-changing array of people, but you'll have less control over who provides the care and how they do so. You'll also need to ensure that their apartment or room is kept clean and safe. You'll most likely help with or fully manage their finances, and living in a facility can be expensive. Very frequent in-person visits will be crucial, so you'll need to plan for time at the facility in conjunction with your work schedule. Your role just got more complicated.

In this chapter you'll learn about:
- Housing options for your loved ones.
- How to make a facility their home.
- Your role when loved ones live in a facility.
- How to handle problems with the facility.

Housing Options

Levels of Care

You will find a wide range of facilities where your loved ones might live, with many different levels of care. Staffing, services, and policies can vary greatly. Be aware that there are different names for these levels of care in different states, as well as varied state regulations and monitoring systems. Not every community will have all of the options, and some may have only one nursing facility or one assisted living to choose from; others will have numerous options. Within a 10-mile radius of my parents' home, we have probably 50 or more facilities to choose from, but in the rural Ohio town where I grew up, there are fewer than five—and not every level of care is available.

Each type of housing option offers a different level of care and support, so it's important to understand what kind of care your loved ones will receive at each level. And they may go back and forth between different levels. At times they might temporarily need to move to a higher level of care due to a health condition, and then go back down to a lower level of care. Conversely, you may think that a move to a higher level of care will be permanent, but then see your loved ones improve with better care and become more independent again.

Wherever the people you care for live, make sure to visit the facility to get a *realistic* picture of the level of care and supervision and the quality of life. You'll also want to review the facility's detailed policies.

Independent Living

In independent living facilities, residents have their own apartments with some services provided, such as meals, housecleaning, and activities. Some facilities also offer transportation for shopping and errands, medical appointments, or group social activities. Some have security and offer additional services that you pay for a la carte, such as medication reminders and help with bathing and laundry. Some independent living facilities have medical professionals on staff; others don't. Residents aren't usually monitored because they are able to live independently, so unless your

loved ones participate in group activities or meals, no one may be aware
of how they are doing.

Assisted Living

Assisted living is higher level of care than independent living. Services
and costs can vary greatly. Services may be included in a flat fee based
on your loved ones' level of functioning or offered a la carte. Some staff
will be in the facility 24 hours a day, but many residents are still fairly
independent. Your loved ones may have a small private room with a small
sitting area or kitchenette; share a room or suite with another resident;
or live as a couple in larger rooms. Most assisted-living facilities have
common areas where residents eat, watch TV, and engage in activities.

Generally, staff provides assistance in the morning and evening with
bathing and dressing as well as medication management, meals, and some
activities. Other times of the day, you'll find varying levels of staff interaction. Don't assume someone will check on your loved ones constantly,
or that staff will be at your loved ones' beck and call. A resident will have
a call button to get help, but in reality I've observed response time can be
a half hour or more. Some facilities have a staffed front desk at the main
entrance, but others don't. For most facilities, residents can come and go
as they please, so don't assume someone will know if your loved ones
wander off. It's really not 24-hour hands-on care or attention; it's just, as
its name implies, assistance. Depending on your loved ones' needs, you
may still need to hire additional care.

Skilled Nursing Facilities

Often referred to as nursing homes, skilled nursing facilities offer 24-hour
medical care and provide meals and activities like other levels of care but
more monitoring (at least in theory). Residents' capabilities will vary, from
people who are bedridden or ambulatory and living there permanently to
those who are there for short-term rehabilitation, recovering from surgery,
a fall or illness. Facilities offer small private or shared rooms. You'll usually find a dining room and perhaps activities and living rooms. Skilled
nursing facilities usually offer on-site physical, occupational, and speech
therapy and may have other therapists, such as recreation, activities, or

music therapists. A social worker will be on staff to help with social services and payment methods. Residents have call buttons for help, but again, I've seen it take at least a half hour before someone responds. Even if facilities meet state staffing standards, the staff have many residents to care for, so they may not be able to provide as much attention to your loved one as you'd think. When Mom was in a skilled nursing facility for rehab, she went as long as two hours in her room with no one checking on her.

Memory Care

Many facilities offer special units for people with Alzheimer's disease and other forms of dementia, generally with a higher staff-to-resident ratio, more supervision, and security measures so residents don't leave the grounds and get lost. But again, don't expect that your loved ones will have someone constantly paying attention to them unless you hire extra private care. Memory care units provide meals, assistance with bathing and dressing, medication administration, and specially designed activities for those with dementia.

Continuing Care Retirement Communities (CCRC)

Continuing care retirement communities usually, but not always, include independent living, assisted living, and skilled nursing on one campus, and residents can move between levels of care as needed. These facilities often offer some extra services to residents in independent and assisted living because they already have nurses and other health practitioners on staff. Residents may pay a large flat fee to buy into the community, along with lower monthly fees that increase according to the level of care. With this arrangement, residents are guaranteed care in the CCRC for the rest of their lives. At other CCRCs, residents don't buy in but just pay monthly fees that increase with higher levels of care. Under this arrangement, residents receive preference for rooms in the various levels of care but are not guaranteed placement.

Group, Residential Care, or Board-and-Care Homes

These types of homes are generally in neighborhood settings, where a homeowner or staff live in and care for several people. While sometimes called assisted living, they generally cost less and are in very different settings from the assisted-living facilities I describe above. Services can vary greatly from home to home but generally cover meals and help with bathing, dressing, and medications; they may offer some activities. They usually don't offer medical services. The one-to-one care may be greater because they are smaller; on the other hand, it may be less because they have fewer staff. The attention your loved one receives may vary a great deal from home to home.

Choosing a Facility

You can find facilities through the local area agency on aging; an online search; local senior-living catalogues; or an assisted-living locator service, which may also help find other types of facilities as well. If your loved ones have been in the hospital or rehab, the social worker or discharge planner can be extremely helpful in locating short-term or permanent facilities. In the Resources section, I point you to specific checklists for different types of facilities, but in general, when making housing decisions, you'll want to take these steps:

- Evaluate your loved ones' needs thoroughly to determine the level of support they currently need to remain as independent as possible for as long as possible.
- Think about long-term needs. It's impossible to predict the future, but you can base decisions on what you know about their desires and the projected progression of their illnesses and conditions.
- Help the people you care for prioritize their wants and needs, including location (a safe neighborhood and proximity to doctors, other service providers, and favorite stores), ambiance, outdoor environment, opportunities to socialize, abilities of people who live there, activities, exercise options, size of the living space (square footage and number of rooms), common living areas, cooking options, quality of food, laundry facilities, help with personal care, transportation, rules about pets, and staff attitudes.

- List factors that are important to you, such as proximity to your home or work (this could be a pivotal factor in visiting daily to check on your loved ones), amount and quality of care, monitoring or supervision, communication with staff, staff's attitude toward working with caregivers, transportation to doctors and stores, and ways you can monitor care and progress remotely.
- Visit facilities more than once. To ease decision-making, consider visiting many facilities yourself and then taking your loved ones to just a few. You'll need to visit at different times of day, and I suggest at least one unannounced visit so you get a true picture of a typical day. Any facility that doesn't allow you to drop by would raise questions in my mind, although it's reasonable for staff to require you to be escorted around the facility. Here's what I look for:
  - **Quality of life:** What is the environment like? Are there gardens, water features, calm areas, social areas? Does it feel like a nice place to live? Do people socialize? Are the elements of whatever makes your loved ones happy there? What is the lifestyle like—boring, exciting, serene, calm, happy, stimulating, nurturing?
  - **Residents:** Are the residents people your loved ones can relate to? Do they seem happy to be there? Are they functioning at similar ability levels as your loved ones? Are they happy with the administration, food, and activities? Try to talk with residents away from staff. Ask what they like and don't like about the facility. Are the residents' rights posted?
  - **Staff interactions:** Are they having fun? Talking to each other? Do they seem to like each other? Do they seem to like their work and be happy there? Or are they grumpy, impersonal, and short with one another?
  - **Staff-resident interactions:** Do you see residents and staff talking, joking, being affectionate and respectful, and enjoying each other? Does it feel like a community or is there a sense of "us against them"? What is the staff-to-resident ratio?
  - **Family involvement:** Are families and friends encouraged to visit and engage in the community? Is there a family council? Do you see families visiting? Are visitors of all ages welcome? Are there

places on-site appropriate for family visits? Talk to the family of a resident and get their honest perspectives.

○ **Safety:** Is there 24-hour on-site security staff? Is the facility kept up? Can people with disabilities get around everywhere safely? Do you see any fall hazards? Are fire extinguishers, smoke alarms, and sprinklers in place and working? Is there an emergency call service? How do residents get help when needed?

○ **Medical, therapeutic, and personal care:** Are medical professionals (doctors, nurses, and nurse practitioners) on staff? Are therapeutic services offered on-site? Who provides personal care assistance? How are they trained, qualified, and monitored? What is their level of experience? Do they provide the level of care your loved ones need?

○ **Activities:** Are the activities interesting and varied? On- and off-site? Do residents attend them regularly and appear engaged? Are activities offered at times your loved ones are likely to be able to go? Are activities offered for residents with different cognitive abilities? Are there special amenities on-site, such as swimming pools, hot tubs, pool tables, exercise facilities, horseshoes, putting greens, and walking paths?

○ **Transportation:** Is transportation included or provided at an extra fee? Where does it go? How difficult is it to arrange? Are vehicles safe and well kept? Are they accessible for people with walkers or wheelchairs? Does an escort accompany residents to appointments? How much do drivers help?

○ **Food:** Have a meal at the facility—the quality of the food tells you a lot. Would you want to eat there every day? If not, why would your loved ones? Is there variety in the menu? Does it meet your loved ones' nutritional needs? Are there plenty of fresh fruits and vegetables? Are serving portions reasonable? Are mealtimes flexible?

○ **Odor:** Are all rooms free of offensive odors? Or does the odor tell you people aren't being well cared for? You should not detect ongoing unpleasant odors in any facility.

- ○ **Restrictions:** Are pets allowed? Are guests allowed, including overnight? Is smoking and drinking allowed? Are there noise restrictions? Can your loved ones decorate their rooms however they wish?
  - ○ **Costs:** Can your loved ones afford this? What are payment options (insurance, frequency, mode of payment, automatic payments)? How often do rates increase?
- If you are considering a skilled nursing facility, compare local Medicare- and Medicaid-certified options at Medicare.gov's Nursing Home Compare website at www.medicare.gov/nursinghomecompare.
- To learn about a facility's licensing, certification, other requirements, and complaints, contact the local area agency on aging at www.eldercare.gov. If there are complaints against the facility, find out how they were resolved.

Payment Assistance

All the housing options I've outlined are costly, so carefully evaluate your loved ones' ability to pay along with how much you and family members can afford to contribute. Medicare, Medicaid, and private medical insurance don't cover independent living, so your loved ones will have to pay the costs themselves. Medicare doesn't cover assisted living either, but Medicaid may cover some assisted-living services for those who qualify. Medicare will cover only a limited amount of skilled nursing costs under certain circumstances if your loved ones are eligible. While Medicaid does cover skilled nursing, not all facilities accept Medicaid.

If your loved ones have long-term care insurance and need extra home health care in independent living, they may qualify for benefits just as they would in a private home. Most long-term care insurance policies cover assisted living and skilled nursing care, but keep in mind most policies have certain "triggers" or qualifications in terms of eligibility for benefits, as well as a waiting period before payments start. In addition, if Medicare or another form of insurance is paying for care, long-term care insurance won't also pay benefits. (See more about long-term care insurance in Chapter 7.) Some assisted living or group homes may accept Social Security's Supplemental Security Income (SSI).

Downsizing, Moving, and Making It Home

Once you've helped your loved ones choose a new home, it's time to tackle the move. A move can take a great deal of time—preparing, packing, unpacking, and settling in. Your loved ones will need your help, so if possible, plan the move at a time when you are able to be away from work. Sometimes these moves are made suddenly with little time to prepare, such as after an accident or an illness. Many people go straight from a hospital to a new living situation. Other moves are more leisurely. Either way, here are some tips for making this process go as smoothly as possible.

- **Consider hiring a professional organizer or relocation, downsizing, or moving service:** These professionals specialize in helping people, including older adults who have been in their homes for many years, move. They've got it down to a science, so it might be worthwhile to have a consultation or get an estimate for the whole service. Ask the facility where your loved ones are relocating for suggestions or contact the National Association of Senior Move Managers at www .nasmm.org. Check with the Better Business Bureau at www.bbb.org or with an online service that shares customers' experiences and ratings of professionals you are considering.
- **Have two or three movers conduct an in-home estimate, and get it in writing:** Ask about any hidden charges, such as added costs for extra help or travel time. You might save money and stress by moving during the week or packing and transporting some precious items (such as jewelry or family heirlooms) yourself.
- **Sort, pack or toss . . . repeat:** The first step of moving, especially if the people you care for are downsizing, is sorting. Have them, if they are able, go through their belongings and decide what will go to their new home. This can be an understandingly overwhelming task, so they'll need your help or they may wait until the last minute. Start

by creating spaces in their current home to make stacks in these five categories:

1. Give to family and friends.
2. Donate to charities.
3. Throw away.
4. Put in storage (you should have a very good reason to store anything—like perhaps seasonal decorations or off-season clothing).
5. Pack and move.

Try to start this weeding-out process long before the move. You can even start before a move is imminent (when stress is lower) to prepare for "someday." If you're on a short time frame and don't have to empty out their current home immediately, focus on the items your loved ones will immediately want and deal with the rest later. If you can keep both homes for a while, you'll likely decrease the stress level.

- **Map out where things will go:** I used large flip-chart paper so my parents could easily see a diagram of the space, and then I used proportioned pieces of paper cut to symbolize various pieces of furniture so we could decide what furniture to move. Storage is often an issue, so keep in mind closet and cupboard sizes. Get a good idea of what will fit and what will not.

- **Buy something new:** When my parents moved, I found I could infuse fun and excitement into the process by helping them buy a few new things, such as bathroom shower curtains and towels. Mom and Dad picked out their own things, which helped them feel some sense of control over a new phase in their lives.

- **Manage the stress of moving day:** Determine what will make your loved ones most comfortable. Don't assume it's better for them to know less about it or not be involved—for most people, some sense of control and participation will be important for "buy-in." But other people will just want you to take care of everything for them.

  - If it's important for them to absorb the move, and if they are up to it, they can observe the process and even help with unpacking and arranging their new home.

- ○ If they aren't up to the hectic pace of moving day, arrange for them to be elsewhere: at an activity that is part of their normal routine, or at a relative's or friend's home, out to lunch or shopping, getting a haircut or manicure, or other treat. Then they will come home to a new place all set up for them.

- **Make it home:** Keep in mind from the start that wherever your loved ones live is their home. They may not be in their private home in the community, but it is their home, whether it's half of a small room or a tiny apartment. You can help them immediately settle in and feel a sense of security and ownership with their own furniture, keepsakes, clothing, toiletries, food, and other necessities in place. Even if they have a small room, their favorite chair and some family photos can make it feel homier. When my parents moved to an independent living apartment, I helped them decorate their patio and all the rooms just like their previous home, only smaller. I noticed that other residents enjoyed seeing my parents' patio fixed up with flowers and seasonal decorations; most didn't have family members helping them do these things, and they missed that aspect of their lives. I could tell Mom and Dad felt more at home than many of their neighbors.

- **Resume the routine:** As soon as possible, help your loved ones get back into their routine to give them a sense of security and help them weather the change. While there may be some new elements to their day—such as organized activities—try at first to pick up their old routine, including waking, eating, and going to bed at normal times; watching favorite TV shows; exercising; and phoning family and friends.

Your Role

When the people you care for live in any type of facility, your role will be different than when they were in their home. You'll be communicating with the facility's staff and coordinating care. You'll need to advocate for your loved ones so they get the best care and quality of life possible.

You'll also want to build relationships with other residents and help your loved ones make new friends.

Be Specific About Care

It's good to have clear ideas of what is and isn't OK with you in terms of care. For example, if your loved ones become combative, are physical or chemical restraints acceptable? How do you want staff to handle any emergencies—for example, do you want them to call you before they call the emergency squad or after? Is there a way to get your wishes on record in the facility? Each facility may have specific policies that you may or may not agree with, so get familiar with them and make sure the facility knows your loved ones' wishes as well as yours.

Visit Regularly

Your loved ones are living in a place where other people live and work. People are in and out every day. Staffing may change without your knowledge. Your loved ones' conditions may change, and you'll need to be sure things are adjusted as needed. You cannot rely entirely on staff to notice everything. The frequency of your visits will depend on how independent your loved ones are. The higher level of care your loved ones are receiving, the more you'll need to track the details of their care in person. I believe the goal is a face-to-face visit every day—yes, *every* day if at all possible, no matter how short the visit is; if not daily, then as frequently as possible, and absolutely not less than once a week. It's amazing how much your loved ones' care and condition can change in just one day.

If you can't go, you'll need to arrange for someone else to visit. Many caregivers—especially working caregivers—have a very difficult time getting there in person, so they ask another family member or friend to go, or hire someone to drop in daily. A geriatric care manager, professional caregiver, or perhaps a concierge you carefully train can play this role. Visit unannounced and at different times of the day, such as before and after work or at lunchtime. With these regular visits, you can monitor physical and mental health status, cleanliness, laundry, and food, and catch small problems before they become huge downhill spirals—and believe me, that can happen quicker than you think. As you, or your designee, observe your loved ones' care, don't hesitate to ask staff about details.

Anne Samaan was a loving caregiver for her husband, Dick, who had early onset Alzheimer's disease. When he lived in a nursing home, she visited him every day or arranged for others to do so, making sure everything from the lighting and noise level in his room to his personal care were right. Some staff adored her zest for life and support of their good work. Others avoided her; she always had questions when most other families passively accepted mediocre and even poor treatment. But she didn't care; her job was not to be best friends with the staff; it was to care for her beloved Dick. So she routinely reviewed his chart and progress notes and participated in treatment plan meetings before that was common. She kept a notebook in his room for visitors to record notes about their interactions as well as observations of his care. Anne was like a second mom to me growing up, and she, more than any other personal or professional influence in my life, taught me to be a fierce advocate for those who are vulnerable. I saw firsthand the difference in Dick's care compared to others—he was left alone less, helped with eating more, kept cleaner and safer, involved in a variety of activities, and nurtured far more.

Build Relationships

When loved ones live in a facility, building relationships with the staff is a crucial step to ensuring quality care. You'll want to become a known presence there. If staff knows you are on top of your loved ones' care, they will invariably get better care. Here's a tip: Identify the people at the facility who *really* get things done. Depending on what you need help with, sometimes the facility administrator isn't the go-to person—it may be the social worker, head nurse, receptionist, aide, or certified nursing assistant.

Pump Up the Care

Even when your loved ones live in a facility, they may need more one-on-one care than they are getting. Lining up more support for the people you care for may mean advocating for better care in their current setting, if the care is simply not up to par. Or it may mean moving them to a higher level of care or hiring additional care in their current setting. It's sometimes less expensive to hire additional caregivers than to go to a higher level of care, and even a higher level of care might not provide the kind of care you'd expect or they need. Do the math—it's all costly—and weigh the alternatives for the best care options as needs change. Find out the facility's policies on hiring additional help from individuals or agencies. Most facilities will allow you to hire more care, but some may have restrictions. Facilities will not be responsible for care from practitioners you hire separately. You'll need to monitor their work, just as you would in a private home setting. It won't be the facility's responsibility to do so. See Chapter 9 regarding how to find and hire paid home health aides, professional caregivers, nurses, other home care, and hospice and palliative care.

When There Are Problems with the Facility

While a facility may be top-notch and provide generally good care, there may be times when you have concerns. It's not unusual for caregivers to disagree with care decisions, quality of care, and facility policies. Here are ways to handle the situation if that happens:

- **Participate in care plan and family council meetings:** Take advantage of any options the facility provides for family involvement. You'll stay more on top of things, and when you do have issues, staff will know you and you'll better understand procedures as well as who can best fix the problem.
- **Document problems:** Keep track of concerns in writing. Record dates, times, people involved, and specifics of what happened, including consequences as a result of the problem. If your loved one had a fall, for example, make note of when and how you found out, how the fall occurred, who was present at the time, what was done, medical diagnoses, office visits, tests and results, associated expenses, prognosis, outcomes, and actual changes in your loved one's life as a result.

- **Keep lines of communication open:** Discuss your complaint with the facility administrator, social worker, director of nursing, resident coordinator, or other staff in charge of the area for which you have concern.

- **Register a complaint with the ombudsman:** Every state has a long-term care ombudsman whose job is to advocate for people in assisted living, nursing facilities, or group or board-and-care homes. Ombudsmen provide information about long-term care; educate people about residents' rights; accept and investigate complaints and work to resolve them among the facility staff, residents, and families; and, if applicable, report complaints to the agency that monitors and qualifies facilities. Look for a notice posted in the facility with the ombudsman's contact information, contact the local area agency on aging, or visit www.ltcombudsman.org to find the local ombudsman's office.

Your Job Description: Housing Coordinator

You've done it again! You've learned to handle yet another facet of caregiving and earned this very important component of your job description.

Assists loved ones in accessing and maintaining appropriate housing. Assesses needs and available options; facilitates decision-making. Assists with downsizing and moving as necessary. Monitors success of facility-based living from practical and subjective health and lifestyle perspectives. Develops relationships with facilities staff, serves as an advocate, and coordinates problem-solving.

CHAPTER 11
CRISIS MANAGEMENT 101

Every time I think I've got all the ducks in a row, another crisis presents itself—health crisis, scheduling crisis, financial crisis, housing crisis, work crisis. When I first started this intense phase of caregiving in 2009, I kept trying to establish a sense of routine, only to be foiled. I'd set my schedule for the day and then a caregiver wouldn't show up; Mom would have a fall and off to the hospital we'd go. I'd make plans to watch a movie with Mom and Dad, and then I'd get a last-minute work assignment to blog about a breaking story. I'd plan to spend time with my boyfriend, and end up spending hours paying bills or working on an insurance claim.

I handle a crisis well—I kick into problem-solving mode and focus on the tasks at hand. But the effort can leave me drained, constantly feeling like I've failed because I didn't prevent the crisis. I finally realized it was futile to long for a sense of stability on a daily basis.

Now, instead of feeling disappointed and frustrated every time my semblance of order crumbles and my planned respites are thwarted, I've changed my mind-set: My goal is simply to ride the waves and roll with the punches. I may get knocked down by a crisis, but I have become more resilient; I view that as success. I actually expect a crisis and actively prepare for it. Crises are my accepted norm, so now if we go a week without a crisis, it's like icing on the cake.

Introduction

In a crisis situation, your caregiving schedule may be less predictable than when you are handling day-to-day issues. Your responsibilities may escalate, so you may need to make some adjustments to other areas of your life. If you are also working at a paid job, your workload or deadlines may need to change temporarily. If so, keep your employer informed.

You have many roles as a caregiver, but in a crisis situation, your role as advocate rises to the top. Up to now you may have kept a lower profile, but in a crisis you may need to step in and take a stronger role in looking out for those you care for. Be sensitive to their needs and desires, and ensure that they get the best possible care and help with making decisions. You may need help, too, to understand the choices and steps needed to manage the crisis, so don't hesitate to ask for support from family, friends, and appropriate professionals.

The best thing you can do is to prepare backup plans for your own life as well as for your loved ones' needs. It's hard to know how long a crisis situation will last, so take it one day at a time and focus on the things you can have influence over versus the things that are out of your control. Your focus may be the people you care for, but remember to take care of yourself, too—stress heightens in a time of crisis, and while you may not be aware of it at the time, often your mind and body will show the effects once things calm down.

In this chapter, you'll learn about:
- Preparing for a variety of caregiving crisis situations.
- Implementing your crisis plan.
- Dealing with and transitioning after a hospitalization.

Crisis Preparation

Plan ahead for the unexpected. You'll be under a great deal of stress at the time and grateful to have something to fall back on. These are some things to consider.

Contacting Your Team

Create a list of people to inform in a crisis. Your list may be different depending on the type of crisis. Determine the fastest, easiest way to contact everyone, such as phone or a phone tree, email, text, Facebook, Twitter, or other social media or apps. Decide who is responsible for passing on the word and under what circumstances the contact plan will be activated.

Medical Crisis

A health crisis is probably the most common caregiving crisis. If the people you care for are lucky, you'll be able to deal with the crisis from home, with mobile health-care practitioners and tests (see Chapter 8). For more serious health crises, you may be managing a hospitalization, which I go into later in this chapter. Either way, be prepared:

- **Keep a list of emergency contacts:** Post your emergency contact list in your loved ones' home and keep a copy in their wallets. If your loved ones live in a facility, post the list in their room and provide a copy for their file or chart. Give a copy to family and professional caregivers.
- **Get paperwork lined up:** Set up a system for quick access to key documents (medical history, medication list, insurance cards, and legal documents, such as advance directives and a DNR), electronically or with a system like the appointments/hospital folder I mentioned in Chapter 4. Be aware of specific instructions, such as those in the advance directives.
- **Stay current on health matters:** You can't see into the future and know what health crises will develop, but you'll have little time to do research in the middle of a crisis, so familiarize yourself with your loved ones' health conditions, illnesses, and prognoses so you have an idea of crises that could occur. Discuss with your loved ones and ask doctors for recommendations on how these crises should be handled.
- **Know health-care preferences:** Decide which hospitals or other health-care facilities your loved ones will go to and which health practitioners will treat them (if you have a choice.) If your loved ones

have an existing condition, find out where the physician treating them has hospital privileges.

Financial Crisis

Finances can get out of control when, for instance, expenses suddenly increase due to a health crisis, income decreases, or investments shift. What if the money to pay bills just wasn't there? Do your loved ones have a backup plan? Create a budget and form a good idea of what resources would be available if needed. Consider the following:

- Drawing on savings accounts.
- Tapping into investments.
- Withdrawing or borrowing from retirement accounts or banks.
- Using credit card advances.
- Taking advantage of a home equity line of credit or a reverse mortgage.
- Using credit to pay bills.
- Getting financial assistance from family or friends.
- Asking for help from financial managers, debt counselors, or debt attorneys.

Housing Crisis

Emergencies happen at home too, and our loved ones may be more vulnerable and unprepared. Think about how you would handle the following crises and what systems you need in place to deal with them.

- **Loss of electricity:** Is there a backup generator? Flashlights? Automatic backup lighting? (I found great flashlights that plug into an outlet and come on automatically when electricity is lost, which worked perfectly when we lost power recently. But I also found that I needed some large, battery-operated lanterns because Daddy was very anxious about being in the dark.) If there's no electricity, what happens to oxygen or other medical equipment? If the heat or air conditioning went out, where would your loved ones go?
- **Natural disasters such as hurricanes and floods:** Do you or the facility where your loved ones live have evacuation plans? Is there a

safe place in their home they can get to easily if there is a tornado? Keep in mind your loved ones' disabilities or mobility issues that may make a sudden evacuation or maneuvering to safe haven difficult. How would those situations be handled? How will you be in contact in the aftermath if phone and email aren't working?

- **Fire:** If there was a fire, could the people you care for get out of the home by themselves, or would they need help? How would you help them? Is there an easily accessible wheelchair? Do they know where to go? Have you ever had a fire drill at home or in the facility where they live?

- **Loss of home:** If your loved ones' home was ruined, where would they go? Is there a family member who would take them temporarily or permanently? If they live in a facility, would the facility be responsible for finding them a new home, or would you as their caregiver have that task?

If your loved ones have pets, be sure to include them in disaster plans. The Humane Society has tips at www.humanesociety.org/issues/animal _rescue/tips/pets-disaster.html.

Care Provider Crisis

If your loved ones are cared for by family members, volunteers, or paid professionals, you'll need a backup plan for when their schedules fall through. In addition, if an emergency occurs for a loved one you are caring for, you may need to quickly find backup care for another person you also care for. This happened to me many times when Mom had to go to the emergency room and Dad couldn't be alone for long. Whether due to emergencies, illness, transportation problems, unreliability, or your own work crises or other complications, your loved ones' care plans may fall through at all hours. Have a backup plan.

- **When your care providers cancel:** Give care providers a list of emergency contact people. If providers can't work their shift, any time day or night, they are responsible for calling down the list until they reach someone. If you are working with an agency, ask about their procedures when workers can't report for their shift. Request as much advance notice as possible.

- **Backup care providers:** Make a list of care providers who might be able to serve as backup in case of an emergency. (Your employer may offer backup care as a benefit; see Chapter 5.) If an agency is providing care workers and one of its workers can't report to work, the agency should be responsible for getting a substitute. But you may have to fill in until they get a replacement. Keep in mind the specific tasks the missing care provider usually performs, and make sure substitutes are qualified to do the same. It's a good idea to have backup providers who are familiar with your loved ones' needs and routines—otherwise you'll need to spend time training them.

- **Dealing with frequent problems:** If your provider or agency frequently cancels at the last minute, ask if there is a problem you should know about. If there is no good explanation, don't hesitate to change providers or agencies. If they aren't doing their job or are making it too hard for you to manage, there are other fish in the sea. Training new workers can feel daunting, but it's better than constant cancellations or unsatisfactory work.

Getting Backup for Your Life, Home, and Family

A caregiving crisis can demand your full attention, and everyday tasks may fall to the wayside. But neglecting these areas of your life can complicate life even more. Look at your team list (see Chapter 3); this is when your "one-time contributors" or "backup players" can step in. Create a simple checklist of top-priority tasks that need to continue with or without you and have a good idea of who might do these things, including:

- caring for children
- retrieving and sorting the mail
- picking up the newspaper
- paying bills
- taking care of plants and the yard
- cleaning
- caring for pets

Your Work

If you're also working at a paid job, a caregiving crisis for your loved ones may affect your ability to go to work or accomplish work goals, so you'll need a backup plan at work.

- **Communication:** Before a crisis strikes, talk with your employer (whether human resources or personnel manager, supervisor, or owner) about how you should handle it. If a caregiving crisis meant you had to leave work suddenly or miss a deadline, what would your employer like you to do? Most employers will appreciate your commitment to maintaining your work responsibilities in the event of a crisis, and taking steps ahead of time may mitigate negative consequences of missing work.
- **Flexible work options:** Ask about emergency leave, telecommuting, or other flexible work options discussed in Chapter 5. Get clear about how much notice your employer needs before you could take advantage of these options—in a crisis, that's crucial.
- **Redistribution of your work:** You may work in an environment where co-workers could pick up your slack if you need to be away from work for a while. Ask your employer if that would be acceptable, and then line up co-workers who would be willing to help you out in a crunch. Offer to do the same for them.
- **Variable plans:** Your plan should include options for various levels of crises, depending on the type of crisis, the length of time you'll need to deal with it, and potential loss of work time.
- **Adjusting the plan:** Over time, your work duties, employer (or your direct supervisor), work location, or schedule may change. Be sure to adjust your crisis backup plan accordingly as changes occur—don't wait for a crisis to realize your plan is no longer valid.

Maureen Statland was in crisis mode the final six months of her dad's life. The ups and downs were filled with hospitalizations, and that prolonged stress took its toll. "I had to focus on Dad, despite working, and learned a lot about advocating for him, dealing with hospital staff, and striving for his comfort," says Maureen. "It's tough to make health care decisions under the pressure of a crisis situation. My sister's support made all the difference, but many months later I'm still recovering from the intensity."

Implementing Your Crisis Management Plan

You've done your preparation, but when a crisis occurs, you may be overwhelmed with the emotions, fatigue, and stress of the situation. That's why it helps to have a simple plan in mind. Here are seven basic steps to follow.

1. **Assess the situation:** This may be a split-second assessment if your loved one has been injured or suddenly taken ill and you need to call 911. Or you may have more time to decide on a course of action. A crisis can be overwhelming. Stay calm. Take a deep breath and focus on the most immediate and important aspects of the situation.

2. **Consider your role:** You may be suddenly thrust into a stronger advocate role for your loved ones. This is when they need you the most. Sometimes it could be temporary until they get through the crisis; other crises will signal a major ongoing shift in the level of responsibility. Either way, just focus on now.

3. **Alert your caregiving team:** Use your phone tree, email list, social media channels, or whatever works for you to let them know about the crisis. Assign any new team roles and responsibilities, adjusted for the crisis situation as needed.

4. **Access key documents and resources:** Gather or make sure you have access to pertinent information. If your loved ones have a health crisis and are in the emergency room or admitted to the hospital, grab your hospital survival kit (see the appendix).

5. **Get help:** Every caregiver needs help managing a crisis. Remember that you are not expected to be an expert at every aspect of caregiving or your loved ones' life and needs. If appropriate, enlist the help of professionals, family members, and friends in everything from researching options to making decisions.

6. **Deal with work:** If a caregiving crisis is going to affect your work:
   ◦ Tell your employer you're dealing with a crisis.
   ◦ Implement the backup plan you've made if you'll need to miss work hours or deadlines.
   ◦ Get clear direction from your employer about the top priorities that need to be accomplished and focus on them.
   ◦ Stay in contact with your employer to show you're doing your best to get back to work or accomplish your work in other ways during this crisis time.
7. **Arrange backup help for home and other loved ones:** If you're like me, you have more than one person to care for, so you'll need to arrange for their care as well. If you'll need to be away from home, kick in your plan to make sure all the basics keep rolling while you are tied up with the crisis.

Susan Sligo Karageorge was shocked at the small amount of attention her mother received in the hospital the night after pacemaker surgery. "I was in her room with her, and I tracked the times she was supposed to have medications and treatments," Susan says. "They were always late, and I often had to ask the nurse about them. We were in her room for hours at a time with no one checking on Mom. She could have been lying on the floor and no one would have known!" Susan says it made her realize how important it was for her to be there looking out for her mom for most of her hospital stay.

Managing a Hospitalization

You've prepared all you can ahead of time, but when your loved ones are in the hospital, there is a lot to deal with. Be sure to check out my Hospital Survival Kit in the appendix. And here are some tips for managing the complications that are a part of any hospitalization. Note that you may not have access to all the medical information if you don't have a health-care power of attorney for your loved ones.

- **Emergency room:** According to the Centers for Disease Control and Prevention, there are about 130 million emergency room visits per year. If the people you care for need to make a trip to the emergency room, keep these things in mind:
  - Do everything you can to avoid sending them by themselves. If they need to be there, they likely aren't able to manage their own care. This is especially critical for patients with dementia. If your loved ones live in a facility, be aware that they will likely be sent off the hospital alone—very rarely do staff from facilities accompany residents to the hospital. If you cannot be immediately available, have a plan for someone to get there quickly (a geriatric care manager or paid caregiver who is familiar with your loved ones may be necessary if you don't have family or friends who can step in).
  - Bring their ID and other pertinent documents (which you've already planned for by creating a folder with copies or have available through technology).
  - Don't bring their money, jewelry, or other valuables. Bring a credit card only if you'll need it to pay.
  - If they have dementia or hearing or vision loss, inform emergency room staff right away.
  - Settle in. I've lost track of how many ER visits I've made with Mom and Dad, but I can tell you that no matter what time of day we've gone, we're there on average six hours. It's a long process that doesn't speed up (and believe me, I've tried) unless the people you care for are viewed as being in life-threatening situations.
  - Be a nudge. Tell ER staff if your loved ones' condition worsens, or if you'd like an update on status. Remind ER staff that you're waiting for test results.
- **Who's in charge:** If your loved one is admitted to the hospital, get the name of the attending physician—the doctor who will coordinate the care—along with the best contact information. Always find out the nurse in charge of the floor, as well as the nurse and aides who will be caring for your loved ones on every shift. Most hospitals have

whiteboards for staff members to write their names, but they are very busy and don't always get that done.

- **Check the chart:** Make sure your loved ones' chart includes your name and phone number, advance directives, special information about how to interact with them, and any important instructions. Your access to the chart will depend on your health-care power of attorney status. When Dad was admitted to the hospital very ill and in a state of confusion, I told the nurse, and had her note in his chart, not to use any chemical restraints because in the past they had made him more anxious and active, rather than calmed him. I had her leave specific instructions in the chart to call me if there were any problems. But in the middle of the night I got a call that they were having trouble calming him down. I went to the hospital, but before I could get there they gave him a sedative—and as I had informed them, it made matters worse. Apparently, the prescribing doctor gave the orders over the phone and hadn't even seen Dad or his chart. I was furious, but since then, I know to speak directly with the attending physicians and ask them to write specific orders in the chart prohibiting chemical restraints or any other medications without my consent. A physician's orders are the best assurance that such requests are followed.

- **Ask questions and share information:** Don't hesitate to ask questions of physicians, nurses, therapists, or other health-care practitioners about your loved one's condition, lab and other test results, prognoses, and treatment options. Let staff know if you see a change in your loved ones' status or if you have important background information. You are there to advocate, and often a suggestion or comment from a caregiver can make all the difference in their loved ones' treatment.

- **Watch for mistakes:** You've read the news reports: Mistakes happen—even in hospitals. People are given wrong medications or doses; charts get switched; the wrong body parts get operated on; important treatments are skipped; orders don't make it to the charts; therapy sessions are missed . . . the list goes on. Part of your role is to observe and keep track of your loved ones' care. I frequently ask to see my parents' medication lists because I've found items accidentally deleted, and one time a medication was listed twice and the nurse was giving Mom a double dose!

- **Take notes:** Document everything: conversations with doctors, nurses, and therapists; medication changes; treatments; tests and results; changes in your loved ones' condition. In the hospital, staff constantly changes. Even the attending physician can change or have a day off, and a substitute will not have as much knowledge; they will ask you about the details, and the electronic records won't likely include as much as you have noted. Time and again I have updated doctors and pointed out changes and trends—it's a crucial part of your role. You may also need to go back to your notes later, after your loved ones are discharged and they are seeing new doctors who may not get a detailed hospital history. Sure, they may get a record of the medications your loved ones were discharged with, but they probably won't know about a reaction to the medication your loved ones received. That history is invaluable, and you are the keeper of it.

- **Watch for shift changes:** When the shifts change for nurses, doctors, and aides, new people are on the floor and caring for your loved ones. Just when you've got a system going with nurses and aides, they leave and new staff come in—and you have to start over. It's a reality of hospitals, so beware of shift changes and assist in orientation as needed. Shift change is also not a good time to have a room full of visitors, as new staff will have to evaluate your loved ones.

- **Make wishes known:** If the people you care for are ill but capable of making decisions, they have the right to decide about their treatments (and refuse treatment), even if you and their physicians don't agree. If your loved ones are incapable of making decisions and you are designated as health-care agent via a health-care power of attorney, be familiar with their living will or other advance directives so you are sure to act according to their wishes.

- **Insist on a cot or a room with a built-in couch or bed:** If you end up spending the night with your loved ones, you may not sleep much, but you'll sleep better if you have a bed of some sort. Who can sleep in the horrible chairs in the hospital room? I usually have to ask for a rollaway bed, as they are rarely offered, but they have *always* materialized when I ask (although I've recently heard about hospitals that don't have them). More hospitals are building rooms now with built-in sleep couches, too. The nurses like caregivers to stay overnight and help care for loved ones because it eases the staff's load. Even if you don't spend the night, the days are long, and it might be helpful to be able to rest.

- **Get more help:** You might have the idea that when your loved ones are in the hospital they have constant care, that someone is always watching over them and responding to their needs. While the intensive care unit has more one-to-one care, it's not usually the reality on other units. Depending on your loved ones' needs and ability to ask for assistance, you may even need to get private duty nurses or other paid care providers—especially when you need a break or a good night's sleep. I never left Mom alone in the hospital. If I had to leave, I always made sure I had a friend or a paid caregiver with her because she was unable to communicate or advocate for herself.
- **Spread the word:** Keep family, friends, and professional caregivers informed about your loved one's condition and progress. Use your plan to keep your caregiving team involved and supporting your loved ones.
- **Show appreciation:** When hospital staff are helpful, be sure to thank them. They are likely working hard, and a little bit of positive feedback can go a long way.

Back to Normal—or a New Normal

After a hospitalization, your loved ones will likely be facing one of these transitions:

- Going back home, maybe needing more help than before.
- Temporarily going to a short-term rehabilitation program or family member's home for more recovery time.
- Moving to a new home or facility better equipped to meet their needs.

Discharge Planning

When your loved ones are in the hospital, ask to speak to the hospital discharge planner (who may be a social worker or nurse), who can help you and your loved ones create a plan together to make decisions about the next best steps. The discharge planner should have an idea of what kind of care your loved ones will need and provide the names of facilities, costs, and other pertinent information to help you make decisions. They should also facilitate your loved ones' transfer to a new location and help you find additional home- and community-based supportive services. Make sure the discharge planner arranges for outpatient or home-based therapies, home health, and home-care physicians if your loved ones aren't going to a rehab facility.

Instructions and Training

Hospitals are discharging patients quicker, and patients may be discharged while still needing significant medical care and support. AARP's 2012 *Home Alone: Family Caregivers Providing Complex Chronic Care* study reported that almost half of family caregivers are providing medical care, such as caring for wounds, using medical equipment, and monitoring and managing medications. Many caregivers say they were given very little training for these tasks. Be sure to get clear, specific directions and training regarding medications, home health equipment, diet, exercise, and follow-up appointments. When Dad was discharged from the hospital with a feeding tube, I was given less than five minutes of training on how to clean the tube, operate the equipment, and change the bags. The hospital arranged for a home health nurse to come just once a week to my parents' home to monitor his health and the feeding tube. Whenever we had problems with the feeding tube, I called to request a special visit, but we still ended up in the ER three times with a clogged tube.

Rehabilitation

If your loved ones go to a short-term rehabilitation facility, be sure to choose one that fits their needs. Some are hospital-based, some are independent, and still others are co-located with skilled nursing facilities. The pace of the rehab program is important: Some are geared toward more aggressive therapy schedules that challenge healthier people to a more intense recovery program; others are slower-paced with more resting time between therapy sessions. You'll want your loved ones to be challenged enough to progress and get stronger and more independent, but you do want the program to be a good match for their needs and abilities.

For more information about how to support your loved ones when they are living at home and need help, see Chapter 9. For more information about facilities where your loved ones may live, see Chapter 10.

Your Job Description: Crisis Manager

Whew—you've gotten through crisis preparation and probably several crises by now. You're a full-fledged crisis manager! Here is the latest component to your job description:

Prepares and plans for emergencies and other crisis situations related to caregiving responsibilities; adjusts plans as needed as crises occur. Identifies crisis situations and implements plans. Proactively stays informed of health, financial, housing, and other key issues to enable nimble response when emergencies arise. Communicates plans and updates to key team members.

CHAPTER 12
HANDLING THE END OF LIFE

*O*ctober 2013, Mom suddenly became extremely ill when she was in the hospital with a urinary tract infection that entered her bloodstream (sepsis). As I described in Chapter 6, without my knowledge, the physicians put a breathing tube down her throat when she coded. Despite heroic efforts in the ICU, she was not responding to treatment, and my sisters and I made the decision to remove the tube and other support her heart and kidneys were receiving. I knew Mom's advance directives and wishes and adhered to them as quickly as I could.

We made our beloved Mom's passing as calm and beautiful as possible in a hospital. In her final two days I played beautiful music in her room in ICU, massaged her hands, sang to her, prayed for her. I slept in her room, as did my sister, Susie, when she arrived from California. Dad came for a visit and held her hand and sang "Let Me Call You Sweetheart" to her. My sister Linda flew in from Ohio and my boyfriend, Bill, flew in from Baltimore. Although she seemed to be mostly unconscious, we made phone calls to my sister, Karen, in Maryland, Mom's four grandchildren, her brother and her sister—and all spoke to her on the speaker phone. We felt that perhaps on some level she could hear them, and it also was so important for them to be able to say their goodbyes. We talked to her, told stories about her, and thanked her for being a wonderful wife, mother, and friend. My sisters and I sang silly songs of our childhood to her. We

209

gathered around her bed—family, friends, Jackson, Karen on the speaker phone, our very caring ICU nurses, and a hospital chaplain—as we said prayers, and let her move on, surrounded by love. When we knew she had let go, we felt we should sing, but not a sad song, as our belief was that she was in a joyful place, despite our sadness and grief. So we all sang "Joy to the World"! I'm sure Mom was laughing at us singing a Christmas song as she transitioned, but it felt right.

Introduction

The end of your loved ones' lives can be emotionally, mentally, and physically challenging for you as a caregiver. Your time, emotions, and energies are catapulted in all directions. It is an important time for you to reach out for help—from professionals, family, and friends. The end of life can be a drawn-out process, or it can be very sudden, with no warning or chance to talk about important issues. As early as possible, talk with the people you care for about their wishes for the last part of their lives. Knowing their wishes can be a great comfort at a difficult time. If you work, be sure you understand how your employer will want you to handle taking time off.

In this chapter you will learn about:
- Handling your emotions.
- Talking with the people you care for about the end of their lives.
- Ensuring their wishes are respected.
- Securing compassionate care for them.
- Dealing with final rituals.

Handling Your Own Emotions

The last phase of your loved ones' lives can bring on a tumult of confusing, intensified emotions. You may experience some of these feelings as you help the people you care for navigate their final days; I assure you that these are all normal responses, so be patient with yourself.

- **Guilt or regret:** You've probably, at times, felt so tired, depleted, discouraged, and overwhelmed that you've wanted relief; you may hope for an end to the stresses of caregiving. At the same time, you don't want your loved ones to be gone. Now, as they face the end of their lives, you may feel guilty about those feelings or you may wish you'd done things differently. You may regret not having done more to support them. Or perhaps your relationship hasn't been ideal, and you're panicked at the thought of it ending on bad terms.

- **Denial or anger:** You may find yourself avoiding the reality of the situation, fighting the inevitable, or grasping for control to keep your loved ones alive. You may even feel angry that this is happening and you can't control it, or that you've been abandoned.

- **Frustration and anxiety:** The end-of-life process can be long and drawn out, and you may feel impatient. You may struggle to have health-care practitioners provide the kind of care your loved ones want. You may have conflicts with other friends and family members about decisions and your loved ones' treatment. Fears about the future and the pressure of making difficult decisions can cause anxiety. You may feel anxious about your job as well—about getting the work done when you're out, or holding onto your job given your absence.

- **Sadness and depression:** You are in the process of experiencing a loss, and grief may overwhelm you even before your loved one dies. Someone you care for is slipping away. An important era in your life is coming to a close.

- **Shock:** You may be stunned by a sudden turn of events, but even when death is not unexpected, shock can set in when we realize it's really happening: the feeling of the finality of death, realizing your time here with your loved ones is ending. Some caregivers may even go into a physical state of shock and need medical support.

- **Relief:** You may have seen the people you care for suffer and feel that their death will be a welcome release for them. You may even feel relief that your own stressful situation as a working caregiver is coming to an end.

If you're experiencing these and other deep emotions, here are some actions to consider:

- **Accept your feelings:** It's natural to have many conflicting emotions at this time. Allow yourself to feel them all. Go with the flow of your feelings. While you will want to be a calm and reassuring presence for your loved ones, it's also fine to feel whatever you are feeling, including sadness, anger, relief or distraction.
- **Let your world become smaller:** It may be difficult to focus on work or other family responsibilities or personal areas of your life at this time. It's normal to narrow your focus to your loved ones, so implement your crisis planning (Chapter 11) and let yourself be fully present.
- **Take care of yourself:** Go back to the list of ways you can care for yourself, like eating healthy foods, getting even a few minutes of fresh air, or taking a hot shower. You may choose being with your loved ones over sleep, but prioritize getting at least some sleep; when you're tired, it's even harder to cope.
- **See yourself as a companion:** It is a privilege and honor to accompany loved ones through their final days. You are there to support them through their journey, but remember that while you can empathize and offer compassion, it is their journey; your life is going on. When Mom passed on, I had to fight back my internal panic to focus on making her transition as easy as possible, and just being with her. When my sister Karen died, I was numb and in shock, but focused on being there for her and supporting my two nieces.
- **Say the important things:** If you can, tell your loved ones what you'd like them to know—things that will bring them comfort or relief. Share thoughts and feelings: Thank you, I love you, it's OK to let go, forgive me, I forgive you, I'm happy to be here for you, everything will be alright, you've made a difference in my life, you will be remembered, I will live my life so you'd be proud. You can also ask if there is anything they want to tell you. Even if your loved ones are apparently unable to hear you, tell them whatever you need to say or write a letter to send with them; it will help you to express

your feelings. When my sister Karen was in her final hours, although she was in a coma, I made sure that all family members and close friends had time alone with her to express their thoughts and feelings in privacy. It helped all of us to be able to let go.

- **Talk with someone:** Get support from people trained in end-of-life issues and transitions. When Mom and Karen passed on, the hospital social workers, chaplains, and nurse supervisors were incredibly helpful, both with practical support around decision-making and arrangements and as comfort and sounding boards. Counselors or your faith community leaders can also be very helpful. If the people you care for are in hospice, hospice workers may be available to help you or provide grief counseling. If you belong to a support group, take your feelings there. Go to friends or family members who've been through this experience and ask for their support and guidance.

- **Find out what to expect:** It can be helpful to talk with doctors and other health-care professionals so you know how your loved ones' final days, hours, and moments will progress. Knowing what to expect can help you weather the changes. Nurses and hospice care workers can be very helpful in this regard. Mom's ICU nurses allowed us to ask many detailed questions so we would be prepared when she passed. After my sister passed, I realized I should have asked the nurse to prepare her daughters, both in their 20s, a bit more for exactly what would happen, as some of it is natural but can be shocking. Knowing just enough (although not too much) of the physical specifics can make a big difference in how we experience death emotionally.

- **Engage in end-of-life rituals:** Rituals exist for a reason—they help people through life transitions. You may find yourself doing traditional things you've not done in a long time, such as praying, singing, gathering with family, telling stories, and attending religious services. You may want to videotape your loved ones and take photos to record their thoughts. Do what you need to do; there are no right and wrong things to do at this time.

Laurette Bennhold-Samaan knew very well what was important to her beloved husband, Cornelius, at the end of his 17-year battle with cancer, because they'd often talked about their desires for this stage of their lives. She created for him as loving and peaceful an atmosphere as was possible in the hospital. A friend played the violin while family, colleagues and close friends sang his favorite songs and prayed. His hands and feet were massaged with lavender scented lotion. Their daughter brought her dog to visit. Knowing that she was complying with his wishes about medical treatments as well as the quality of the end of his life was a great comfort to Laurette; it was a loving gift she could give him. She also felt that he had given her the gift of knowing what he wanted. She didn't have to struggle to make decisions in the midst of that very difficult time.

Talking About the End of Life with Your Loved Ones

Many caregivers find themselves at the end of their loved ones' lives uncertain of what to do. In Chapter 6, I outlined advance preparation: how to specify the medical care they do and don't want; who they want to make decisions for them if they are unable; the details of how they'd like to be cared for; and funeral or burial plans. This can be a starting point for more in-depth conversations about your loved ones' wishes. Essentially, the more you have discussed what they want, the more comfortable and reassured you'll feel about caring for them at this crucial time. While my sister's paperwork wasn't terribly well organized, I had talked with her enough to feel completely certain I knew what she wanted. This lightened the burden of decision-making.

If you see your loved ones' lives coming to an end and haven't talked about their vision for their end-of-life care, you can still do so if they are able. If they are in the hospital or receiving palliative or hospice care, a counselor or spiritual leader may be available to facilitate the conversation. (You can find a local palliative or hospice agency through the National Hospice and Palliative Care Organization at www.nhpco.org.)

10 Questions to Ask Loved Ones About the End of Life

Ideally, you'll want to talk about end-of-life wishes far in advance, although sometimes a crisis occurs and you realize you've not discussed these matters. Either way, when you have these discussions, you might want to have family members or an objective witness present, and make written notes or an audio or video recording you'll be able to go back to, especially if the discussions happen at an emotional time. Use various print and online tools (see Chapter 4) to record and keep track of their wishes. Follow up with a lawyer to create the appropriate legal documents if they don't already exist (see Chapter 6).

Here are key questions you can ask about.

1. **What kind of medical treatment do you want?** Do you have advance directives? Where are they, and what do they cover? Would you like to change any of your advance directives? Do you have additional guidance? Are there specific things related to your current condition you know you'll want or not want?

2. **What other kind of care do you want?** Do you want certain foods? Alternative therapies (such as acupuncture or massage)? Any favorite clothes you want to wear? Do you want your hair or nails done? Makeup?

3. **Who do you want to take care of you?** Family members? Certain health-care workers? Hospice? Would you prefer men or women?

4. **If you have a choice, where do you want to be, and with whom?** At home, or in a hospital or medical facility? In a certain room at home? A favorite bed or chair? Indoors or outdoors? Is there someplace you want to visit? Are there certain people you want to be there, or who you don't want to be there? Is there anyone you want us to contact for you? Do you want a beloved pet with you? Is there a religious leader you'd like to be there?

5. **What atmosphere do you want?** Do you want people all around, talking to you, telling stories? A quiet, calming atmosphere? Music, and if so, what kind of music? TV on or off? Would you like us to massage your hands or shoulders, cuddle close or give you space?

Do you want certain belongings, favorite pictures, or flowers around you? Do you want prayers?

6. **Do you want a service to honor or celebrate your life?** Where would you like the service to take place? Do you want religious or secular services? Who would you like to officiate, speak, and attend? What would you like to be said or read, such as a poem or spiritual reading? What music would you like? Would you like flowers, and what kind? Is there certain food you'd like to have served or a caterer you'd like to use?

7. **How would you like to be remembered after you've passed on?** Would you like specific rituals on your birthday or anniversary of your passing? Is there a charity you'd like people to contribute to? Would you be pleased with a specific type of memorial, such as a tree planted in your name, an education scholarship, a bench in your favorite park, or another structure dedicated to you?

8. **What about your remains?** Do you plan to donate any organs or tissues to science? Have prepaid funeral services? Or how much money would you want to be spent on your funeral services? Burial or cremation? If buried, open or closed casket? Where do you want to be buried? Do you have a burial plot—and is it still where you want to be buried? Do you want your ashes kept in a specific container or columbarium, scattered in a place meaningful to you, or buried? Mom wished her body to be donated to science at a specific university, but after she passed they refused her body because of her health condition (sepsis). So the hospital social worker helped us find another organization that accepted her body. I felt good that we were able to follow through with Mom's wishes even though our original plan wasn't possible.

9. **How do you want your assets and belongings distributed after you die?** Do you have a living trust or will or other written instructions for how you want your belongings distributed? Do you have additional guidance? Who is designated as the executor of your estate?

10. **Is there anything else you want us to know?** Who would you like us to contact upon your death? Any other specifics about how you'd

like us to view your passing? Anything you want to discuss before you die? Anything you want to do or anyone you want to see before you die? Is there anything else we can do to bring you peace and comfort? Is there anything that you need closure on? Any loose ends you want to take care of?

Respecting and Enforcing Their Wishes

If you've been made your loved ones' agent via their power of attorney, or if you're designated executor of their estate, it may feel like an ominous responsibility. Making decisions for them when they can no longer do so themselves can be tough. You may not agree with their wishes, and family members may disagree. Family conflict, hurt feelings, and even feuds can arise from such disagreements. If you are entrusted with this responsibility, remember that you are carrying out *their* wishes, not yours. If you have strong disagreements with the way they want to be treated or how they want their estate to be distributed, and you don't feel confident you'll be able to carry through their wishes, you may want to ask them to designate someone else. If family conflicts come up around these issues, it's very helpful to keep going back to your loved ones' documents or other proof you have of what they wanted.

If you are not providing the direct care for your loved ones, you'll also want to ensure that those who are providing treatments and care are adhering to your loved ones' wishes. This is another opportunity to step up your advocacy skills.

Shoshana Tova's mother died after a long good-bye and with the support of hospice care. "The hospice nurses were angels: gentle, kind, intuitive and strong," says Shoshana. But her family struggled with an enormous wall of animosity that developed because Shoshana felt her sister didn't adhere to their mother's wishes for good pain management. "At a time when we needed each other the most, it drove us apart."

Compassionate End-of-Life Care

When your loved ones' health is deteriorating and the end of life is near, arranging for compassionate care to keep them comfortable and maximize their quality of life will be vitally important to you. As a caregiver, you may have concerns about your loved ones' increasing needs and your ability to meet them while keeping up with other aspects of your life and perhaps a paid job. You'll probably need increased help during this time. In Chapter 8, I described two options or approaches that you may find for your loved ones: palliative care and hospice care. Whether the people you care for are at home or in a hospital, nursing home, or other type of facility or treatment center, palliative care approaches and hospice care programs may be available.

10 Questions to Ask Health-Care Practitioners About End-of-Life Care

Ask health-care practitioners, including palliative care and hospice agencies, these questions to evaluate the options and discuss end-of-life care:

1. **What is your philosophy about end-of-life care?** How would you describe the way you'll approach my loved ones' care as their condition deteriorates? What kind of medical treatment do you think they should get? Can my loved ones get curative treatments while under your care? Can they continue to pursue life-prolonging programs, including chemotherapy, radiation, and surgery? Will you address my loved ones' physical, psychological, social and spiritual needs? How will you manage pain and symptoms? Will you follow my loved ones' wishes? How can I be sure?

2. **What are your credentials?** Are you, or is the program, certified and state licensed? How is the program monitored? How do I know you are providing good care?

3. **Do you work with an integrated team?** Who are members of that team? What health-care and alternative approaches are included? Do you work with physicians, nurses, home health workers, nursing assistants, respiratory therapists, social workers, pastoral counselors

and other faith-based professionals, physical and occupational and creative arts (such as music, art, dance, and theater) therapists? Who leads the team, and how do team members communicate for well-rounded and smoothly administered care?

4. **What care will my loved ones get regularly?** How often does a doctor, nurse practitioner, nurse, or aide see my loved ones? Will they see the same professional every time? Is care provided 24 hours a day, 7 days a week? Just once a day? Periodically throughout the day? Is someone on call at any time if we have problems or need help? Do I need to arrange for other care in addition to your services?

5. **Does your approach include volunteers?** What will they do for those I care for? How are they recruited, trained, and managed?

6. **How long will you care for my loved ones?** Will they be under your care until they die? Is there a circumstance under which you will no longer treat them or they would move into another program? If so, how do you help transition us to another program?

7. **How do you support and involve family and friends?** Do you consider family and friends members of the team? Do you involve us in decisions about care and treatment? Can we continue to help care for our loved ones? Do you offer supportive services for family and friends and specifically caregivers?

8. **Where do you provide care?** Will you care for my loved ones at home? In the hospital? In a nursing or assisted-living facility? In a hospice facility? Where is a hospice facility?

9. **How are your services paid for?** Does Medicare, Medicaid, or private insurance cover your services and medications? If not, what is the cost?

10. **How soon can you begin caring for my loved ones?** Is there an intake or referral process? Do you have to wait for insurance precertification?

Planning Final Rituals

When a loved one dies, your final act of caregiving may be to manage the final rituals: memorial service, funeral, burial, or cremation. You've hopefully talked ahead of time about your loved one's wishes and have a general idea of what to do. But you're certainly dealing with grief and loss, probably fatigue, and perhaps shock. You may need to make many decisions, even if the bigger decisions have been taken care of.

I've found it's a helpful part of the grieving process to temporarily throw myself into planning and holding my loved ones' final rituals. On the other hand, you may be unable to deal with these logistics while in the throes of grief. For the first few days after Mom passed on, it was too much for me to even discuss a memorial service. I had to allow myself time to adjust.

We eventually held a church service and, a few days later, a Celebration of Life service outdoors. Seven months later, I brought Mom's ashes to Indiana, where we had an extended family gathering and graveside service at the family cemetery, where her cremains were interred. ("Cremains" is the technical term for remains that are cremated.) We did what felt right and comforting to us, though holding three different events wasn't necessarily the traditional way to do things. But we felt Mom deserved an extended send-off.

When my sister Karen died, there were logistical issues in terms of family in town and work schedules. Her many friends needed to acknowledge her death and honor her. I knew the ritual, while difficult, would help all of us. We decided to hold a memorial service just a few days later at her local faith community fellowship. It was too soon and too emotional for her daughters to handle much of the planning, so my sisters and I did most of that. But her daughters will hold another celebration of her life for family and close friends at a later date to scatter her cremains at the ocean as she wished.

Remember, there is no one "right" way to do this. Go with what works best for all of the people closest to your loved ones who have passed on.

Dealing with Death: A Checklist
Use this checklist as your guide for the steps to take going forward.

People to Contact
The following people can help you navigate the tasks or should be notified after your loved ones pass on.

- Family, friends, and neighbors
- Funeral director
- Faith leader
- Attorney
- Executor or "personal representative" of the estate (if not you)
- Accountant
- Health-care providers
- Alumni, veteran, or professional groups or clubs.

Obituary
Writing your loved ones' death notice can be a loving gift and cathartic process. Most large funeral homes will help with posting obituaries in the newspaper, but if not, you can contact the newspaper where your loved ones live or lived as well as former employers, if appropriate. When Mom passed on, we honored her with obituaries in newspapers in both Arizona and Athens, Ohio, where we had lived for many years and where she still had friends. We did something similar for my sister. The university where Dad taught shares obituaries in its newsletter. You may also want to post notices on social media sites. A friend told me that when her brother-in-law died, relatives and friends posted messages on his Facebook page. Through just that, an online newspaper obituary, and word of mouth, more than 60 people showed up at his funeral to honor his life. Most funeral homes and newspapers will also create a permanent online guestbook where people can post tributes. Since we tragically lost my niece, Shaelee, who suffered from bipolar disorder, to suicide at age 19, we treasure the online comments of her friends and family celebrating her many wonderful qualities.

Arrangements for Your Loved Ones' Remains

- **Funeral home:** Call a funeral home, or ask the hospital or hospice social worker to do so. If your loved ones didn't choose one, ask the hospital, friends, your faith-community leaders, hospice, or other health-care practitioners for recommendations. The funeral director can point you to resources that will help you with a variety of issues associated with your loved ones' death.

- **Prepaid funeral plans:** Prepaid funeral plans may cover funeral home services, burial plot, coffin, and other aspects of a traditional funeral. Many plans do not include all expenses, so be sure you know what the remaining costs will be.

- **Remains:** Find out how those you cared for wanted their remains to be taken care of. If they have donated their body to a science, research, or teaching facility, find out where their remains should go. Find out if burial, entombment in a mausoleum, or cremation has been chosen. Find out the costs associated with each so you can plan accordingly. For example, if your loved ones donated their bodies to science, there is usually no charge for cremation.

- **Out-of-state:** If your loved ones' remains are to be transported to another state, you'll need to work with a local funeral home and one in the destination location. The funeral homes will coordinate transportation, unless the remains have been cremated. (You can transport cremains yourself along with any necessary paperwork the funeral home or organization that handles body donations provides.)

- **Death certificate:** Ask the funeral director for multiple certified original copies of the death certificate to manage the estate—for everything from life insurance policies to checking accounts to safe deposit boxes. You can also get certified copies from the appropriate government agency in the state where your loved ones die, such as the Department of Public Health. There is a fee for certified copies, and often photocopies aren't accepted, so try to determine how many certified copies you'll need from the start. If your loved ones' remains are donated to science, the organization may handle submitting information for the death certificate, but you will likely need to order certified copies directly from the designated government agency.

- **Cemetery:** If the remains or cremains will be buried or entombed at a cemetery, you will need to contact a local funeral home to make necessary arrangements. Although Mom died in Arizona, her cremains are buried in Indiana, and a local funeral home prepared the grave and provided us with a tent, tombstone engraving, and other services. You may also want to plan for upkeep of the plot or tomb. You can hire grave maintenance services if you or other family and friends live elsewhere or otherwise can't get to the site regularly.
- **Veterans' services:** If your loved ones were veterans, you may get some assistance with the funeral, burial plot, headstone, or other benefits. Ask the funeral home, or contact the U.S. Department of Veterans Affairs at 800-827-1000.

Services

- **Viewing, wake, shivah:** Some families hold visiting hours—opportunities for people to come and pay their respects, view the body, pray, and offer support to the family.
- **Gravesite:** If your loved ones' remains or cremains are to be buried, will you hold a graveside service after a service elsewhere?
- **Timing:** Some people wait to hold services until they have time to plan, or faraway family and friends can arrive. Some religions, however, dictate a time frame for when burial and services should take place. Every family has a unique set of circumstances to determine when to hold services.
- **Planning:** Unless your loved ones specified they did not want a funeral, memorial, or celebration of life service, you will probably be planning a gathering in memory of them. If they didn't stipulate who should put together the service, work with your family, friends, and caregiving team to decide who takes on which tasks. This is also a time when friends are often willing to step in and take on tasks, as family members are dealing with grief.
- **Music and readings:** Perhaps your loved ones had wishes for specific music, or reading of a favorite poem, story, or scripture.
- **Eulogy:** For some people, delivering the eulogy is more difficult than writing it; perhaps another family member or friend could read

what you've written or vice versa. You may want more than one person's reflections on your loved ones. For my sister Karen's service, we encouraged people to speak up and share their memories in any way they chose, which was especially meaningful. One friend sang a beautiful song for her.

- **Create a photographic memory:** Go through old photographs of your loved ones and pull out your favorites or create collages, slide shows, and videos. These can be shared at calling hours, wakes, funerals, memorial services, and on social media sites to bring back memories, help you feel connected to your loved ones, and provide great comfort.
- **Presence of military or other forms of service:** If your loved ones were veterans of the military, police, or fire department, ask the funeral director about obtaining a color guard, military fly-by, or other representation of their branch of service. When Granddaddy C.V., a veteran of World Wars I and II and a retired Air Force officer, passed on, the funeral director arranged for a 21-gun salute and a fly-by from the nearby Air Force base. It was the most important and meaningful part of his services, and I'll never forget it. I only wish video cameras had been more readily available back then.
- **Pallbearers:** Your loved ones may have designated who they'd like to carry their coffin, if that is a part of their service.
- **Unique commemorations:** In recent years, services often go beyond the traditional. My friends Laurette and Jenny brought a variety of their mother's jewelry to her service and encouraged attendees to take a piece to remember her by. After my sister Karen's service, we held a potluck! She loved potlucks, and we felt she would approve. For Mom's celebration of life, we polished her silver service and served coffee and tea with it. You may feel you can more suitably honor your loved ones by including something that is indicative of their personalities.

Financial and Legal Matters

- **Notify the Social Security Administration:** If your loved ones were collecting Social Security benefits, immediately notify the Social Security Administration to stop benefits. You may find the funeral home or body donation organization already notified SSA, but it's a good idea to make sure. Find out about benefits for a surviving spouse.

- **Notify the health insurance company:** Find out about continuing coverage for family members covered under the same policy.
- **Notify the long-term care insurance company:** If your loved ones were receiving payments, you'll need to notify the company to stop them; if your loved ones had long-term care insurance but had not been receiving payments, notify the company of the death and cease paying premiums.
- **Notify the life insurance company:** You'll need the policy number and an original death certificate, as well as beneficiary information. If the beneficiary is a living trust, you'll need certain documents from the trust, and you'll likely need a trust checking account to deposit the life insurance claim check. Some life insurance companies will also want a copy of the obituary.
- **Remove the deceased persons as beneficiary:** Check all insurance policies, pensions, and financial accounts that list your deceased loved ones as beneficiaries.
- **Notify employers:** If your loved ones were working, let their employers know and find out about any death benefits, pension plans, or employee credit union accounts.
- **Notify credit card companies and other debtors:** You'll need a death certificate. If your name is also on the account, find out about retaining use of it.
- **Notify frequent buyer groups:** They may allow transfer of points; for example, some airline frequent-flyer programs will allow you to roll over miles to a family member's account upon receipt of a death certificate.
- **Talk to a financial adviser about taxes:** Speak with an accountant about filing taxes for your loved ones after their death.
- **Look into bank accounts:** Find out what you need to do about bank accounts; if your loved ones had a living trust, were the accounts in the trust? If your name is also on the account, speak to the branch manager about having your loved ones' names removed. Some accounts will be frozen so they can't be used at all pending probate court or

other proceedings. This can pose a problem if those funds are needed to pay for funeral and other services.

- **Determine next steps for investments:** Ask their stockbroker or accountant what to do about stocks and bonds. Were they in a living trust? Is your name on the accounts?
- **Pay bills:** Make sure important bills continue to be paid, such as the mortgage or utilities. Talk with the accountant about how to manage bill paying.
- **Deal with the home:** If your loved ones lived in a private home and no one else is living there, forward mail and stop newspapers. Turn off utilities as appropriate. Determine how your loved ones' personal belongings will be distributed, according their wishes. Decide what to do about their house.

You'll find excellent guidance about managing the legal and financial issues when loved ones die in *A Checklist for Family Survivors: A Guide to Practical and Legal Matters When Someone You Love Dies* from the American Bar Association and AARP, by Sally Balch Hurme.

Your Job Description: End-of-Life Coordinator

This is perhaps the most difficult time in your caregiving journey, and you have learned to cope, follow your loved ones' wishes, and provide end-of-life care for them. Here is a new component to your job description:

> Discovers, understands, and adheres to loved ones' wishes for compassionate care at the end of life. Selects, monitors, and coordinates an interdisciplinary team of care providers. Evaluates ongoing quality of care. Makes frequent decisions as conditions and care plans change. Creates atmosphere of comfort. Maintains caregiving role while managing personal effects of grief and loss. Follows through with final care after death of loved ones, including planning and implementing funeral services and dealing with estate matters.

CHAPTER 13
LIFE AFTER CAREGIVING

*A*fter both of my paternal grandparents died, six weeks apart, I was busy helping Dad plan their memorial services and prepare their house for sale. But when these tasks were done, for the first time in quite a while I had a weekend all to myself. Instead of relishing the freedom, though, I stayed in bed and cried. The reality hit me hard: losing them both so close together, feeling defeated that I hadn't been able to keep them in their home in their final days, wishing I could have been with them when they died, and having nothing more to do for them. I couldn't believe the world kept revolving and the sun kept rising, as if nothing significant had happened. I didn't know how to resolve this deep sense of loss.

Returning to work helped. I was able to start back at a slower pace, thanks to a supportive supervisor at the Ohio Department of Aging, where I was employed at the time. Work gave me something to do every day, a reason to get up in the morning and back into a routine, a sense of accomplishment. It also helped that I could apply the new skills I'd attained as a caregiver to my job. And I soon realized that there were others in my life who needed support: I was able to spend more time with my other grandmother and my parents.

Twenty years later, when Mom passed on, I encountered a similar situation. I had to handle grieving her loss while still caring for Dad. But this time I was overwhelmed with grieving and very intensive caregiving at the same time. Recently my sister died, and the responsibilities have piled up. It has been very difficult for me to fully grieve, but Dad also *keeps me going. It seems there are always others to help. As I've heard other caregivers say: Once a caregiver, always a caregiver.*

Introduction

If you're like me, you may have adjusted every part of your life to care for your loved ones. Caregiving was your role, and it, along with all the job descriptions that came along with it (as reflected in this book), was a big part of your identity. Now, for whatever reason, your time as a caregiver has changed or come to a close. You may feel unsettled. You may feel a sense of loss, both for your loved ones and for the role you no longer play. Take time to grieve on both fronts, and know that grieving is a process—not something you do quickly and then finish and close the door. Find ways to channel your grief and redirect your caregiving wisdom and energies to your work, family roles, or other activities. Know that the process might, often unexpectedly, affect your work and other parts of your life for quite some time. Allow yourself to go through this time as *you* need to—there is no "right" way to grieve, no set timetable. Through it all, allow a sense of hope and peace to emerge and honor the incredible gift of love you've given. Life will keep unfolding, and you will engage more fully in its many aspects when you are ready.

In this chapter you'll learn about:
- Dealing with loss and going through the grieving process.
- Remembering and honoring your loved ones and the care you gave them.
- Moving forward with your life and work.

Dealing with Grief and Loss

Loss of a Loved One
You may be experiencing a deep and intense sense of loss if the people you've been caring for have died. Whether you've been caregiving

for a short or an extended time, their passing may have been somewhat expected—or it could have been a shock. Either way, it can feel devastating. You'll need time to grieve and get your own life back on track.

Loss of Your Role as a Caregiver

Perhaps your caregiving role changed because those you've been caring for passed on or have recovered from an injury or illness. Or perhaps they receive more help from others or have moved to a facility, and you are no longer as deeply engaged in their day-to-day or hands-on care. Maybe you had to step down from your role, perhaps because you had to move away for your own or your partner's job, or you've experienced a health problem of your own. Regardless of the reasons, and even if you feel a measure of relief, it is normal to feel a sense of loss when caregiving is no longer a leading role. Many caregivers tell me they just don't know what to do with themselves after a prolonged period of focusing their energies on caregiving. Your life—and possibly your identity—has changed drastically, and any type of loss can trigger the grieving process. You may feel a bit lost and need to thoughtfully redirect your energies.

The Grieving Process

Grieving is an individual task, and no two people grieve exactly the same way. Some withdraw, freeze, or find it hard to get through an hour, much less a day. Others jump into other responsibilities and demands on their lives, in a conscious or unconscious attempt to skip the grieving process. Many caregivers tell me they don't have time to grieve because they've put so much aside while caregiving, and they now need to catch up with their work and lives. Everyone grieves differently, but if you try to stifle grieving, it will likely come back around and catch you unaware at some point. Remember these two key points:

- Grieving is a process with many phases and stages. It can feel messy and chaotic because it doesn't take one clear, straight path. Expect ups and downs. All you have to do right now is breathe—take it one minute at a time.

- There is no prescribed period of time by which you should be done grieving. You can't rush it. Just allow it, and you will progress through it. You don't have to look into the future until you're ready.

Experts have many theories about grieving, and I find merits to them all. It might be helpful for you to read more about these and other theories to help you through the grieving process.

- Elisabeth Kübler-Ross identified five stages: denial, anger, bargaining, depression, and acceptance.
- Roberta Temes and Geoffrey Gorer outlined three phases: numbness, disorganization, and reorganization.
- J. William Worden outlines four tasks of grief: accept the reality of the loss, process the pain of grief, adjust to a world without the deceased, and find an enduring connection with the deceased in the midst of embarking on a new life.
- Sidney Zisook describes four stages: separation distress; traumatic distress; guilt, remorse, and regret; and social withdrawal.

The Emotions of Grieving

No matter how you look at grief, it is a journey we all travel at some point in our lives, and it can be incredibly painful and exhausting. Those who have been intimately involved in the care of loved ones often grieve differently from other friends and relatives. Caregivers who have witnessed a great deal of pain and suffering may feel relief in knowing their loved ones are no longer in distress. You can miss them terribly and at the same time be glad they are no longer in pain or discomfort. That is how I felt when Mom died. I was also comforted by the fact that I knew I did all I could for her before she died; I have no big regrets. That doesn't undermine my love for her or how much I miss her. Nor does it invalidate what I went through as a caregiver.

Grieving feels unpredictable; our feelings often astound us. Emotions can get stirred up at unexpected times, including at work, in relationships with our families and friends, and even in simple interactions.

I remember being at the grocery store soon after my niece Shaelee died in 2012 and growing incredibly impatient with the clerk who was taking his time ringing up my purchases. I was shocked at the level of my emotions, but I quickly realized the mundane task of buying groceries felt so meaningless compared to the loss our family had suffered, and I resented the clerk's laid-back attitude when I was feeling such pain. Of course, the emotions during grieving don't always make perfect sense, and the kid behind the counter didn't deserve my impatience. The extreme emotions leveled out over the months. Today the shock has subsided, and I feel acceptance more often than I used to, although the grieving process continues.

Our emotions tend to jump all over the place when we're grieving, so be prepared to go from relieved to angry, to lighthearted, to denial, to acceptance, to guilt, to disbelief, and back to angry again—maybe all in one day or even an hour. You may feel unfocused, un-needed, hollow, purposeless, and numb. Or you may feel liberated, calm, relieved, and at peace. Exhaustion could catch up with you, or you could feel tense and still on the alert because you've grown accustomed to that feeling—it can be hard to turn off. These feelings are all normal.

But if you feel overwhelming sadness and depression or have suicidal thoughts, DO NOT just wait for it to pass. Get help immediately. Call the National Suicide Prevention Lifeline at 800-273-TALK (8255) or the National Hopeline Network at 800-442-HOPE (4673).

Tips for Grief Support and Healing

Remember that this is a delicate and important time for you. You may be very vulnerable and emotionally fragile. You'll find your own unique grieving path and supports, but here are a few suggestions that may be helpful to you. (See the Resources section for information about how to find support.)

- **Take extra good care of yourself:** Get plenty of sleep, eat well, exercise, take a hot bath, or do whatever you do to comfort yourself. If you're having trouble sleeping, talk with your doctor. It's hard to cope when we are physically exhausted.

- **Try to maintain some of your usual routines:** Something as simple as feeding or walking a pet or watering plants can be comforting. If your routines mostly involve loved ones you've lost, try doing some of those things to honor them, but avoid activities that would be too painful right now.

- **Get help with responsibilities:** This is a time to reach out to family and friends for help. You may need extra assistance with everyday tasks until you get your bearings again.

- **Journal:** Write or make audio or video recordings of your feelings, thoughts, memories, and reactions to the process you are living through.

- **Talk with family and friends:** Most people get through grieving with the support of family and friends. You'll know who you can talk to about your feelings. Line up at least one or two people you can call at any time of the day or night. Talking about your loved ones can be very helpful, so let people know it is OK to bring up the subject—they will take their cues from you. Enjoy the memories.

- **Don't let others rush you:** As a survivor, you are grieving, and at first some people may be patient and kind. Over time, they may become impatient, feeling it's time for you to get back to "normal." Assure them that you are doing your best, but grieving takes time. If your family and friends are especially concerned that you might be experiencing complications of grieving, you might seek professional help.

- **Put off decision-making:** When you are grieving may not be the best time to make important life decisions. In fact, you may feel very indecisive. You may notice that at work, too.

- **Connect with your caregiving team:** This is a time to gather your caregiving team and support each other in the grieving process. Most people report that they take comfort in expressing their feelings to people who may be experiencing similar emotions.

- **Find support through work:** If you're working a paid job, contact your employer's human resources or personnel office to find out if there are employee benefits or services available to you through an Employee Assistance Program (EAP), support groups, or counseling benefits.

- **Contact your caregiving support group:** If you've been involved in a caregiving support group, reach out to your fellow caregivers. Many of them have experienced a similar loss or gone in and out of the caregiving role.
- **Join a grief support group:** Some grief support groups focus on grieving in general, but many focus on specific types of loss, such as losing a parent or spouse, losing a child, or losing someone to suicide. (See the Resources section for how to find in-person or online grief-support groups or organizations.)
- **Get grief counseling:** Some people experience what mental health professionals call "complicated grief": that is, if your grief is extreme, worsens over time, or leaves you unable to function for a prolonged period; if you experience other symptoms (such as illness) instead of processing grief; or if another life event triggers grief from an earlier, unrelated loss. If so, find a psychiatrist, psychologist, social worker, or counselor who is trained in this area.
- **Care for others:** When my niece Shaelee died, I still had to focus on my parents' care. I would have liked to have stopped everything to grieve, but I couldn't. Turns out it was a good thing: My parents gave me something to focus on. It was my reason to get out of bed every morning.
- **Work or volunteer:** After a loss, paid or volunteer work can be a positive way to re-engage with the world. It can give us a break from thinking about the loss, redirect our energies, and provide social interaction. A friend told me she was glad to go back to work because for those hours every day, she didn't think about the loss of her husband. When she was home alone, his absence was too overwhelming.
- **Start a new project:** Creating something new or organizing your home or work environment may be a great way to distract yourself and jump-start your ability to look to the future. Set a goal—something achievable with visible results—and work toward it. You'll feel good about your accomplishments, and something you can throw yourself into might help you feel a sense of purpose again.

Memories and Tributes

Every person finds his or her own unique method of tribute. Some people at first find visual reminders too painful; others want memories all around them. That may likely change over time. My friend whose husband died four years ago keeps a life-size photograph of him in her dining room. She says it makes her feel like he's still there at mealtime; she likes to acknowledge his importance in her daughter's life and hers. I keep a big photo of Mom in our family room, not far from where she used to sit, and it's a comfort and joy to see her smiling face there. We also created a memorial scholarship fund in Mom's name at a local children's theater she helped to found many years ago. On occasions such as her birthday and holidays, I make a donation to her fund. I've created a special place on our fireplace mantel honoring my niece Shaelee with a photograph, many angel statues, and an engraved candleholder with her name on it. My sister Susie, Shaelee's mom, and her husband, Dean, have created a lovely garden at their home in memory of Shaelee.

20 Ways to Remember Loved Ones
Here are 20 ideas I've gathered for memorializing our loved ones.

1. Dedicate a religious service or provide flowers in their names.
2. Donate to a favorite charity in their names.
3. Create a scholarship fund in their names.
4. Plant a tree in their names.
5. Volunteer for a cause that was dear to their heart.
6. Honor the anniversary of their death by taking time alone to reflect or pamper yourself, visiting their burial site or a favorite place, holding a gathering of family or friends, or lighting a candle.
7. Celebrate their birthdays, wedding anniversaries, or other important dates.
8. Create a scrapbook (you can even do this online), memory folder, or box with pictures, mementos, notes about your loved ones, and even letters you write your loved ones after they have passed on.
9. Make a photo collage of your loved ones to hang in your home.

10. Donate a holiday gift they would like in their name, or hang a Christmas stocking or other holiday decoration for them and leave them notes or a list of gifts you would have given them.

11. Have fun doing what they loved to do—attend a music event, visit a museum, go to a ball game, take a walk, nurture a garden.

12. Create a photo pin of your loved ones and wear it on special occasions such as their birthday, Mother's Day, or Father's Day.

13. Write the story of your loved ones' life.

14. Create a monument, such as a fountain or statue in your backyard, or go all the way with a monument in a public place.

15. Share memories and encourage others to post theirs on a social media site, such as Facebook, or memorial guest books provided by many newspapers.

16. Create a work of art in their memory—a painting, sculpture, wood carving, or craft project that communicates their unique personality.

17. Toast them with their favorite drink, make their favorite meal, or eat at their favorite restaurant.

18. Get a tattoo! Okay, this isn't for everyone, but I'm surprised at how many people get memorial tattoos. The boy who bagged my groceries recently had a tattoo in memory of his grandmother, who had died; a woman I met had a tattoo identical to her father's so she'd feel close to him after he passed on.

19. Talk about them. It's the best way to ensure they will be remembered. Tell younger generations stories so the memories will carry on for future generations.

20. Live. Honor their lives by living *your* life to the fullest. Learn from your loved ones' best qualities and be the best you can be. Most of us know that our loved ones would want us to go forward, remembering them but continuing to live.

Moving Forward

You've probably been so focused on those you've been caring for (perhaps for an extended period of time—months or years) that you've had little time for yourself. You may have felt a lack of freedom as you committed yourself to their all-consuming care. Your world got smaller. You probably saw less of family and friends, so your relationships may have suffered. You may have taken time off work and now need time to transition back. Many of us are not fully aware of how much we've put aside to care for loved ones; we often become numb as we automatically do the next thing, day after day, trying to keep up with the roller coaster of emotions and the complications of caregiving. You also may not be aware of how important your role as a caregiver was to you.

Reflecting on and Celebrating Your Caregiving Experience

You have just been through a life-changing experience. No one goes through caring for loved ones without it changing the core of their being. You have learned new skills; stretched and grown mentally, emotionally, and spiritually; and gained useful knowledge that can help others. Taking time to reflect on your caregiving experience can be a cathartic and uplifting exercise.

It may seem counterintuitive since you are grieving a loss, but give yourself permission to celebrate the amazing gifts you have given your loved ones by caring for them. You did what you knew to be right. You provided care for them in your own unique way. Celebrating your contributions can help you through the grieving process. You have something to feel good about, and that can be a great comfort.

You will always carry your caregiving experiences with you as you go forward in your life. Validate your contribution, dedication, commitment, and caring. Here are some ways to reflect upon and celebrate your caregiving contributions—now that you probably have more time to do so.

- **Do something great for yourself:** Acknowledge, honor, and commemorate the life transition you are currently going through. You could have a gathering of friends to mark this shift in your life. I met a woman who had cared for her mother for two years until her death. After the funeral, she went straight to a spa for two weeks of pampering, reflection, and recuperation. She said the time away gave her great peace and prepared her for the transition back to work.

- **Document your story:** Write about what you've learned and how you grew through your caregiving experience. Sometimes it's easier to see these things when we look back than when we are going through challenging times. You might also document your story visually, through photos.
- **Publish your experiences:** Publish online or in print your journal, notes, or blog so other caregivers can learn from you.
- **Listen, reinforce, and advise:** Through casual conversations, in-person support groups, or online groups and message boards, help others who are caregiving.
- **Talk about your experience:** Speak at support and community group meetings; provide input to employers who are striving to help their employees who are caregivers; or speak with reporters writing stories about caregiving.
- **Advocate:** Volunteer with advocacy groups, testify in a hearing, or attend other political events geared toward garnering more supports for caregivers.
- **Make a caregiving résumé:** List the skills you developed as a caregiver. Use the job descriptions at the end of each chapter of this book to help you hone in on how fabulous you really are. It will give you a sense of accomplishment, and it may help you with your work.

Your Changing Role

When the intense external focus of caregiving is no longer needed, you may feel a great sense of freedom to do whatever you want to do; or you may feel uncomfortable and self-centered, since you are unaccustomed to focusing on yourself. You may lack direction and feel at a loss as to what to do next. When you were caregiving, you probably put your health, interests, career goals, activities, and relationships on the back burner. Now you can put energies back into these vital parts of your life again.

Laurette Bennhold-Samaan took care of her mom, dad, and husband, who have now all passed on. "What is my role now?" she asks. "My role as a wife and daughter are gone; my role as a caregiver is completed. Decades of caregiving in one way or another are over, and I'm a different person because of that role. What will the future look like?"

Continuing to Care for Others

Many of us are grieving the loss of one loved one while simultaneously caring for another. While in some ways this may give you a much-needed sense of purpose, it can also be difficult to dig down deep and come up with the energy to care for others when you're mourning. If this is your situation, try to get some extra help for a time. You may not need extra help for long, but you do need time to adjust and grieve. For three months after Mom died, I had extra support to help take care of Dad.

Work

If you have a paid job, life circumstances may demand that you deal with work sooner, but go at your own pace as much as possible. I can't emphasize enough: There is no set time line for grieving or for life transitions. You'll need to replenish your personal emotional and physical reserves. Here are some things to consider as you transition back to work.

- Once you're back at work, it may feel difficult to focus. At first it's OK to just get through the day when grieving. You may feel like nothing really matters anymore, including your work. But eventually you will gain more satisfaction from your work. You might allow work to be a respite from sadness.
- If you've been gone awhile, you may need more education and training. Look into online courses, read, connect with work groups and professional organizations, and catch up on new developments in your field.
- Bring the skills you've developed as a caregiver into your work life. You're probably a wiser and more confident person. You've gained new competencies and proficiencies as a caregiver. (See the end of each chapter for more on the skills you've developed.)

Laura George cared for her husband, who was injured in an accident, for many years before he died. "I've had so many people tell me what I can and cannot do with respect to playing the grieving widow, to the point I started getting angry," she says. "I am young. I can, have the ability to, and will move on and be successful. People can either cheer me on or get out of my way. There will be days I just cry, but I realized that the purpose of my husband's life was to give life to others, and I am the conduit that is going to make that happen." After her husband's death, Laura took a job as an emergency management disability liaison. She also volunteers at a spinal cord injury rehab program in his memory. She says her experience caring for him taught her how to be a strong advocate and prepared her for her work helping those with disabilities.

The Benefits of Caregiving

It's so common to focus on the challenges of caregiving because there are so many: the stress, responsibilities, and time pressures. But caregiving also brings many positives to our lives. Caregivers and researchers have reported many benefits, including these:

- Better memory and cognitive functioning than non-caregivers
- Stronger physical performance than non-caregivers
- Improved confidence
- Sense of competency
- Personal life satisfaction
- Improved sense of meaning and purpose
- Improved relationships
- Increased practical life skills.

As a caregiver, you have grown. I, too, see my experiences as a caregiver enriching my life in many ways:

- **My relationships with my parents have been even closer than they were before.** Mom and Dad knew that I made sacrifices for them, and they appreciated me and knew I appreciated them. We had a mutual respect and love that was stronger and deeper than at other phases of our lives. I grew to know them in ways I never could have if I'd not stepped up to the caregiving plate when they needed me. I am so glad to have had the time with them, knowing and connecting with them in a different way. Even now, when Dad doesn't always know who I am in overt ways, he is generally more happy and calm when he is with me, and I can see that I provide a certain sense of security for him that Alzheimer's hasn't destroyed.

- **I have the great joy of a multitude of special moments with them.** I would never have had so many moments if I had not committed to intimately accompanying them through this time. We've created joy and memories together when I've taken them to concerts and the theater, stores or restaurants. Even more special for me has been noticing—being mindful of—the little things that happen on a daily basis: kissing them goodnight regularly; sharing meals and hearing Dad say grace; seeing Mom's face light up when I brought her flowers just as Dad used to do; bursting into song with Dad as we take a walk with Jackson; enjoying spontaneous hugs; sharing favorite foods; having good company; and seeing their stress levels go down and their sense of security go up. They have given me the gift of a special connection with them.

- **My conscience is clear.** I had the great good fortune to be able to make their lives easier, more comfortable, and more meaningful, and I have witnessed that on a daily basis, whether I've helped them with personal care, made sure they had intellectual stimulation, arranged for medical care or therapies, or found the perfect item of clothing. No words can describe the fulfillment that brings. I choose to care. It has made their lives better. I will have no regrets.

- **I know I've made a difference.** The things I do matter. They have had a positive effect on my parents and, I believe, in a bigger sense, as I have contributed to the stream of love in this world. My life has meaning. I know that living up to my responsibility in caring for them—being of service, as imperfect as my care is—has made a difference, and that feels good. I could be volunteering in other ways, but I believe that, as the saying goes, charity begins at home. I will help others in the future, but for now I make a difference in my own family, where I'm needed the most.

- **I am stronger and more confident.** After some of the caregiving experiences I've been through, I feel like there isn't much I couldn't survive. Sure, I get thrown about in the winds of change and challenge, but somewhere deep inside I know I will get through it—I've learned that I always do. I feel successful because I am resilient. It's also easier for me to make decisions, prioritize, and juggle multiple tasks. I do what I have to do, I don't have time to fool around, and most of the time I get to the point and get things done.
- **I have grown personally.** I've developed mentally, emotionally, and spiritually as a result of caring for others. It is often through challenge that we learn, and caregiving is a life experience that has few parallels when it comes to that. I know myself better: my personal resources, my limits, my values, and my priorities. I've had, and will continue to have, many opportunities to strengthen my ability to manage my negative thinking or feelings of being overwhelmed. I've learned to reboot myself as best I can in any given situation.
- **I have developed skills and competencies.** I know that I've improved in all the skill areas outlined in this book. And, like other caregivers, I can apply many of those skills to my work or other areas of my life. I am now an even stronger advocate than I was, and that's saying something, because my entire career has been built around helping those who are vulnerable or have special needs, especially older adults. I'm sure I'm stretching my cognitive skills at a key time in my life as I, too, am aging. Caregiving has been preparing me for the next phase of my own life.

Caregiving and Your Life Plan

As you've realized the incredible depth of skills you've accumulated, perhaps you're ready to reimagine your life. Ask yourself: Is it time for a change? In what area of your life? Consider making work changes—is it time for your encore career? If caregiving necessitated a change in your career path, what direction do you want to go now? Are there new ways to integrate your work, your caregiving, and the rest of your personal life?

Here are some steps you can take as you contemplate the benefits of caregiving and how you might imagine, or reimagine, your life.

- **Where are you now?** Go back over your 360-degree assessment from Chapter 1. Has anything changed? What are your needs now? What resources are at your disposal? What is most important to you in life now?
- **Open your mind:** Think about what your life might look like going forward. Envision how you *want* your life to be. Write down what you'd like in terms of your time, who you are with, where you live, your work, hobbies, relationships, health, finances, and how you want to *feel*—every aspect of your life. Write it as if it has already happened, as if it presently exists. This exercise will help you shift your mind-set to the future.
- **Create goals:** Write down your goals for each of these areas and revisit them regularly. Think about your life goals from the new perspectives you've gained as a caregiver.
- **Get some help:** A life or career coach, counselor, or therapist may be helpful. Ask friends for input and support.
- **Create an actionable plan:** Set a realistic, doable path toward achieving your goals.
- **Get started!** When you are ready, get started, one step at a time.
- **Revisit, reinforce, and validate your plan:** As your dreams and desires change, continue to be clear about what you want—imagine it and make it happen! You have cared for loved ones—you can do anything!

Have faith. You will be able to move forward in work—and with life—with new skills and depth, and you will always treasure your memories of your loved ones. Take comfort in knowing you took care of them, and honor their memory by moving forward and living your life to the fullest.

Your Job Description: Life Transition Coordinator

This component of your job description is the most personal of all. You have learned to manage your own life transitions after caregiving ends. This can be a challenging task, but you have learned and grown. This component rounds out your caregiving skills competencies.

Understands the emotional and practical aspects of grieving. Obtains assistance as needed in navigating the grief process. Creates memorials and remembrances of loved ones who have passed on. Engages in personal reflection regarding caregiving role and coordinates internal and external commemoration of such. Acknowledges role changes and actively coordinates resulting life transitions. Recognizes the ways that caregiving has enriched life experience.

APPENDIX A
TIPS FOR CHALLENGING CONVERSATIONS

As a caregiver, you'll likely need to talk with the people you are caring for about decisions regarding their skills and abilities, health care, finances, legal matters, living situations, and safety. These conversations can be difficult, but here are some tips I've found helpful.

- **Talk early and often.** The more you've discussed and planned for the future, the easier it will be when it's time to make decisions.
- **Be supportive.** You're not here to take over their lives. Even if you're caring for your parents, you will never be their parent—you'll always be their child. If you're clear that you just want to help and support them, they will feel less threatened. Don't make this a power play. Talk about ways you can support their independence, even if it means making some changes.
- **Do your homework *first*.** Observe their situation, identify specific areas of concern, and talk with other family members and people in their support network so you have examples to discuss. Research the options for support and care.
- **Start by expressing your love and concern.** Be clear that your thoughts and actions are motivated by your love and your desire to help them be as independent as possible for as long as possible. Be

sincere; they'll see through a snow job right away. Strive for honest, caring, clear communication.

- **Use "I" statements:** Anytime you start a sentence with "you," be aware of how your loved ones will react. "You need to . . ." or "You just have to . . ." will put people off. Instead, try "I am concerned about . . ." or "I want to help you . . . ."
- **Ask them to say how they think they're doing.** Don't just dive in with your opinions. Ask for theirs as well. If they say everything is fine as is, patiently express your own concerns.
- **Ask specific questions.** If it's hard to get the conversation going, ask questions like these:
  - Do you ever think about the future and how to plan for a time when you may need more support?
  - Are you ever worried about or tired of taking care of the house and yard?
  - Do you ever feel unsafe, isolated, or uncomfortable being alone?
  - What would you like to do more of? What would you like to do less of?
  - Would a bit of help ease your stress? Help with what?
- **Validate their feelings.** Change is hard, and the unknown is a big fear for all of us of any age. Tell them that you understand any reluctance, fears, or even anger they might feel and that you want to help make change easier for them. Sometimes they just need acknowledgment that this is hard stuff to deal with.
- **Involve the right people in the conversation.** Include trusted family members or, if needed, an objective third party to facilitate the conversation. If your parents always take your brother's advice, for example, be sure he's there. If they trust their doctor, financial adviser or lawyer, then arrange for an appointment and go along.
- **Try an indirect approach.** As a more casual conversation starter, talk about a friend who has talked with his or her loved ones about future plans, an article or book you've read, or a movie or TV show you've seen. If a friend or family member dies, talk about what your loved ones want when they die. Casually ask their opinions and whether you could help them plan.

- **Offer specifics and alternatives.** Especially if you want the people you care for to give something up, have resources and options lined up so they know a replacement or alternative is available. For example, if you notice that it's not safe for them to cook any more, propose other options for meals.

- **Pose various scenarios and talk about the options.** It may be easier to discuss their desires and plans if you describe "what if" possibilities in the future and ask how they would like things handled. It's a good way to get them talking about their current situation, too. For example, you could say, "If someday you have a health issue that makes it impossible for you to use stairs, would you like to adjust to living on the first floor, or would you like to move?" or "If in the future you should need more care and your savings run out, would you want to sell certain assets you own?"

- **Try empathy and sympathy.** If they are reticent to talk about their personal affairs, the changes they're experiencing, or their fears or worries, you might try explaining yours. If you open up to them, perhaps they'll be more likely to share with you. And a little guilt trip isn't always a bad thing; tell them you're worried they might need you one day, and you need to know what to do if that time ever comes. They likely don't want to cause you any trouble.

APPENDIX B

IS IT TIME TO STOP DRIVING?

Of course you want the people you care for to continue driving for as long as they can do so safely. But for many people, a time will come when they must limit or stop driving, either temporarily or permanently, due to their health, skills, or abilities. **Remember that it's all about safety. Safe driving is a matter of health and skills—not age.** Here are my tips for approaching the subject.

- **Watch for signs that it's time to have a conversation about modifying driving habits or hanging up the keys.** Monitor loved ones' driving. Ride along with them. Then you'll be able to discuss facts and personal observations, not generalizations or vague worries. Note AARP's list of the top ten signs that it's time to limit or stop driving:
  1. Frequent "close calls."
  2. Mild fender benders, evidenced by dents and scrapes on the car and on fences, mailboxes, garage doors, and curbs.
  3. Getting lost, especially in familiar locations.
  4. Having trouble seeing or following traffic signals, road signs, and pavement markings.
  5. Responding more slowly to unexpected situations, having trouble moving their foot from the gas to the brake pedal, or confusing the brake and accelerator pedals.

6. Misjudging gaps in traffic at intersections and on highway entrance and exit ramps.

7. Experiencing road rage or causing other drivers to honk or complain.

8. Easily becoming distracted or having difficulty concentrating while driving.

9. Having a hard time turning around to check the rear view while backing up or changing lanes.

10. Receiving multiple traffic tickets or warnings from law enforcement officers.

- **Have the conversations about driving early and often—before a crisis occurs.** That can help desensitize the subject and give you a chance to put solid plans in place. The United States is difficult to navigate without a car, especially in suburbs and rural areas. Approach the subject in terms of how *we* will deal with a time when they won't drive anymore. For information about broaching the topic, consider taking AARP Driver Safety's free "We Need to Talk" online seminar at www.aarp.org/weneedtotalk.

- **Choose who will talk.** Determine the best person to address this sensitive topic. Dad's doctor broached the subject for us after discussions about his memory, vision, and hearing problems. Anyone is better than a police officer; that's your last resort.

- **If they can still drive, help them drive more safely.**
  - Suggest they refresh their driving skills. You'll find many classroom and online programs to choose from, including the at www.aarp.org/drive.
  - Help set up an assessment from an occupational therapist who can help them make sure their car is adjusted properly for them.
  - Help arrange for ongoing car maintenance to ensure the car is running well.
  - Talk to them about modifying activities to sync with changes in driving. For example, if night driving is a concern, help them find daytime instead of evening activities. Offer to take them grocery shopping when you go to share gas costs and save them a trip. Ask if their friends can pick them up when they go out in the evening.

- **Be careful about the language you use.** Try approaching them this way: "I know you don't want to hurt anyone else much less yourself, and I know how terrible you would feel if you did hurt someone. I love you, and I don't want you to get hurt either. How can I help you plan for modifying your driving habits or not driving at all?" Discussing "hanging up the keys" is much less adversarial, belittling, or threatening than saying, "I'm taking away your keys."

- **Remember the meaning of driving: freedom, adventure, flexibility.** Reluctance to give up driving is often about the changes it will signify. Be compassionate and help your loved ones work through their fears and concerns. Transportation can be key to ensuring that people remain productive, happy, and connected to their family, friends, and community. Lack of transportation can lead to social isolation, which can cause depression and health problems.

- **Line up alternate means of transportation.** Gather information about public transportation; driving services; taxis; friends, family, members of their faith community, and neighbors who could drive them; transportation for older adults; facility vans; and volunteers. Help people you care for make choices about what will work for them. Remind them that they can afford to spend money on alternative transportation now that they no longer will be paying for insurance, car payments, maintenance, and gas.

HOSPITAL SURVIVAL KIT

Over the years, I've spent many days and nights in hospitals with my parents, and now I know what we need to lessen the stress for us all and maximize their comfort and healing. I'm sharing with you my time-tested 20 must-have items to take a hospitalization from miserable to manageable. I keep many of these items on the ready in an easy-to-grab, large tote bag so I'm prepared for a crisis.

1. **Electronics and their chargers:** They're first on the list. Most hospitals, even in the emergency room, allow use of cell phones (if you can get a signal) and offer free Wi-Fi. I use my iPad to take copious notes on everything that happens and create a list of questions; I then email this to my note-taking account while copying my sisters to keep them apprised. Facebook posts also bring lots of virtual support from friends and family and have helped me through many a tense and lonely time in the hospital. And my trusty iPad is loaded with movies, calming music, and favorite tunes (big band for my parents).

2. **Healthy snacks:** The hospital cafeteria and vending machines are usually packed with unhealthy comfort food, which, yes, is sometimes absolutely necessary, but I just end up feeling worse if I eat too much of that stuff. So I bring my own nuts, air-popped popcorn, brown rice chips, and granola.

3. **Magazines, books, and photo albums:** I brought magazines for Mom and me to look at and books for me to read to Dad. Looking at family photos or scrapbooks is also a good way to pass the time.

4. **Stuff to stay warm and comfy:** I wear sweatpants and long-sleeve shirts. No jeans—loose is more comfy when spending hours in hospital chairs and sleeping on cots. I bring warm jackets for all of us because it's always so darned cold in hospitals. I never forget Dad's hat (his head gets cold) and slippers and robe for them. I also take my lightweight, easy-to-wash slippers I keep just for hospital visits and travel; I can stay more relaxed in their room if I wear my slippers. Psychological? Perhaps. But if it works, do it. I also bring hairbrush, ponytail holders, and hair clips. I always brought a colorful shawl or throw blanket for Mom; hospital rooms are so dull—a cheerful color goes a long way.

5. **Really good moisturizers:** It's so dry in hospitals! Lip balm is a must. Good, thick hand cream can be used every time we wash our hands (which is often) and is great for hand or foot massages.

6. **Nose protection:** Keep the nose moist to prevent infections, headaches, and other discomfort in the dry environment. Saline spray works well and can be used frequently (I like a brand with Xylitol. It can prevent any bacteria in hospital air from adhering to the nasal passages.) Mentholatum or Vicks ointment helps too. Sometimes these measures aren't enough. When Dad started to develop sinus problems during a hospital stay, a doctor agreed to let me bring in a vaporizer. And ditch the rough and scratchy cheap tissues the hospital supplies; I splurge on the good, soft tissues from home.

7. **Nicely scented antibacterial hand gel:** You'll constantly be cleaning your hands to stop the spread of germs, so hand gel is a must. The stuff available from wall units in hospitals often dries your hands and smells nasty. I like the lavender-scented gel. It makes us all feel special.

8. **Warm blankets:** I bring my soft, fuzzy green blanket my best friend gave me. The texture is soothing, the color is calming, and it feels like a hug from a friend. Mom and Dad got lovely heated hospital blankets, and I wasn't shy about asking for fresh ones frequently.

9. **My own pillow:** I am more comfortable with my favorite pillow, with a good cover on it and soft pillowcase for protection from germs. The hospital has pillows, but they are far from comfortable. Unfortunately, the hospital wouldn't usually let Mom and Dad use their own pillows.

10. **Homecoming clothes:** I threw in clean clothes for Mom and Dad to wear for their triumphant homecoming when they left the hospital.

11. **A small flashlight:** With a flashlight, I can read or find things in the room when Dad is asleep.

12. **Eye mask:** With all the flashing hospital lights and doors opening and closing (which seems to happen constantly—how does anyone get rest in the hospital?), an eye mask helps us get to sleep during the day or at night.

13. **A sound machine:** A portable sound machine is great, or a smartphone or iPad app with calming nature sounds, music, or white noise. It blocks out the beeping and other disturbing hospital noises, and we sleep more soundly.

14. **Room spray or essential oils:** A friend gave Mom a beautiful scent when she broke her hip, and it's amazing how a little aromatherapy obliterated hospital odors and lifted our spirits. Make sure no one is allergic to it.

15. **Mom's teddy bears:** Mom had a collection of teddy bears, and for an extended stay I always brought in a few. They kept her company, comforted her, and made her laugh. Any familiar item from home can be helpful.

16. **Portable CD player:** For extended hospital stays, I bring in a CD player and Dad's favorite CDs. It's great when I don't have enough tunes on my iPad, and nurses can also turn on a CD player when I'm not there. Sitting alone in a hospital room can be so depressing— music can lift the mood, calm, soothe, relax, or energize.

17. **Flowers:** Some blossoms really brighten the room as well as our spirits. Intensive care and certain hospital units don't always allow live flowers, but silk flowers might be acceptable.

18. **Pictures:** I bring tape, beautiful nature pictures, and copies of family photos. I tape them on walls or mirrors along with get well cards. It's

easy to take down when we get to go home. When Mom fractured her spine and couldn't stand on her own, I posted photos of her standing tall and strong as inspiration while she recovered from surgery.

19. **Pocket yoga:** Many hours in hospital chairs leaves me stiff and achy. I bring a small set of simple yoga stretches and positions I can easily do in small places; many of these can be done while seated. Sometimes I could get Mom and Dad to join in, too!

20. **Chocolate!** This is my most important hospital survival tip: When your or your loved ones' spirits need a lift, there is nothing like chocolate. I prefer dark chocolate—and lots of it. (Of course, check to make sure it doesn't conflict with your loved ones' diet plans.)

APPENDIX D
MUSIC AND CAREGIVING

As a music therapist, I have used music as a tool to help people who have a wide variety of conditions, such as dementia, Parkinson's disease, strokes, and cancer. Now I use music frequently as I care for my parents.

Music can soothe the soul, bring joy to our lives, and ease stress. It can also help lower blood pressure and bring healing; encourage social interaction, communication, and physical activity; boost self-esteem; and stimulate memories and emotions. Dad, who has Alzheimer's disease, sometimes can't produce the word he wants to speak. But he can sing words to songs he's known most of his life.

Music therapists are specially trained and credentialed health specialists. They assess clients' needs and create individualized treatment plans using music as a therapeutic tool, working in private homes, hospitals, or facilities. You can find a music therapist through the American Music Therapy Association (www.musictherapy.org).

As a caregiver, you can consult with a music therapist, and you can also integrate music into your everyday activities. First, think about the people you care for. Do they need to talk, move, eat, interact, focus, remember, or relax more? Do they need activities to stay engaged and have fun? Do they respond well to music? If so, you can use music as you address those needs.

Here are a few tips:

- Identify music your loved ones enjoy—tunes from when they were in their teens or 20s will strike a note, or a particular type of music, such as big band, classical, religious, country, or rock-n-roll.
- Play music on a CD player or create a playlist on an iPod or other MP3 player.
- Use a music app such as Amazon Prime Music, iHeart Radio, or Pandora to stream music for your loved ones. You can create stations or playlists based on their favorite type of music.
- Use an app like SingFit that has songs and adjustable features such as a guide singer, word cues, and the ability to record yourselves singing along.
- Create a soundtrack for the day: light music for waking up, stimulating music to get them going, dance music or military marches for exercise, soothing music for bedtime.
- If the people you care for experience anxiety or agitation, try distracting them with a humorous song or a quick dance, or try some massage with relaxing music.
- Watch musicals (one of the few things Dad still enjoys on TV) and YouTube music videos.
- Play musical instruments or sing together. Don't worry about how it sounds; it's about the process, not the product!

Consider using music for yourself, too. As caregivers, we feel a great deal of stress and fatigue. Use music to relax, energize, or lift your mood. I also find playing music with guided imagery at night helps me sleep better.

Resources

Accompanion guide to this book, *Checklist for Family Caregivers: A Guide to Making It Manageable*, by Sally Hurme, from AARP and the American Bar Association (AARP.org/ChecklistCaregivers), is a simple how-to guide that helps caregivers get and stay organized throughout their caregiving journey.

(Many of the following resources and organizations listed here have information in both English and Spanish.)

AARP Caregiving Resources

AARP Caregiving Glossary (www.aarp.org/home-family/caregiving /info-05-2012/caregiving-resource-center-glossary.html)

AARP Caregiving Resource Center (www.aarp.org/caregiving)
Tools, worksheets, and tips on how to plan, prepare, and succeed as a caregiver. Includes information on caregiving options, housing, legal issues, financial matters, care for the caregiver, and more.

AARP Caregiving Support Line
877-333-5885
Free call center available weekdays from 7 a.m. to 11 p.m. Eastern time. Call for help finding local and national resources, services, and support groups.

AARP Caregiving Take Care Blog (http://blog.aarp.org/tag/takecare)
Blog posts from Amy Goyer and others with personal stories, up-to-date information, and practical tips.

AARP Checklists and Information About Assessing Facilities

- **Independent Living** (www.aarp.org/home-family/caregiving/
  info-05-2012/talking-about-independent-living.html)
- **Assisted Living** (assets.aarp.org/external_sites/caregiving/checklists
  /checklist_assistedLiving.html and www.aarp.org/relationships/
  caregiving-resource-center/info-09-2010/ho_assisted_living_weighing
  _the_options.html)
- **Nursing Homes or Skilled Nursing Facilities** (assets.aarp.org/
  external_sites/caregiving/checklists/checklist_nursingHomes.html
  and www.aarp.org/home-family/caregiving/info-05-2012/caregiving-
  resource-center-asking-right-questions.html)
- **Memory Care for People with Dementia** (www.aarp.org/
  relationships/caregiving/info-10-2010/the_high_costs_of_caring_
  for_alzheimers_patients.html)
- **Continuing Care Retirement Communities** (www.aarp.org/
  relationships/caregiving-resource-center/info-09-2010/ho_what_to
  _ask_retirement_communities.html and www.aarp.org/content/aarp
  /en/home/relationships/caregiving-resource-center/info-09-2010/ho
  _continuing_care_retirement_communities.html)
- **Adult Day Services** (www.aarp.org/relationships/
  caregiving-resource-center/info-10-2010/pc_adult_day_services_
  checklist.html)

AARP Prepare to Care (www.aarp.org/home-family/caregiving/
info-07-2012/prepare-to-care-planning-guide.html)
A caregiving planning guide for families.

AARP YouTube Channel (www.aarp.org/takingcare)
Helpful videos about a wide range of caregiving topics.

Advance Directives

AARP Advance Directives by State (www.aarp.org/advancedirectives)
Free advance directives forms for every state.

Aging with Dignity Five Wishes (www.agingwithdignity.org)
888-594-7437
Information and instruction on developing a living will and having conversations with family.

Physicians Orders for Life Sustaining Treatment (POLST) Paradigm (www.polst.org)
503-494-9550
An approach to end-of-life plan that emphasizes patients' wishes about the care they receive.

Animals

International Association of Canine Professionals (www.canineprofessionals.com/find-a-professional)
512-564-1011
Find a dog trainer or other canine professional in your area.

Animal-Assisted Therapy

Pet Partners (www.petpartners.org)
425-679-5500
Registers handlers of multiple species as volunteer teams providing animal-assisted interactions.

Therapy Dogs International (www.tdi-dog.org/About.aspx)
973-252-9800
Dedicated to regulating, testing, and registering of therapy dogs and their volunteer handlers for the purpose of visiting nursing homes, hospitals, and other institutions and wherever else therapy dogs are needed.

Pets

American Association of Housecall Veterinarians
(http://homevets.org/Find_A_Mobile_Vet.html)
Lists local veterinarians who make house calls.

Banfield Charitable Trust (www.banfieldcharitabletrust.org)
503-922-5801
Programs to help pet owners struggling to care for their pets or facing
difficult life circumstances.

Service Animals and Guide Dogs

These organizations may provide service animals such as guide dogs
and training for individuals and/or for professionals, volunteers, or
facilities.

Animal Assisted Intervention International (www
.animalassistedintervention.org/AnimalAssistedIntervention.aspx)

Assistance Dogs International (www.assistancedogsinternational.org)

Bergin University of Canine Studies (www.berginu.edu)

Canine Companions for Independence (www.caninecompanions.org)
800-572-BARK (2275)

Eye Dog Foundation for the Blind (www.eyedogfoundation.org)
800-393-3641

Guide Dog Foundation for the Blind (www.guidedog.org)
800-548-3347

Guide Dogs of America (www.guidedogsofamerica.org)
818-362-5834

Paws'itive Teams (www.pawsteams.org)
858-558-7297

Caregiver Support

Area Agencies on Aging (www.eldercare.gov or www.n4a.org)
800-677-1116
Local agencies that provide information and referral, services, and supports for older adults and caregivers.

Assisted Living Federation of America (http://www.alfa.org/alfa/Consumer_Corner.asp)
703-894-1805
Information and resources for consumers on senior living options and how to find them.

Caregiver Action Network (http://caregiveraction.org)
202-454-3970
Provides education, peer support, and resources to family caregivers of all ages.

CareZone (www.carezone.com)
Organize care and communicate with caregiving team online or using a mobile app.

Caring Connections (www.caringinfo.org)
800-658-8898
A national engagement initiative and helpline to improve care at the end of life.

Case Management Society of America (http://www.cmsa.org/Consumer/tabid/61/Default.aspx)
800-216-2672
Find a case manager to help assess your loved ones' situation and manage care in their Care Management Industry Directory (http://caremanagemesntindustrydirectory.com/).

The Eden Alternative (http://www.edenalt.org/resources/ for-consumers)
583-461-3951
An international organization dedicated to creating quality of life for elders and their caring partners, wherever they may live.

Family Caregiver Alliance (www.caregiver.org)
800-445-8106
Support for caregivers through education, services, research and advocacy.

LeadingAge (www.leadingage.org)
202-783-2242
Consumer information on facilities and services for older Americans and how to access them.

Lotsa Helping Hands (www.lotsahelpinghands.com)
Connects caregivers who need help to people who want to provide help and offers tools to help caregivers coordinate their caregiving teams online or with a mobile app.

National Alliance for Caregiving (www.caregiving.org)
301-718-8444
A coalition of national organizations dedicated to improving quality of life for families and their care recipients through research, innovation, and advocacy.

National Association of Professional Geriatric Care Managers (www.caremanager.org)
520-881-8008
Searchable database of private geriatric care managers.

National Association of Social Workers (www.socialworkers.org)
Maintains an online directory of licensed social workers at www.helppro.com/nasw.

Rosalynn Carter Institute for Caregiving (www.rosalynncarter.org)
229-928-1234
Supports professional and family caregivers through advocacy,
education, research, and service.

SAGECAP (www.sageusa.org/programs/sagecap.cfm)
212-741-2247
Counseling, information, and support groups for gay, lesbian, bisexual,
and transgender caregivers.

Veterans Affairs Caregiver Support Program (www.caregiver.va
.gov)
855-260-3274
Services and supports for veterans and their caregivers.

Caregiver Support Groups
Find support groups through local hospitals, the facility where your loved
ones live, local faith-based communities, the local area agency on aging
(www.eldercare.gov), or these resources:

AARP Caregiving Online Community (www.aarp.org/
online-community/groups/index.action?slGroupKey=Group92)
Online community to share advice and challenges, find comfort, and
gain support and understanding.

AARP Caregiving Message Board (www.aarp.org/online-community/
forums.action/relationships_caregiving)
Online forum used to discuss caregiving issues.

Family Caregiver Alliance support group listing
(www.caregiver.org/caregiver/jsp/content_node.jsp?nodeid=347)
800-445-8106

Illness-specific organizations, such as these:

- **The Alzheimer's Association** caregiver support group listing (www
  .alz.org/apps/we_can_help/support_groups.asp)
- **CancerCare** caregiver support group listing (www.cancercare.org/
  tagged/caregiving)
- **National Association for Mental Illness** listing of support group for
  family and caregivers (www.nami.org/Local-NAMI/Programs?class
  key=72e2fdaf-2755-404f-a8be-606d4de63fdb)
- **National Parkinson Foundation** listing of local resources (www
  .parkinson.org/Search-Pages/Chapter-Locator)
- **National Stroke Association** stroke support group listing (http://portal
  .stroke.org/a_supportgroupsearch)

Respite Care

ARCH Respite Network (www.archrespite.org/respitelocator)
919-490-5577
Local programs and services that help caregivers take a break from
caregiving.

Family Care Navigator (https://caregiver.org/family-care-navigator)
800-445-8106
A service provided by the Family Caregiver Alliance to help find local
programs.

National Adult Day Services Association (www.nadsa.org)
877-745-1440
Listing of local adult day services center where loved ones can go,
providing a break for caregivers.

National Family Caregiver Support Program (www.eldercare.gov)
800-677-1116

To find local respite programs funded by the Administration on Aging (www.aoa.gov), contact the local area agency on aging or aging and disabilities resource center.

Veterans Affairs' Caregiver Support Line (www.caregiver.va.gov)
855-260-3274
Help finding local respite services and, in some cases, free respite care for veterans.

Driving and Transportation
AARP Driver Safety Program (www.aarp.org
/home-garden/transportation/driver_safety)
877-846-3299
Refresher courses for older drivers as well as driving tools and tips and the "We Need to Talk" program for talking to loved ones about their driving.

American Automobile Association (www.seniordriving.aaa.com)
Information for older drivers, including a self-test and transportation resources.

Beverly Foundation (www.beverlyfoundation.org)
A state-by-state list of programs providing transportation options for older adults.

National Center on Senior Transportation (http://seniortransportation
.net)
866-528-6278
A partnership of Easter Seals and the National Association of Area Agencies on Aging (n4a), with transportation resources for older adults and caregivers.

Elder Abuse
Note: To report suspected elder abuse, call 911 or local police, or contact the local Adult Protective Services agency.

National Center on Elder Abuse (http://ncea.aoa.gov)
855-500-3537
Information about elder abuse.

National Adult Protective Services Association (www.napsa-now.org/
get-help/help-in-your-area)
217-523-4431
Listing of public Adult Protective Services (APS) agencies by state to
report abuse online.

Finances
AARP Benefits QuickLINK (www.aarp.org/quicklink)
Fast, private, and secure online tool to help easily navigate the maze of
public benefit programs.

AARP Foundation Tax-Aide (www.aarp.org/money/taxes/aarp
_taxaide)
888-687-2277
Free tax assistance for those with low to moderate incomes.

AARP Money Tools (www.aarp.org/money/money_tools)
Free online calculators to help plan, save, and budget.

AARP Reverse Mortgages (www.aarp.org/money/credit-loans-debt/
reverse_mortgages)
Sets out how reverse mortgages work and their pros and cons.

AARP Social Security Benefits Calculator (www.aarp.org/
socialsecuritybenefits)
A calculator that estimates benefits to help determine the best time to
start taking Social Security.

AARP Social Security Q&A Tool (www.aarp.org/ssqa)
An easy-to-use tool that provides answers to your most frequently
asked questions about Social Security retirement benefits.

American Association for Long-Term Care Insurance (www.aaltci .org)

818-597-3227

Provides information about but does not sell long-term care insurance.

U.S. Department of Agriculture America's Health Insurance Plans, Guide to Long-Term Care Insurance (www.publications.usa.gov/ USAPubs.php?PubID=5879)

719-295-2675 (questions only—no new orders)

Download or order print publication that outline costs, limitations and exclusions, and coverage options of long-term care insurance.

Grief and Loss

American Foundation for Suicide Prevention (www.afsp.org)

National Suicide Prevention Life Line: 800-273-TALK (8255)

General line: 888-333-2377

Support for those who have lost loved ones to suicide.

Association for Death Education and Counseling (www.adec.org)

847-509-0403

Database of counselors trained to work with the dying and bereaved.

Compassionate Friends (www.compassionatefriends.org)

877-969-0010

A national network of support for those who have experienced the death of a child.

GriefNet (www.griefnet.org)

Online grief support network for adults.

Kids Aid (www.kidsaid.com)

Online grief support for children.

National Alliance for Grieving Children (www.childrengrieve.org)
866-432-1542
A locator connecting families with support in their communities.

National Widowers' Organization (www.nationalwidowers.org)
800-309-3658
Support for surviving spouses.

Health

AARP Health Tools (www.aarp.org/health/health_tools.html)
Free online tools to help you manage health records, keep track of
immunizations and screenings, look up information on drugs and
health conditions, calculate long-term care costs, and more.

Alzheimers.gov (www.alzheimers.gov)
Information about caring for someone with Alzheimer's disease.

Alzheimer's Association (www.alz.org)
800-272-3900
Information to enhance care and support for all those affected by
Alzheimer's disease and other dementias.

Alzheimer's Foundation of America (www.alzfdn.org)
866-232-8484
Services and supports for those with Alzheimer's disease or other
forms of dementia. Includes toll-free helpline.

American Cancer Society (www.cancer.org)
800-227-2345
Information and support for those dealing with cancer and their
caregivers. Find local services and programs.

American Diabetes Association (www.diabetes.org)
800-342-2383
Services and information for those affected by diabetes.

American Heart Association (www.heart.org)

800-242-8721

Information and support regarding cardiovascular disease and stroke, including caregiver support.

American Lung Association (www.lung.org)

800-586-4872

Education, advocacy, and research about lung health and preventing lung disease.

American Stroke Association (www.strokeassociation.org)

800-478-7653

Information and support for those who have suffered a stroke and their caregivers.

Centers for Medicaid and Medicare Services (www.cms.gov, www .medicare.gov and www.medicaid.gov)

800-633-4227

Information about Medicare and Medicaid.

Health Screenings and Vaccines After 50 (www.aarp.org/ healthscreenings and www.aarp.org/vaccines)

Health screening and vaccination recommendations.

Mental Health America (www.mentalhealthamerica.net)

800-969-6642

Information, services, education, advocacy, and research about mental health.

National Alliance for Hispanic Health (www.hispanichealth.org)
866-783-2645
The Hispanic Family Health Helpline and its Su Familia hotline provide
free and confidential health information for Hispanic families.

National Alliance on Mental Illness (www.nami.org) 800-950-6264
Helpline, information and support for those with mental health issues
and their caregivers.

National Cancer Institute (www.cancer.gov) 800-422-6237
Information about caring for someone who has cancer.

National Institutes of Health (NIH) Senior Health (www
.nihseniorhealth.gov)
Fact sheets on a range of health topics.

National Institute on Aging (www.nia.nih.gov)
800-222-2225
Research-based information and resources related to health and aging,
including clinical trials and information about Alzheimer's disease, at
www.nia.nih.gov/alzheimers/topics/caregiving.

National Kidney Foundation (www.kidney.org)
855-653-2273
Information and support regarding prevention and care for those with
kidney disease.

National Parkinson Foundation (www.parkinson.org)
800-473-4636
Information and referral to local resources for those who care for
people with Parkinson's disease.

National Stroke Association (www.stroke.org)
800-787-6537
Information and helpline for stroke survivors and their caregivers.

Hospice and Palliative Care

National Association for Home Care and Hospice (www.nahcagencylocator.com)
202-547-7424
Local home care and hospice programs.

National Hospice and Palliative Care Organization (www.nhpco
.org)
703-837-1500
Consumer information on hospice care and referrals to local hospice
and palliative care providers.

Legal Assistance

American Bar Association (www.findlegalhelp.org)
Online state-specific guide to finding legal help in your state.

American Bar Association Commission on Law and Aging (www
.americanbar.org/groups/law_aging.html)
Online information on legal issues affecting older adults and referrals
to lawyers in your area.

Legal assistance for older adults (www.eldercare.gov) 800-677-1116
Help finding local programs that offer legal assistance.

National Academy of Elder Law Attorneys (www.naela.org)
703-942-5711
Listing of local elder law attorneys.

Life After Caregiving

Life Reimagined (www.lifereimagined.aarp.org)
An online resource to help you take the mystery out of change and
discover your path to new possibilities after—or during—caregiving.

Local Services and Supports

211 (www.211us.org)

Dial 211 on your phone.

A collaborative information and referral service provided by United Way and the Alliance for Information and Referral Systems to find local community services such as homemaker services, congregate and home-delivered meals, transportation assistance, home health care, and respite care.

Eldercare Locator (www.eldercare.gov)

800-677-1116

Searchable databases to find community resources, including a local area agency on aging, local aging and disabilities resource center, and community resources that serve older adults and their caregivers, such as home-delivered meals, legal services, and volunteers.

National Adult Day Services Association (www.nadsa.org/locator/)

877-745-1440

Searchable database of local adult day services centers.

National Center for Creative Aging (www.creativeaging.org)

202-895-9456

Lists local arts programs serving older adults and intergenerational programs.

Meals

MealCall (www.mealcall.org)

Searchable online database of local providers of meal programs.

Meals on Wheels Association of America (www.mowaa.org/findameal)

888-998-6325

Searchable database of local programs that provide home-delivered meals.

Mediation

Academy of Professional Family Mediators (www.apfmnet.org)
Local family mediators listed by ZIP code or state in online database.

Eldercare Mediators (www.eldercaremediators.com)
303-268-2282
List of eldercare mediators by state.

Mediate.com (www.mediate.com)
541-345-1629
Search for a local mediator by specialty area, including family and
eldercare mediation.

Therapeutic Services

American Art Therapy Association (www.arttherapy
.org/upload/LOCATOR2.15.11.pdf)
888-290-0878
Local arts therapists.

American Music Therapy Association (www.musictherapy.org/about
/find/)
301-589-3300
Local music therapists.

American Physical Therapy Association (www.apta.org/apta/findapt/
index.aspx?navID=10737422525)
Online database of local physical therapists.

American Speech-Language-Hearing Association (www.asha.org/
proserv/)
800-498-2071
Local audiologists, speech therapists, and speech-language pathologists.

Veterans and Military

Military OneSource (www.militaryonesource.mil)
800-342-9647
Free resources and support from the U.S. Department of Defense for active-duty, National Guard, and Reserve service members and their families anywhere in the world.

National Resource Directory (www.nrd.gov; caregiver support at www.nrd.gov/family_and_caregiver_support)
Support for wounded warriors, service members, veterans, their families, and caregivers.

U.S. Department of Veterans Affairs (www.benefits.va.gov/ PENSIONANDFIDUCIARY/pension/aid_attendance_housebound.asp)
Information about Veterans Aid and Attendance benefits and Housebound benefits.

U.S. Department of Veterans Affairs' Caregiver Support (www .caregiver.va.gov) 855-260-3274
Support for caregivers of veterans.

U.S. Department of Veterans Affairs Guide to Long-Term Care (www.va.gov/GERIATRICS/Guide/LongTermCare/index.asp)

U.S. Department of Veterans Affairs Regional Office Locator (www2.va.gov/directory/guide/home.asp?isflash=1)
800-827-1000
Find your local veterans affairs office.

Work

AARP Work Resources (www.aarp.org/workresources)
Key resources for job-hunting and starting a business. Includes www .aarp.org/jobs, a free job-search tool, and information about AARP Best Employers for Workers Over 50 (www.aarp.org/bestemployers), with information on employers that offer flexible schedules, part-time

opportunities, time off for caregiving needs, and other benefits useful to caregivers.

National Partnership for Women & Families (www
.nationalpartnership.org)
202-986-2600
Information about the Family and Medical Leave Act and paid sick leave.

U.S. Department of Labor (www.dol.gov/whd/fmla)
866-487-9243
Information about the Family and Medical Leave Act and Military Caregiver Leave.

U.S. Equal Employment Opportunity Commission (www.eeoc.gov)
800-669-4000
Information about filing complaints for discrimination, including discrimination on the basis of family responsibilities.

Work Life Law Family Discrimination Hotline (www.worklifelaw
.org)
415-703-8276
A free service from the University of California Hastings College of Law to help parents and other family caregivers who may be facing employment discrimination because of their family responsibilities.

Select Sources

AARP Public Policy Institute and United Hospital Fund: *Home Alone: Family Caregivers Providing Complex Chronic Care*, 2012, http://www.aarp.org/home-family/caregiving/info-10-2012/home-alone-family-caregivers-providing-complex-chronic-care.html.

AARP Public Policy Institute: *Understanding the Impact on Family Caregiving on Work,* 2012, www.aarp.org/home-family/caregiving/info-10-2012/understanding-the-impact-of-family-caregiving-and-work-fs-AARP-ppi-ltc.html.

AARP Public Policy Institute: *Valuing the Invaluable*, 2011 Update, www.aarp.org/relationships/caregiving/info-07-2011/valuing-the-invaluable.html.

Gallup Consulting: *The Well-Being of the Working Caregiver Survey,* 2010, www.gallup.com/poll/145115/working-caregivers-face-wellbeing-challenges.aspx.